LOVELY IN EYES NOT HIS

Homilies for an Imaging of Christ

WALTER J. BURGHARDT, S.J.
Theologian in Residence
Georgetown University

PAULIST/PRESS
New York/Mahwah

To the worshipers
at Georgetown 12:15
and
Holy Trinity 5:30
whose human warmth and Christian devotion
are largely responsible for
whatever wit and wisdom
these pages possess

Paulist Press gratefully acknowledges the use of "Fire and Ice" by Robert Frost, copyright 1923 and renewed 1951 by Robert Frost. Reprinted from *The Poetry of Robert Frost* edited by Edward Connery Lathem, by permission of Henry Holt and Company, Inc.; "The End of the World" by Archibald MacLeish has been reprinted from *New and Collected Poems 1917–1982* by Archibald MacLeish. Copyright © 1985 by The Estate of Archibald MacLeish. Reprinted by permission of Houghton Mifflin Company.

Illustrations by Mary K. Burt.
Cover by Tim McKeen.

Library of Congress Cataloging-in-Publication Data

Burghardt, Walter J.
    Lovely in eyes not his : homilies for an imaging of Christ /
Walter J. Burghardt.
      p. cm.
    Bibliography: p.
    ISBN 0-8091-2981-7 (pbk.)
    1. Catholic Church—Sermons. 2. Sermons, American. I. Title.
BX1756.B828L68 1988
252'.02—dc19
                                             88-2505
                                                CIP

Published by Paulist Press
997 Macarthur Boulevard
Mahwah, NJ 07430

Printed and bound in the
United States of America

TABLE OF CONTENTS

MEDLEY

I say more: the just man justices;
    Keeps grace: that keeps all his goings graces;
Acts in God's eye what in God's eye he is—
    Christ. For Christ plays in ten thousand places,
Lovely in limbs, and lovely in eyes not his
    To the Father through the features of men's faces.

Gerard Manley Hopkins, S.J.

PREFACE

This fifth collection of homilies within nine years demands, if not an apology, at least an explanation. The warm reception accorded to four previous collections (1980, 1982, 1984, 1986), scores of addresses and workshops on preaching across the country, and exposure to thousands of the laity confirm my conviction that as in theology, so in homiletics, our practitioners can profit from "models." Not that any given model, such as mine, is *the* answer to every preacher's prayer. Not that a set of published sermons is fair game for priestly piracy. Rather that a collection of carefully crafted sermons—whether from the pen of a Buechner or a Fosdick, Leo the Great or John Henry Newman—often reveals what manner of homiletic art has in fact proved effective, may cause a creative dissatisfaction with one's own efforts, can provide stimulus, inspiration, ideas.

My main title, *Lovely in Eyes Not His,* is borrowed (as the facing page reveals) from Gerard Manley Hopkins (1844–89), the Jesuit whose poetry was symbolic of his agonizing effort to grow into an image of the Christ who never did his own will but always the will of his Father, even unto crucifixion. For years these lines of a sonnet that bears no title but begins "As kingfishers catch fire" have captured for me, more lyrically than any others, the Christian struggle to express our human imaging of the divine.[1] I am persuaded that, in the last analysis, my homilies have this as their primary thrust: to help Christians recognize their dignity, their likeness to Christ, and move them to live its awesome responsibilities from dawn to darkness, from childhood to final cross. Hence my subtitle, *Homilies for an Imaging of Christ.*

With this as prelude, my prayer for each gentle reader is a twin prayer. May you increasingly discover in yourself the experience of St. Paul: "It is no longer I who live, but Christ who lives in me" (Gal 2:20). And may you find Christ playing "in ten thousand places," in ten thousand persons, find him "lovely in eyes not his," lovely especially and paradoxically where the grime and the grit on the face of humanity hide from us the features even of Christ crucified.

Walter J. Burghardt, S.J.

ADVENT

1
SHOPPING FOR CHRIST
Second Sunday of Advent (A)

- Isaiah 11:1–10
- Romans 15:4–9
- Matthew 3:1–12

For Christians, one word recaptures the essence of Advent. One word: We are "waiting." But that very word (1) creates a problem. The problem (2) compels me to recall our human experience of waiting. And that experience (3) just might make our Advent considerably more Christian.

I

First, the problem. For a moment, let me play the not so grand inquisitor. Don't raise your hands, but . . . right now, how many of you are waiting? And if you are, waiting for what? Oh I know, here and across the earth, countless folk are saying "I just can't wait for Christmas to come." For all sorts of good reasons: dear faces too long absent, a reprieve from classroom tyranny, Wrangler jeans fashioned for your figure, wassail on your lips and in your heart, carols invented by angels, another ruthless assault on Tom Turkey. Good reasons indeed. But how many here and round the globe are saying "I just can't wait for *Christ* to come"?

The problem is, why *should* you wait for Christ to come? You don't wait for someone who has already come, someone who is actually here. Christ came one midnight clear, came in the imprisoning bands of a baby. And when he left us, paradoxically he stayed with us. He took from us the sensible charm of his presence: the face his mother eyed, the voice that was music to his disciples, the feet Magdalene grasped at his grave. And still he is here. You heard him in his word proclaimed; you glimpse him in your gathering together; in a short while he will touch your tongue or rest in the hollow of your hand. What could you possibly be waiting for? For the final coming of Christ on a pink cloud, separating us saved sheep from those damned goats? If you are, it would be wise not to hold your breath.

The problem? No Christ to wait for. Little wonder Advent means so little to the average Christian, plays second fiddle to the ads for Christmas buying. Understand me: I am not saying we should not celebrate the first Christmas, remember it lovingly each year, relive it in our liturgy. I am asking whether "waiting for Christ" makes any sense when he surrounds us, when he rests within us, when he lies each day on every Eucharistic table on earth. Waiting made sense for the Hebrews of old yearning for a promised Messiah. Waiting made sense for John the Baptist preparing the people for him "who is coming after me" (Mt 3:11). But to wait for a Christ who is here: Is this not to pretend, to playact, to engage in make-believe?

II

The problem compels a second point: the human experience of waiting. Take two levels of that experience. We experience waiting on one level when the other is simply not here. A poignant example is a diary in a recent book titled *The War*.[1] The diary focuses on the pain of the narrator, a woman of the French Resistance, as she waits for her husband to return from a Nazi concentration camp, from infamous Dachau. "The story of Marguerite's waiting is a very human one, filled with an anguish at times verging almost on despair. . . ."[2] As the Allies advance in Germany, the realities of the Nazi camps filter back to Paris. She does not know what to think, what to make of the rumors and speculation. Paris is jubilant, but how can Marguerite rejoice when her husband may be dead in a ditch somewhere in Germany? The City of Light is literally lit up again, but without her husband "It is a sign of death, of a tomorrow without [him]." Peace? "It's like a great darkness falling, it's the beginning of forgetting." It's the experience of waiting for someone you love, but you're not at all sure he or she is coming; the other may even be dead.

There is another experience of waiting, quite different from Marguerite's. It is the experience of Mary, told by an angel that God wants her to bring His Son into the world—and from her very flesh. From the moment Gabriel left her, Mary knew that Jesus was there—inside her. But she had nine months to wait. To wait for what? For her child to transpire, to appear, to show himself. For her to see him, touch him, cradle him, kiss him.

What was it like for Mary to wait for Jesus? As a man, I can merely imagine it; only you mothers experience what it was like. He was indeed there; and still he was not yet there—not the way she wanted him to be, not the way he would be in a stable 97 miles away. In the meantime, there was the paradox of pregnancy: hours of ecstasy offset by days of discomfort, by anxiety and fear, by sleepless nights.[3]

And one dear night, amid the cattle dung and all the litter of a Palestinian stable, Jesus was actually born of her. He came to light, came *from* her *to* her; she looked into his eyes, heard him wail, held his shivering flesh, bussed him roundly. Of course he was hers before, but what a difference one night makes! This, this is what Mary has been waiting for; here is where Jesus becomes real to her as never before. Before, she believed with her mind, even felt with her body; now, she experiences Jesus with all her senses: eyes and ears, touch and taste and smell.

III

This summons up my third point: How can the experiences of Marguerite and Mary make your Advent more Christian? The point is, your Advent should reflect the experience not so much of Marguerite as of Mary. Like Mary and unlike Marguerite, you need not wait for someone to simply come where you are. As I've said, the Lord Jesus is here, all around you and deep within you. The question is, how alive is he—for you?

If Christ is thrillingly alive for you, as pulsating a person as the man or woman beside you, you have my permission to doze through the rest of this homily. But if Christ is within you only like an embryo, if you haven't felt him move or been surprised by his kicking, if he hasn't warmed you with his presence or sickened you for your sinning, if above all you do not embrace him like the best of brothers, then his birth in you is overdue. If he is someone you sup with on Sundays because it's a family ritual, and the rest of the week is Christless (not sinful, just Christless), you have a tough job these next 18 days.

You see, it's not enough to just wait for something to happen. You may remember Samuel Beckett's devastating play *Waiting for Godot*.[4] Godot is a diminutive for God. Didi and Gogo are pathetic creatures, two halves of a single mentality, two absurd clowns who wait each evening at the same tree, wait for Mr. Godot to come along and give meaning to their meaningless existence, killing time before it kills them. As Didi remarks, "habit is a great deadener."[5]

No, if you want Christ to come alive in you, you get off (to put it delicately) your haunches. What did Mary do when the angel went winging away? She did not (as one priest supposedly suggested) go into chapel and say her beads before the Blessed Sacrament. Luke tells us what she did: "Mary arose and went with haste into the hill country" (Lk 1:39), went to the home of her kinswoman Elizabeth. Why? Because Elizabeth was six months pregnant with John, and Elizabeth was an old woman. Elizabeth needed her.

So too for you. Here our annual Christmas craze can help. Every store window, every colorful commercial, is seducing you into giving. What does not come through clearly is that the best of gifts is the gift that is a symbol, pregnant with a depth of meaning not always explicitly stated. A gift is most perfect when it stands for me, when in the gift I am giving myself; the underlying gift is I.

What am I urging? That, like Mary, you activate your waiting, energize it, dynamize it. If you want the Christ within you to come to living birth, stop waiting listlessly at the same old tree for Mr. Godot. Give yourself, bring your Christ, to your sisters and brothers, especially those who look like Jesus only because they are pinned to a cross. Some of you fly to Dominica or Peru, and you do well. But you can spare yourself that expense. Crucified Christs encircle you, from Luther Place to Lorton, from Salvadoran refugees to the family next door, from the bundle of rags on M Street to the fashion plate in your dorm who may be lonely as hell.

I cannot tell you exactly where to go, to whom you should give of yourself, how to go about it. Let the Lord Jesus tell you that— Jesus and your own two eyes, your experience, your sensitivity. What I can tell you is this. If you mirror Mary, if you carry your

Christ to someone who needs your caring, the effect can be an amazing grace. A twin grace. Do you remember how Elizabeth reacted when Mary arrived to help her? "When the voice of your greeting came to my ears, the baby in my womb leaped for joy" (Lk 1:44). Unborn John sensed the presence of Jesus within Mary, and he jumped in joy. And do you recall how Mary responded to Elizabeth's cry? "My spirit rejoices in God my Savior" (Lk 1:47). So may it well be for you. An other, a scarred sister or broken brother, will be touched by you—more accurately, by the Christ within you; *and* when he comes to life in the other, Jesus will come to light for you, at long last a real person more alive even than you—the source of your joy.

This kind of Advent is not easy. Like any mother in labor, you will cry and gasp and pray, have to push and sweat and bleed. Like Marguerite, you may verge at times on despair, wondering if he whom you want so much to love will ever come within the circle of your arms. Like Mary, you will need all the faith, all the hope, all the courage God alone can give if you are to rise up and go "with haste into the hill country," onto the hill where Christ is crucified each day, where a naked cross may await even you.

Rough indeed, but it's worth it if Christ comes alive for you. Otherwise Christmas is a crib, a holy day only a holly day, gifts an expensive round of "oohs" and "ahs." These I do not knock; they can be splendidly expressive of love, of joy in one another. But I shall be sad, terribly sad, if your Christmas is confined to these, defined by them; if your Christmas is not caught up in a Christ who not only was once born for you but at this instant is alive for you; if the Christmas Christ is locked away in you as in some tabernacle but is never let loose so that you jump for joy; if on December 25 Christ does not shine out for you on the faces of the crucified.

Believe me, good friends, I am not playing party pooper. Quite the opposite. You want joy that is deeper than a belly laugh? You want joy that doesn't end with a New Year's hangover, a joy that never ends? You want joy that makes your large and small crucifixions bearable? You want joy that thrills your every sense, oozes out of every pore? Then let the Christ in you come out! Not as an infant; he's grown up; he's risen from the dead, risen from all that is death, risen precisely to be your life, to infuse his life into all the life that is latent in you.

Eighteen days to Christmas. Eighteen days to shop for Christ, for a living Christ. It might be too short if you had to shop for him in Bethlehem or on Calvary, in Salvador or Somalia. The good news for shoppers is that the risen Christ has been seen in D.C. In fact, you can find him anywhere in the District, on any face, if . . . if you want to and if you have eyes to see. Happy hunting.

Dahlgren Chapel
Georgetown University
and
Holy Trinity Church
Washington, D.C.
December 7, 1986

2
EXPERIENCE THE JOY OF SALVATION
Third Sunday of Advent (C)

- Zephaniah 3:14–18
- Philippians 4:4–7
- Luke 3:10–18

Last month I had an unforgettable experience. I was standing in front of the Capitol Building in Honolulu, face to face with the striking sculpture of Father Damien of Molokai. Damien is the famous Belgian who gave all 25 years of his priestly life to lepers—the lepers of Molokai, an island in central Hawaii. To the lepers he was not only pastor but physician and counselor, housebuilder and sheriff, undertaker and gravedigger. This is the missionary who one day in 1885, four years before he died, began his sermon with two unexpected words: "We lepers. . . ."

The sculpture shows Damien with the disfigured face of the leper he had become. When some protested the ugliness of his features, the sculptress, Marisol Escobar, responded in accents that are carved into the pedestal. Working from photographs of the dying priest, what she saw in Damien, what she reproduced, was "the mystery of physical transformation—as if he had become what he wanted to become."

"As if he had become what he wanted to become." As I read and reread those startling syllables, my Advent sermon started to take shape. I saw in a rough sketch the three stages of this homily: (1) the puzzle that is Advent; (2) one clue to that puzzle; (3) the challenge this clue flings out to us.

I

First, the puzzle that is Advent. It is indeed a puzzle. For most Christians, Advent is unreal. Oh yes, we professionals do our best to make it real. Rome authorizes four special Sundays; liturgists organize a month of scriptural readings; parish committees fashion Advent wreaths and candles; angelic choirs implore the clouds to "rain down the Just One." And still the season is strange. Not only because many of us are like cats on a hot tin roof: frantic last-minute shopping; the great grade rush; Christmas cards for all who remembered me last year. The season is strange because we are supposed to be waiting, preparing—in Luke's lovely phrase, "on tiptoe of expectation" (Lk 3:15 NEB).

But what are we waiting for? Whom are we expecting? The answer, you say, is simple: We're waiting for Christmas; we're expecting Jesus. But isn't this naive, a form of make-believe? Jesus is here.[1] He lives, first, in all the world. He is everywhere, in every nook and cranny of his universe. He *has* to be, because he is God the Son. Wherever you look—the sky above you, the earth beneath you, the air about you—wherever your eye falls, he is there. Not indeed with his physical body. He *is* everywhere because he is *active* everywhere, because without him the sun could not shine nor the snowflake fall; without him the grass could not grow nor the seas surge; without him the skylark could not sing, the panther prowl, the shad ascend the rivers.

Jesus lives, secondly, in this church building, in the tabernacle. True, I do not see him as Mary did, bundled in straw. I do not reach for him as Peter did, walking on the waters. I do not speak to him as Dismas did, bleeding on the wood. I do not grasp him as Magdalene did, risen from the rock. I do not see the smile part his lips, the tears moisten his eyes; I do not hear the music of his voice, trace his wounds with my finger. But I know he is there, body and blood, soul and divinity. A hidden Christ, yes; for he hides his face from me. But he is there . . . as truly as you and I are here.

Jesus lives, thirdly, within you. Within you at that sacred moment when the Christ you offer in the Calvary of the Mass cradles within your firm fingers, nestles on your trembling tongue, rests deep inside you. Within you each and every moment, waking or sleeping, as long as you love him, as long as you have faith in his Last Supper promise: "If you love me, my Father will love you, and we will come to you and make our home with you" (cf. Jn 14:23).

Jesus is here. He lives in this enormous universe and in a tiny tabernacle, in your body and in your soul. If on Christmas Day, when angels herald his birth, you do not find him here—in your world and your church, in your flesh and your spirit—do not look for him in the crib. You will not find him there.

II

But if Jesus is so thrillingly here, can we still be waiting for him, preparing for his coming, on tiptoe of expectation? Yes indeed! My second point suggests a clue to the Advent puzzle. You may have missed it a quarter hour ago; it was hidden in the opening prayer of today's liturgy: "Lord God, may we, your people, who look forward to the birthday of Christ, experience the joy of salvation. . . . " Experience it. The heart of Advent is a single word: experience.

You know as well as I how living experience differs from abstract knowledge, from book learning, from simply hearing about something, talking about it, looking on from the sidelines. I preach about marriage—eloquently, enthusiastically; but only you who live it can feel what marriage is, swirl in its currents and drown in its depths, actually touch its heavens and its hells. It's one thing to watch Redskin Riggins burst off tackle; it's quite another thing to hit that line yourself. If I want to sell you on Oysters Rockefeller or Veal Piccata, I don't hand you a recipe; I let you smell it, taste it, savor it. If you are to grasp the horrors of the Holocaust, it's not enough to read "six million were exterminated"; you must see the gas ovens, the mountains of human bones. To appreciate Handel's *Messiah*, the score is not enough; you have to drink it in with your ears. Naked knowledge is not unimportant, but it's only a beginning. You know best when you are one with what you know: with the things of God, with the people of God, with God Himself. You know best when you love.

And so it is with Advent, so it is with the Lord Jesus. It is one thing to know intellectually, to be convinced, to believe that Jesus is in the general area—hidden in a Host or "hanging out" in Healy Circle; that he may even be inside you, closer to you than you are to yourself. It is quite another thing to be aware of his presence, feel it, sense it, thrill to it, shiver with it. I take it that most of you have been in love, perhaps still are. Do you remember the early days, that unbelievable first day? Didn't you tremble in the presence of "the other"? At that initial lovers' touch, didn't you go slightly or thoroughly mad, forget who you were and where you were, lose some of that iron self-control we rational animals prize so highly?

This is what Advent hopes to accomplish: to take Jesus out of the catechism, out of theology, out of the tabernacle, and have him touch you, have you touch him. He is indeed here, all around you, deep inside you; but that is simply not enough. He did not take your skin, walk your dust, die your death so that you might know him like a chemical formula, a historical event, a dogma to be memorized, a creed to be recited after the homily. He became all that you are, hid the glory that was his as God, that you might experience him somewhat as you experience the man or woman dearest to you in all the world—with understanding and passion, with laughter and tears, with anxiety when he seems far from you, with delight when he shows his face again.

That, my friends, is Christmas, whatever the day: when Christ is born for you. Not as a baby cuddled in straw, but as a living, throbbing God-man, the risen Christ, held lovingly in your mind and heart. And this is Advent, whatever the season: when you strain and sweat to make a living Christ come alive, when you mirror the maiden in the Old Testament Song of Songs:

> I sought him whom my soul loves;
> I sought him, but found him not;
> I called him, but he gave no answer.
> I will rise now and go about the city,
>   in the streets and in the squares;
> I will seek him whom my soul loves.
>   (Cant 3:1–2)

This is Advent: actively waiting, intensely preparing, on tiptoe of expectation, to experience the joy that is Jesus.

III

All of which leads into my third point. If one clue to the Advent puzzle is experience—experience of a living Christ—what concrete challenge does this fling out to us? This brings us back to our beginning, the statue in front of the Capitol building in Honolulu, the sculpture of Father Damien—Damien as leper. I mean in particular the words carved into the pedestal: "as if he had become what he wanted to become." And what was that? A leper with lepers; Christ as Christ looked on Molokai, the Suffering Servant of Isaiah: "He had no form or comeliness that we should look at him, and no beauty that we should desire him" (Isa 53:2).

If your Christmas is to be an experience of Christ, you must first answer honestly a tough Advent question: What do you want to become? Not primarily, what profession: doctor or lawyer, banker or broker, priest or politician? No, the crucial Advent question is: Over and above your workaday vocation, at the very depths of your personhood, precisely as a man or woman baptized into Christ, what do you want to become? Only you can answer the factual question; you are the world's supreme authority on what in fact you want to become. I can do no more than suggest what you *should* want to become.

Very simply, you should want what Damien wanted. Oh, not to become a leper; God rarely calls a man or woman to that. And even becoming a leper was, for Damien, not top priority, not the be-all and end-all of his mission on Molokai. Leprosy was a means to an end. Leprosy made it easier for him to identify with his flock, easier to become brother to the leprous Christs he touched 24 hours a day.

What Damien wanted above all to become was what St. Paul preached to the Galatians: "My little children, with whom I am again in travail until Christ be formed in you" (Gal 4:19). Here each of us confronts a critical Christian question: Do you want, more than anything else in creation, do you want Christ to be formed in you? Do you want to become Christ?

This is not pious poetry, Jesuit twaddle. When I say "become Christ," I do not mean: Get yourself born in a stable, grow up in a hick town, sell your Toyota for a pair of sandals, teach from a hilltop and heal all manner of malady, end your days on a criminal's cross. This is sheer physical resemblance. To become Christ today, in your world, means to mirror his way of looking, his way of loving, his way of laughing.

His way of looking: "Blessed are the poor in spirit and the pure in heart; blessed are the meek and the merciful; blessed are they who thirst for righteousness and make peace" (cf. Mt 5:3–9). His way of loving: "Love one another as I have loved you" (Jn 15:12)— a love without condition or restriction, for the just and the unjust, the likable and the unlovable, color and race be damned—ready to die for each of them. His way of laughing: a joy in living, in being alive, in sharing the very life of God; constantly discovering life as he did, in a glance or a touch, in sailing clouds or waving wheat, in the newborn and the careworn, even in a garden called Gethsem-ane.

Good friends: If your Advent or your Christian existence calls for some adrenalin, I prescribe Escobar's statue of Damien. You need not fly to Honolulu. I've discovered, to my embarrassment, that a replica stands several miles from here: in the National Statuary Hall on the House side of the U.S. Capitol. Fix your eyes on that face, not so much disfigured as transformed. Then lower your gaze to the base, and mull over "the mystery of physical transformation—as if he had become what he wanted to become." Keep yearning for this—to become Christ, to look and love and laugh the way he did—keep struggling for this, and your Advent will turn remarkably real. Keep struggling for this, and one day Advent will turn into Christmas: You will "experience the joy of salvation." Experience it. He will show his face to you. At that moment you will discover why the Christ who became you is the Christ you want to become.

Dahlgren Chapel
Georgetown University
and
Holy Trinity Church
Washington, D.C.
December 15, 1985

LENT

3
WHERE SIN INCREASED, GRACE ABOUNDED ALL THE MORE
First Sunday of Lent (A)

- Genesis 2:7–9; 3:1–7
- Romans 5:12–19
- Matthew 4:1–11

Our Christian vocabulary contains a fair number of *three*-letter words: lie and cry and die; awe and law and war; vow and bow and (now) Dow. But the Lent we are entering reminds me that one three-letter word threatens to disappear from contemporary Christian dictionaries. The word and its problems were confronted courageously back in 1973—not by a fire-and-brimstone preacher but by a calm, cool, collected psychiatrist. That year Karl Menninger produced a heady volume with the unexpected title *Whatever Became of Sin?*[1] Despite the scorn of the early 70s, despite skepticism within his profession, Dr. Menninger was not afraid to speak of sin, did not even hesitate to quote from the First Letter of John: "If we say we have no sin, we deceive ourselves, and the truth is not in us" (1 Jn 1:8). So, at the risk of distressing your digestion, let me lead into Lent by speaking of sin. For unless we speak of sin, we shall not speak sensibly of Easter, of resurrection, of Jesus Christ—even of ourselves.

But what is a Christian scenario for sin? I mean a scenario that weds intelligence and faith. I am not concerned to scare you out of hell, or even to "scare the hell" out of you. I simply want you to see sin for what it is, for what it does; and I want to do it in such style that you will opt joyously for sin's opposite: opt for love, for life, for Christ. Three stages to my quest, three questions: (1) What is this three-letter word all about? (2) What does it have to do with the Christ of Lent? (3) What should it say to today's Christian, in Lent and beyond?

19

I

First, what *is* this thing called "sin"? What is it all about? More expressive than any catechism definition is the Genesis story of the first man, the first woman, and the first sin. It is expressive because it reveals that sin is not a recent phenomenon, was not invented in Rome, was not first carved on my sensitive psyche by a guilt-ridden Sister Mary Ignatius.[2] Sin goes back to the beginning of the human drama. Somewhere in the distant past, a man and a woman shaped to God's own image, the most wondrous work of God's creative hand, turned their backs on their creator. The way Genesis describes it, they ate of the tree of which God had commanded the man "You shall not eat of it" (Gen 3:17).

Whether you see a real red apple in Eden or some sort of symbol doesn't ultimately matter. What matters more is how God's people, under God's guidance, came to understand sin. Sin was rebellion. From one individual's sin to a whole nation's sin, to sin was to rebel, to revolt, to disobey. It meant that a creature said no to its Lord. David, adulterous murderer, finally realized that he had not only profaned the rights of a husband, of Uriah: "I have sinned against *the Lord*" (2 Sam 12:13). And for the nation, for Israel, to sin meant to rupture a covenant, to play the prostitute, to prove unfaithful to a God who had wed the people to Him. Listen to Hosea:

> Rejoice not, O Israel, . . .
> for you have played the harlot,
>   forsaking your God.
> You have loved a harlot's hire
> [the pay of the sacred prostitute]. . . .
> (Hos 9:1)

Listen to the Lord in Jeremiah:

> You [Judah] have played the harlot with many lovers;
>   and would you return to me? . . .
> By the waysides you have sat awaiting lovers
>   like an Arab in the wilderness.
> You have polluted the land
>   with your vile harlotry.
> (Jer 3:1–2)

This, as God's chosen people saw it, this is what sin basically is; this is what sin at bottom does. It ruptures a relationship, intimacy with the God who fashioned you out of nothing—fashioned you out of love alone.

The Gospels are no different. For John's Jesus, sin is separation—separation from God. It means you are no longer a son or daughter of the Father; you are a slave—enslaved to Satan. In John's Gospel, sin has a frightful face: I no longer love God. All this is what Luke's parable of the Prodigal Son portrays so powerfully. To sin, as the prodigal sinned, is not primarily to waste a father's wealth; to fornicate, as the prodigal fornicated, is not simply to violate a biblical commandment. To sin, as the prodigal sinned, is to break a bond. Listen to the poignant confession of the prodigal: "Father, I have sinned against heaven and before you; I am no longer worthy to be called your son" (Lk 15:21).[3]

I am not saying that when we sin we rebel against God face to face. Only rarely does any one of us say to God in so many words: "I no longer love you; in fact, I hate you. I just don't care to be your daughter or your son. I have other gods I prefer to you." Much more frequently we say this silently when we say no to God's images, to our sisters and brothers. Most sins reflect the sin of Cain, who invited his brother Abel into a field, "rose up . . . and killed him" (Gen 4:8). Most sin is "man's inhumanity to man." Most sin, most of our rebellion against God, happens when two world wars take uncounted millions of lives; when Christians shed Christian blood in Christian Belfast; when bombs redden the streets of Beirut; when blacks are second-class citizens whether in Pretoria or D.C.; when a billion humans bed down hungry each night while millions grow fat in their shadow; when uncounted innocents perish in uncounted wombs. Most sin takes place because we do not love our neighbor nearly as much as we love ourselves.

II

Which brings me to my second question: What has all this to do with the Christ of Lent? It may help to go back to St. Paul. You see, Paul was profoundly aware of a "sin" that is almost a personal force. It indeed entered the world through one man's rebellion, Adam's act of disobedience. But it is more than a single act. It is an evil force, a malevolent power that tyrannizes every man and woman born to earth. It is a power hostile to God, a power that alienates us from God. Its works are sinful deeds. Because of it, he confesses for all of us, "I do not do the good I want, but the evil I do not want" (Rom 7:19). It is Sin with a capital S.

But Paul was profoundly aware of a still more powerful reality. He proclaimed it in deathless syllables to the Christians of Rome: " . . . as by one man's disobedience the many were made sinners, so by one man's obedience the many will be made righteous. . . . Where sin increased, grace abounded all the more . . . through Jesus Christ our Lord" (Rom 5:19–21). Through Jesus Christ our Lord. That phrase sums up what you read in the Gospel of John: "God so loved the world that He gave His only Son, that whoever believes in him should not perish but have eternal life" (Jn 3:16).

Lent makes sense only because in Lent we relive a love that has no rival, the love that is more powerful than sin—more powerful than the Sin that dominated human history from the very first rebellion in Eden, more powerful than the countless sins that deface God's image each day on earth. You see, only the God whom sin defies could possibly destroy sin, destroy the death that stems from sin. So what did God do? Send an angel announcing to the world "Sin is dead and your sins are forgiven"? No. God sent His very own Son. And not simply *sent* His Son. His Son was born as we are—born of a Jewish teen-ager pregnant with him nine months. That alone would have been enough to break sin's power. But it was not enough for God. In the divine scenario, God's Son-in-flesh lived as we live, grew as we grow, ate as we eat, got tired and slept as we sleep, sweated as we sweat, laughed our laughter and cried our tears. That alone would have been enough to break Satan's hold. But it was not enough for God. Unbelievably, God had determined to conquer sin on a cross. Pinned to crossed beams, God's own Son would bleed out his life and die like a criminal.

Oh yes, he would rise again. But the man Jesus knew this only by faith. He could not have proved it, even to himself. He had indeed raised the dead—a widow's only son, the small daughter of Jairus, his friend Lazarus—but he had never been dead himself. That is why he sweated blood in Gethsemane, cried out to his Father: "If it be possible, don't let me die!" (cf. Lk 22:42).

Such is the love we relive in Lent: a God-man freely enduring a cruel crucifixion for a world that had sinned against him, was still sinning, would never quite stop sinning. St. Paul himself was amazed, found it hard to credit: "Why, one will hardly die for a righteous man [or woman]—though perhaps for a good man [or woman] one will dare even to die. But God shows His love for us in that while we were yet sinners Christ died for us" (Rom 5:7–8). For us. Not for some misty mass called humanity. For Adam and Eve, for Mary his mother and Mary of Magdala, for John who rested on his breast and Judas who sold him for silver, for Mother Teresa and Ayatollah Khomeini—for each of you and for me. If in Lent I dwell on that alone, fix solely on blood for which like Cain I am responsible, I will be tempted to despair with Cain: "My punishment is greater than I can bear" (Gen 4:13). But if in Lent I lift my eyes to the love that led Christ to the cross, if with Paul I never forget that the Son of God "gave himself for me" because "he loved me" (Gal 2:20), I shall break out in unconfined joy: "What return shall I make to the Lord for all the good He has given me?" (Ps 116:12).

III

And that, good friends, summons up my third question: What should all this say to today's Christian, in Lent and beyond? The problem is this: Though Jesus has destroyed the tyranny of sin, he has not destroyed our ability to sin. Though sin no longer enslaves us, we are still tempted to sin, we are still free to sin, we still sin. What return shall we make to the Lord? Why, it's obvious: Don't sin! But, true as this is, it's dreadfully abstract. How bring it down to earth, down to the earth we walk each day?

Unexpectedly, one concrete answer leaps out of today's Gospel, out of Jesus "led up by the Spirit into the wilderness" (Mt 4:1). Like Israel, 40 years in the wilderness, Jesus, the new Israel, is tempted—tempted when he is weak from 40 days of fasting, tempted to betray his mission. All three temptations are temptations to power. You're hungry? Well then, change these stones into bread! You want the people to pay attention to you? Well then, soar like a bird from the top of the temple and let the angels enfold you! You want to rule over the world? Well then, just worship me and you've got it made!

No, Jesus responds, you've got it all wrong; your way is not my way. It is not bread that gives life; it is my word. It is not by circus spectacles that I reveal myself; look for me among the lowly, the powerless, the crucified. It is not by political power that my kingdom will come; to use worldly power is to worship false gods.

You know, when Matthew wrote of Jesus' temptations, it was his own Christian community he had in mind.[4] Here is a ceaseless temptation for the Church, for the Christian: to use the world's power to win the world. Christians have tried it with the Inquisition and the Crusades, with the wars of religion and with ghettos for Jews. We try it in more modern ways when the Ku Klux Klan put the fear not of God but of man into blacks and Catholics; when unchristian comic strips slander the beliefs of other Christians; when some insist that this is a Christian country (the implication: All others are second-class citizens). The examples are legion, too many to detail; but they all point to a fundamental fact we forget: The kingdom of God is won by love. And that love, at its best, is a crucified love.

For the 40 days of Lent, then, and beyond those 40 days, let a crucial Christian challenge characterize your daily living. Rather than setting your eyes on sin, rather than focusing on the fear that our sinfulness can foment, why not shake loose the love in you, the love that is stronger than sin, the love that "casts out fear" (1 Jn 4:18)? Not a vague or insipid love, not a sentimental or teenybopper love. I mean the kind of love that carried Christ to a cross. I mean a love that can turn the other cheek (at least at times); a love that does not sulk until apology arrives on bended knee; a love that keeps marriage alive through stress and sickness, through dark nights and infidelity; a love that goes out to those who are different from you in race or face, goes out to the homeless and the loveless, to the gross and the grimy, to all who ail from acne to AIDS. I mean the love that, in St. Paul's paean, "is patient and kind, is not jealous or boastful, is not arrogant or rude, does not insist on its own way, is not irritable or resentful, does not rejoice at wrong but [only] in the right, bears all things, believes all things, hopes all things, endures all things" (1 Cor 13:4–7).

Such, my friends, is the Lent that leads to Easter, the crucifixion that ends in resurrection, the dying that is Christian living. In the wake of such love, sin runs a distant second—always a threat because of ourselves we are woefully weak, but never a tyrant because in Christ we are strikingly strong. So then, let not your Lent be simply a physical fasting, an exercise in slimming, John the Baptist's answer to Jane Fonda. Rather, let your Lent be large in loving, in the kind of love that can crucify, that did crucify. I promise you, it will take a lot of weight off you: the weight of sin, the weight of guilt.

> The First Church in Tulsa
> The United Presbyterian Church in the U.S.A.
>   and
> University of Tulsa
> Tulsa, Okla.
> March 4, 1987
>   also
> Dahlgren Chapel
> Georgetown University
>   and
> Holy Trinity Church
> Washington, D.C.
> March 8, 1987

4
IF YOU KNEW THE GIFT OF GOD
Third Sunday of Lent (A)

- Exodus 17:3–7
- Romans 5:1–2, 5–8
- John 4:5–42

Today's Gospel could easily deceive you. You see, it has all the makings of a TV docudrama: two attractive characters, a life-and-death confrontation, a happy resolution. As always, the neon lights spell Jesus. But the actor who steals the show is a woman—a leading lady with five husbands and no name. She comes out of nowhere, and in two days she disappears. But without her—as without Mary of Nazareth and Mary of Magdala—without this nameless woman of Samaria the Gospel of Jesus Christ would be much the poorer.

But how might this Gospel deceive you? If you were to bury the lady in history, see in her a two-day phenomenon in a small Middle East village. No. A perceptive female theologian has put it well: "We all love a good story because . . . in a sense *any* story is about ourselves, and a *good* story is good precisely because somehow it rings true to human life. . . . We recognize our pilgrimage from here to there in a good story."[1] The Samaritan woman is . . . you. Each one of you.

Today I am thinking especially of the "elect" and "candidates" here: those of you who are begging the Lord for his baptism, and those who are craving the completeness of his Christian community. Each of you has a story like hers. Oh, not five husbands; that is a small detail, intriguing perhaps but insignificant. Her story is your story because her story is the drama of faith in a capsule: how you came to believe, what it all means to you, and where it is taking you. I realize, only you can tell the full story, recount chapter and verse; there I am uncommonly ignorant. But this I do know: what your movement to Christian faith means in terms of the Catholic idea,

26

the Catholic vision. Here three paramount principles leap forth from the paradigm that is the Samaritan woman. (1) The gift you have received is "the gift of God" (Jn 4:10). (2) The gift you have received is "living water." (3) The gift is given to be shared.

I

First, the gift you have received is "the gift of God." How do you come to believe, to accept a crucified Jew as your Lord and Savior, to adopt a way of thinking and living and worshiping that contradicts the culture that encircles you? Not because your native intelligence is 4.0 and rising. Not because you've worked out for yourself the "sweet mystery of life" and, like ancient Archimedes, cried out in rapture "Eureka! *I* have found it!" No, not by a long shot. Go back to the city Sychar; walk with the woman to Jacob's well. As always in the drama of faith, it is the Lord who takes the initiative: "Give me a drink" (Jn 4:7). He speaks, and the first act opens. *He* speaks. Not because she was living a high moral life; she was not. Not because she had a Brite smile, a sparkling personality, Mrs. Samaria; that cuts no ice with Yahweh. The Lord takes the first step, and He takes the first step not because we are who we are but because He is who He is: a God whose very name is Love. He takes the first step because, as Jesus declared to his disciples, apart from him "you can do nothing" (Jn 15:5).

Such is the drama of faith as far back as we can reach in history. For a Lenten pick-me-up, read the Letter to the Hebrews, the upbeat chapter 11 on the heroes of the Old Testament, what they were able to accomplish purely and simply "by faith." It was by faith that Abel offered a sacrifice more acceptable than Cain. It was by faith that Noah shaped his saving ark. It was by faith that Abraham left country and kin for a vast unknown, offered his only son in sacrifice. It was by faith that senescent Sarah found power to conceive. It was by faith that Moses confronted Pharaoh, led the Israelites out of bondage through the Red Sea. In each instance it was God who called. Not for any merit of theirs; God calls because He wants to call, and each call is His love.

The same holds true for the New Covenant, struck in the blood of Christ. Oh yes, the actual ways in which God calls are beyond numbering, all but infinite in variety. Augustine hears a voice from a nearby house, "Take and read"; he snatches up his book of Scripture, opens it at random, reads from Romans: "not in reveling and drunkenness, not in debauchery and licentiousness, not in quarreling and jealousy; but put on the Lord Jesus Christ, and make no provision for the flesh, to gratify its desires" (Rom 13:13–14). And Augustine tells us: "I had no wish to read further, and no need. For in that instant, with the very ending of the sentence, it was as though a light of utter confidence shone in all my heart, and all the darkness of uncertainty vanished away."[2] Anglican John Henry Newman plunges deep into the early Church to find the fulness of Christ, and concludes: "The Fathers [of the Church] made me Catholic." Edith Stein loses her Jewish faith as a young girl; she searches for the truth through phenomenology under its masters, Husserl and Scheler, and still she doubts; she reads the autobiography of St. Teresa of Avila and writes therein with exclamatory conviction "This is the truth!" A Georgetown student in love with Dahlgren Chapel asks me to baptize her. Curious, I question her: "How did it happen that you decided you wanted to be baptized?" Her response, very simply: "Because you were so human."

Each of you has your own story. But however diverse the details, one reality abides unchanged, unchallenged—the words of Jesus in John: "No one can come to me unless the Father who sent me draws him/her" (Jn 6:44). Not "compels"; simply "draws"—draws us, in Augustine's fine insight, by the cords of love. Of course, you had to respond—and freely. Like the lady at the well, you had to ask for water. But even this, the ability to ask, to ask in freedom, this too is a gift. Only through God's gracious giving were you able to respond: "Sir, give me this water, that I may not thirst" (Jn 4:15).

II

So much for my first point: The drama that is faith begins with God. The First Letter of John is clear, unequivocal: "In this is love, not that we loved God but that He loved us" (1 Jn 4:10). Which summons up my second point: What concretely is this "gift of God" proffered to the Samaritan woman, promised to you? It is not some filmy, fragile "faith" that embarrasses you in debate with a slick unbeliever. Oh yes, it is wrapped in mystery, so mysterious that God-in-flesh was forced into a metaphor: living water. "Whoever drinks of the water that I shall give him/her will never thirst; the water that I shall give him/her will become in him/her a spring of water welling up to eternal life" (Jn 4:14). But the metaphor does not obscure, does not conceal; it casts a brilliant light on God's gift to you.[3]

Disappoint you it may, but the living water is not baptism, not the flowing, pulsing stream into which many an early believer was plunged. In John's theology two wondrous ideas are wed together in this single metaphor: Living water is at once revelation and the Spirit—and both we owe to the Son of God in our flesh.

Living water is the revelation Jesus gave us. It reminds us of Yahweh inviting His dear people to listen, so that their souls might live: "All you who thirst, come to the waters" (Isa 55:1; cf. v. 3). For all the ages that have thirsted or will thirst for a word from above, the opening sentence of the Letter to the Hebrews sums it up simply and magnificently: "In many and various ways God spoke of old to our fathers by the prophets; but in these last days He has spoken to us by a Son" (Heb 1:1–2). This Son told us secrets unsuspected about God and about the mirror of God that is you. He told us about the secret life of God, where Father, Son, and Spirit live alone without ever being lonely. He told of a God who, uncompelled, clothed His only Son in our flesh, pinned him to a criminal's cross for a world that had said no to His love. He told of a food that would be his flesh, a drink that would be his blood. He told of a unique community that would prolong His presence till time gives way to eternity. He told of a new life, his life in us, a life that gathers up all that is best in our flesh and spirit and transforms it into an image of the Crucified and Risen. He told of seven symbolic acts that would channel divine life to us from our first breath to our last. He told us that this life-in-Christ will not end in dust, will find its perfection in the endless embrace of the God who can no longer live without us.

Thrilling indeed, this living water that is God speaking; for God's word is a life-giving word. But, for Jesus, living water is not simply talk; it is a divine Person. Living water is the Holy Spirit. On this the Gospel of John leaves no doubt. Recall Jesus' remarkable outburst in Jerusalem: "On the last day of the feast [Tabernacles], the great day, Jesus stood up and proclaimed: 'If anyone thirst, let him/her come to me and drink. He/she who believes in me, as the Scripture has said, "Out of his/her heart shall flow rivers of living water." ' Now this [John adds] he said about the Spirit, which those who believed in him were to receive . . . " (Jn 7:37–39).

Think of it! Marvel at it! What happens to you when you believe, when you commit to Christ all you are and have, all you will for ever be? God's own Spirit dwells in you. You are as truly a sacred shrine as is the tabernacle in front of you. No need to moon and moan over what you lack: the vocal chords of Tina Turner or the muscles of Arnold Schwarzenegger, the wit of William Buckley or the wisdom of Mother Teresa, the income of Lee Iacocca, the grace of Tiffany Chin, the name and fame of Abdul Jabbar. You are the new creature God made you to be: a temple of God, a shrine of the Spirit. Indeed, living water wells up in you to eternal life.

III

All well and good: It is God who gives you living water, and the living water is God's revealing word and God's sanctifying Spirit. Excellent exegesis, top-flight theology, highly orthodox and deeply consoling. But a critical question remains: Where should the exegesis and the theology take you—those of you who have professed Catholic faith for decades and those of you who will profess it the evening before Easter? It should take you where the dialogue with Jesus took the Samaritan woman. She "left her water jar," rushed excitedly back to center city, cried out to all and sundry: "Come, see a man who told me all that I ever did. Can this be the Christ?" (Jn 4:28–29). She played the apostle. I mean, she shared with others her own experience of Jesus, urged them to see for themselves. They did. They brought him back with them to Sychar, kept him for two whole days, heard his word from his own lips. The result? "They said to the woman: 'It is no longer because of your words that we believe; for we have heard for ourselves, and we know that this is indeed the Savior of the world' " (v. 42).

So too for you. Not yours to clutch in hot little hands a private pitcher of living water. God's gift—His Son speaking to you and His Spirit dwelling in you—is given you to be given, to be shared. Unless I'm terribly mistaken (possible, I suppose), it was not a vision or a dream that drew you elect and candidates to the well where Jesus was sitting. Most adults are attracted to the community called Catholic because they have experienced its power, sensed its strength, uncovered its saving grace *in others*. They touched Catholic faith, Catholic hope, Catholic love not so much propounded in abstract propositions as lived by pulsing men and women—Christians who do indeed love God above all else, love others as much as they love themselves.

And so for you. Share the gift! Let the living water spill over! Not primarily by preaching, sermonizing; not buttonholing an unwary victim and deluging him or her with a diarrhea of words. Your Catholicism is not in the first instance a philosophy; it is a complete way of life. How can it be otherwise if God's word is your way and

God's Spirit is your life? It is this incredibly new creature that confronts contemporary culture—what sociologists call "economic man, economic woman"—trumpets to it through deeds that *numero uno* is not I but the other: the Other with a capital O, the other with a small o.

Dear elect and candidates, you have been privileged beyond my poor words to describe; for you are sitting with Jesus at the well. It is an enticing temptation to sit there for ever, alone with Jesus—the other disciples foraging for food, this world's Samaritans locked in the city. But you dare not. Part of today's Gospel is an urgent, insistent summons from the Master to his disciples: "I tell you, lift up your eyes, and see how the fields are already white for harvest" (v. 35). Catholic Christians old and new: When you leave the well, when you leave this cherished chapel, lift up your eyes! Lift your eyes from the risen Christ; lift them to the crucified Christian.

Dahlgren Chapel
Georgetown University
February 23, 1986[4]

5
CAN THESE BONES LIVE?
Fifth Sunday of Lent (A)

- Ezekiel 37:12–14
- Romans 8:8–11
- John 11:1–45

Part and parcel of our every day are pairs of monosyllables: love and hate, laugh and weep, war and peace, work and play, run and rest, sleep and wake . . . even hoops and hops. But one pair of monosyllables is perhaps the most crucial of all—always with us, but brought to tragic turns today by fresh fears: fear of being nuked and fear of the Big C, the reign of terrorism and the plague of AIDS. I mean . . . life and death.

It is on this pair of monosyllables that today's liturgy of Lent focuses. Not only will you consume the Bread of life, the antidote to death. Each reading takes up the theme—each in a different way, each with urgent meaning for your existence and mine. The readings are a marvelous movement from Ezekiel to Paul to John, from Jerusalem to our world to the next, from the past to the present into the future. A word on each.

I

The movement opens with the prophet Ezekiel.[1] Now the snippet from Ezekiel, like most passages out of context, can be more confusing than enlightening. "You shall know that I am the Lord, when I open your graves, and raise you from your graves, O my people" (Ezek 37:13). Sounds like a promise of resurrection, doesn't it? It is indeed resurrection, but not from physical death. The context is exile. In 597 B.C., when Ezekiel was about 26, Jerusalem was assaulted and conquered by Babylonian King Nebuchadrezzar. The

32

city survived, but many of its leading families and citizens were deported to Babylon. Among the exiles was Ezekiel. Educated for service as a priest, he found himself in a foreign land, where there was no temple of his faith.

In this context, Ezekiel's prophecy has two startling stages. Through the early years of exile, the Jews in Babylon were still hopeful that Jerusalem and its temple would survive. Ezekiel refused to feed that hope; his task was to bury it. Jerusalem, he prophesies, will not survive; it will be destroyed, and its destruction will be God's judgment on a people that has played the harlot in infidelity to its God. The message did little to cheer his fellow exiles. One large hope made exile endurable: a homeland to which they might one day return. In 586 B.C. the city and its temple were destroyed.

From that point, when the exiles had lost all natural hope, Ezekiel's role was reversed. No longer did he preach "doom to a people who lived on hollow hopes"; he "now preached hope to a people who felt they were doomed."[2] Here is where our snippet fits in. The Jews in Babylon speak of themselves as dead: "Our bones are dried up, and hope is lost . . . " (Ezek 37:11). But God commands Ezekiel to prophesy: "Behold, I will . . . raise you from your graves, O my people; and I will bring you home into the land of Israel. . . . And I will put my Spirit within you, and you shall live, and I will place you in your own land; then you shall know that I, the Lord, have spoken, and I have done it . . . " (37:12, 14).

Once the exiles repent of their infidelities, once they recognize that sheerly human hope is hopeless, once they despair of what they can do by their naked selves, God will give them a new Spirit, His own Spirit, will give them new life, life in a Jerusalem restored, in a temple rebuilt. From death will come life. They will experience once again God's presence among His people in their own dear land.

II

From Ezekiel the readings move to Paul, from ancient Jerusalem to our world, from the past to the present. Again we hear of death and life, of dying and rising. Not the death of exile and hopelessness; not life in a restored Jerusalem.[3] Dead are "those who are in the flesh" (Rom 8:8), who "live according to the flesh," who "set their minds on the things of the flesh" (v. 5). Oh, not "flesh" in its obvious sense: We are all "in the flesh"; each of us is shaped of sinew and skin, of bone and blood. For Paul, "flesh" has a special meaning. It denotes man and woman in their "natural, physical, and visible existence, weak and earthbound . . . ; it connotes the natural human creature left to" its native self.[4]

If you want that abstraction brought out of the clouds, listen to Paul as he spells it out concretely for the Christians of Galatia: "Now the works of the flesh are plain: immorality, impurity, licentious-ness, idolatry, sorcery, enmity, strife, jealousy, anger, selfishness, dissension, party strife, envy, drunkenness, carousing, and the like" (Gal 5:19–21). There are indeed other works of the flesh ("and the like"); Paul is not fashioning a full-blown textbook of morality. But the works he does list should trigger your thinking and mine. What, if any, are the works that sever *me* from God, darken the image of Christ in *me?*

But if this is what it means to be dead, who are alive? In Paul, even more than in Ezekiel, alive are those who are "in the Spirit," in whom "the Spirit of God really dwells" (Rom 8:9). Too vague for you? How do you know that this gossamer "Spirit of God" actually lives in you, acts in you, moves you? Again Paul spells it out, not only for ancient Asia Minor but for contemporary America. You can be reasonably sure you are alive, you can be confident that God is at work within you, if the fruits of the Spirit shine out from you. Paul lists nine (cf. Gal 5:22–23).

You are alive if your life is shaped of *love:* if your life is centered not on yourself but on a whole little world around you. You are alive if *joy* suffuses your whole self—a joy that lends joy to all you touch. You are alive if you are at *peace*—at peace with yourself, at peace with your sisters and brothers. You are alive if you are *patient:* if you can take the slings and arrows of each day with a measure of calm, with a minimum of complaint. You are alive if you are *kind,* not only to your own kind but to such as bore you to tears. You are alive if you are *generous*—not only liberal in giving, a free spender and not a free-loader, but free from meanness in mind, from smallness of spirit. You are alive if you are *faithful:* if you are full of faith in God and your fellows, if you inspire faith and trust in others. You are alive if you are *gentle:* if you are caring, courteous, considerate. You are alive if you are in *control*—not of others but of yourself, master of whatever passions make you less human, less a mirror of the Christ in whose image you were molded.

This it is to be alive in the Spirit, fully alive. Does it sound im-possible to you? It *is* impossible—to you. The glorious thing about life in the Spirit is that it is a gift. It is the Spirit who brings you to life, if . . . if only you *want* to come alive, if only you ask for it with all your heart: "Come, Holy Spirit, fill the hearts of us your faithful; enkindle in us the fire of your love." Here is the dying/rising of these 40 days: dying to the deeds of death you can do all by your lonesome, rising to a kind of life you can scarcely imagine. Now!

III

From Paul the readings move majestically to John, from our world to the next, from the present into the future. The movement is of high significance. For through the centuries that have fled, pseudo prophets of all sorts have told us it doesn't really matter for Christians whether life ends with death—even whether Christ himself rose from the dead or simply corrupted in the "tomb where no one had ever been laid" (Jn 19:41). The big thing is: Live now!

Hogwash! I'm not against living now; I do a fair amount of it myself, freed up for it by the Spirit and three challenging vows. But the "good news," the Christian gospel, is not simply that we are alive now; the good news is that we are destined to be alive for ever. The Gospel of Lazarus tells us in story what Paul proclaimed to the Christians of Corinth: "If Christ has not been raised, your faith is futile and you are still in your sins. Then those also who have fallen asleep in Christ have perished. If for this life alone we have had hope in Christ, we are of all men and women most to be pitied. *But in fact* Christ has been raised from the dead, the first fruits of those who have fallen asleep" (1 Cor 15:17–19).

Tell me: Do you really think the Son of God would have borrowed our flesh, preached a kingdom not of this world, and died brutally between two thieves so that we might live 90 days or 90 years? The story of salvation from Eden to Calvary and beyond makes sense only if you take literally the verse in the Evangelist John that Luther called "the gospel in miniature": "God so loved the world that He gave His only Son, that whoever believes in him should not perish but have eternal life" (Jn 3:16).

Let me be extraordinarily frank with you. I would not have become a priest, I would not have remained a priest these 45 years, I would certainly not have vowed myself to a celibate existence for life, if I suspected there is really no resurrection of the dead. As I have insisted in one immortal line, if heaven is not for real, I shall be madder than hell.

Of course I am ordained to help make this world more human,

a fit place for every man, woman, and child. Of course I want to dry your tears and quiet your fears, lend you a compassionate ear and a strong shoulder. But I am not a social worker, not a therapist. My task, my privilege, my joy is to preach a risen Christ, to lay in your minds and on your palms a living Lord, to promise you who love God "what no eye has seen, nor ear heard, nor the heart of man or woman conceived" (1 Cor 2:9), the thrilling promise of Christ the night before he died: "Because I live, you also will live" (Jn 14:19).

That promise spans your entire life. It began when water bathed your brow and the Lord Jesus made you not merely members of an earthbound community but heirs of heaven. It is repeated Sunday after Sunday, day after day, when your flesh and spirit are electrified not with bare symbols but with the bread of immortality, the bread of which Jesus said in the synagogue at Capernaum: "This is the bread which came down from heaven, not such as [your] fathers ate and died; he who eats this bread will live for ever" (Jn 6:58). The promise courses through your very veins at this very moment, the pledge of days without end: "If [you] love me," Jesus assured you, "my Father will love [you], and we will come to [you] and make our home with [you]" (Jn 14:23). Today's grace is your pledge of tomorrow's glory.

Good friends: Ezekiel, Paul, and John guarantee us in different ways that God can make dry bones spring to life. But, like Lent itself, they remind us that rising involves dying. Now dying is not limited to the end of our earthly existence, to the terminal cancer, the cardiac arrest. Dying in a theological sense begins when living begins; we share in Jesus' dying by sharing his cross through the whole of our lives. Whatever makes for pain—pain of flesh or of spirit—should be part and parcel of our Christian dying. Diverticula or disappointments, schizophrenia or the wrenching of my heart, dying hopes or the death of a dear one, the insecurities of youth and the trembling of the aging—whatever it is that pricks my pride, assails my lustiness, intimates my mortality, takes the joy from my very bones:

> In all these brief moments of [what theologian Karl Rahner called] dying in installments we are faced with the question of how we are to cope with them: whether we merely protest, merely despair (even for brief moments), become cynical and cling all the more desperately to what has not yet been taken from us, *or* whether we abandon with resignation what is taken from us, accept twilight as promise of an eternal Christmas full of light, regard slight breakdowns as events of grace. . . .[5]

You do not need a theologian to inform you that the cross is erected over your world. You spy it every day—from Northern Ireland to South Africa, from Lebanon to Afghanistan, in the slums of your cities and over countless hospital beds, on your own streets, in your own homes, along your corridors, in every heart that cries mutely for bread or justice or love. I see it in the Georgetown graduate student who flung himself from St. Mary's Hall last Monday and, if he lives, will be a paraplegic.

My sisters and brothers in Christ: Lent, the cross, Easter—all tell you graphically that the Christian choice is not between dying and living. The paschal mystery, the salvation story of Christ *and* the Christian, is an incredible duality: dying/living, dying/rising. A paradox indeed, but not a contradiction. It was not by refusing to die that Jesus triumphed over death; it was in his very dying that he gave us new life—his life—now and for ever.

So, too, for you. I cannot promise you a rose garden—only a mysterious wedding of Eden and Gethsemane. Each of you lives, or will live, in the shadow of a cross, perhaps be ruthlessly pinned to it. You may well sweat blood like Jesus, cry out with him to the Father: "Dear God, don't let me die!" (cf. Lk 22:42). Whatever the cross, don't run from it; simply ask the Christ of Calvary to carry it with you. For it is in dying—not only to sin but to yourself, not only to selfish ambitions but to green hopes that have turned to ashes, not only to money and power and fame but to your own plans for human and Godlike living—it is in dying to yourself that you come to life in Christ.

The greatest paradox of all? It will be rough—rough as death— but you will never have known so ecstatic a joy—the joy Jesus promised no man or woman can take from you (Jn 16:22).

Dahlgren Chapel
Georgetown University
and
Holy Trinity Church
Washington, D.C.
April 5, 1987

EASTER

6
ALIVE TO GOD IN CHRIST JESUS
Easter Vigil (C)

- Romans 6:3–11
- Luke 24:1–12

The story of salvation is sprinkled with momentous moments. There was the moment, lost in history, when a God who needed no one shaped a man and a woman in His own image. There was the moment, captured in the Old Testament, when God chose for Himself a special people through whom "all the families of the earth [would] be blessed" (Gen 12:3). There was the midnight when the heavens opened and the very Son of the living God took our bone and blood from a Jewish girl. There was the dark afternoon when God-in-flesh "uttered a loud cry and breathed his last" (Mk 15:37).

But marvelous as all these were—creation and covenant, crib and cross—they pale in comparison with this blessed night. Oh indeed, without them this night would never have been. And still, they are preludes,[1] acts in a divine drama that reaches its climax now. "He is not here; he has been raised" (Lk 24:6). Those slender monosyllables summon us to sheer worship; but they also are so pregnant with meaning that they call for prayerful reflection. A reflection with three questions: (1) What is the Easter faith that Luke's Gospel proclaims? (2) What is the Easter message that 20 centuries of Christian tradition have drawn from the Gospel? (3) What might this blessed night say to you now? Briefly, the Gospel, the Church, and you.

I

First, the Gospel. What is the Easter faith Luke proclaims? In essence, it is surprisingly simple: Our Lord is alive; "he has been raised." But to make those words come alive, to sense their significance for your Christian living, you have to contemplate them in context, replace them within Luke's fine story. In that story women play a remarkable role.

You see, a number of women—we know not how many—had followed Jesus from Galilee, followed him to Golgotha. They had "stood at a distance, looking on" (Lk 23:49). They had seen him pinned to a cross between two criminals; had seen their leaders, Roman soldiers, one of the criminals mocking him; had seen the sunlight fail and darkness cover the land from 12 to three. They had heard him utter a loud cry: "Father, into your hands I entrust my spirit" (23:46). They had seen him breathe his last, seen their Lord and loved one die.

These women were different from "the crowds" (23:48). Both groups, Luke tells us, were looking. But in Luke's vocabulary, in his choice of words, there is a profound difference. The crowds were simply looking at a spectacle, the last hours of a mystery man dying a cruel death. The women—Mary Magdalene, Joanna the wife of Herod's steward, Susanna, many others—the women were witnesses—an important word in Luke's theology. The women were not just looking. Their role was to bear witness; this afternoon on Calvary would be part and parcel of their testimony to Christ.[2]

But the women's witness did not end when the head of Jesus slumped in death. They returned to Calvary on the first day of the week, "at the crack of dawn" (Lk 24:1), as soon as Jewish law allowed. They came with spices and ointments for his battered body. Imagine their amazement, their perplexity: Jesus' body is no longer there! Suddenly two men (Luke will later call them "angels") stand by them, startle them, utter two sentences that have changed the face of the earth: "Why do you look for the living among the dead? He is not here, but has been raised" (vv. 5–6). The men jog the women's memories: "Remember what he told you . . . : [he] must . . . be crucified, and rise again on the third day" (vv. 6–7). The women remember. Remembering, they rush from the rock, back to "the Eleven and all the others" (v. 8). They keep repeating to the apostles what they have seen and heard; but the apostles treat their story "as humbug, so much nonsense" (v. 11), refuse to believe them. Oh yes,

Peter sprints to the tomb; he too finds it empty; but unlike the women, he returns not believing, only "wondering" (v. 12).

The point is, these women are witnesses. They bear witness, not now to a dead Christ, not only to an empty tomb. They bear witness to a Christ who is alive. Not because they have seen him; only because his word has come through to them, has touched their hearts, compels them to proclaim to one and all "He's alive!"

II

So far, my friends, a new song of angels to women, "He has been raised." It rounds out the song of an angel to shepherds, "A Savior is born to you" (Lk 2:11). But that Easter proclamation, what message have 20 centuries of Christian tradition drawn therefrom? What does the empty grave add to the Christ-filled cave? St. Paul put it pungently to the Christians of Corinth: "If Christ has not been raised, then our preaching is in vain, . . . your faith is futile, and you are still in your sins" (1 Cor 15:14, 17). What our faith professes is a truth as thrilling as it is profound, a twin truth Jesus summed up at the Last Supper: "Because I live, you will live also" (Jn 14:19).

"Because I live. . . . " Across the centuries Christians have had to struggle against all sorts of efforts to water down the Easter gospel—and the end is not yet. We are told that Jesus is indeed alive, but only in our unforgettable memories, or as a living example, or as a timeless inspiration, a powerful reminder of what our flawed humanity can be at its best. True, but not true enough. To be a Christian, you must take Luke literally: "He has been raised." That unique morning, the tomb was empty for one reason alone: Jesus had returned to the glorious presence of his heavenly Father.[3] Not simply as eternal Son of God, but in the full richness of the humanity he took from Mary. The Jesus who had died in agony on Friday was alive again on Sunday—as alive as Lazarus emerging from his tomb and rubbing his eyes against the sunlight, as alive as Jairus' little daughter and the widow's sole son sitting up at Jesus' command.

Would you have recognized him? Not right off, not with the naked eye. After all, Mary Magdalene, who had eyes for Jesus alone, saw him and mistook him for the gardener. Two disciples walked miles with him between Jerusalem and Emmaus, talked hours with him, and thought him a stranger. To recognize the risen Jesus, you would have needed a special grace—as when Jesus murmured to Magdalene "Mary," or broke bread with Cleopas and his friend at Emmaus. And still, for all the mystery of this new Jesus, at once seated with his Father in glory and moving magically through the barriers of our earth, he is the same Jesus who was fashioned from a teen-ager's flesh, the same Jesus who walked our dust and waked our dead, the same Jesus who hung three hours between two robbers, the same Jesus who, Scripture proclaims, "always lives to make intercession for [us]" (Heb 7:25). Without *so* risen a Christ, without *so* living a Lord, Christianity is a sham and a scam.

"I live." Indeed he does. But that is only half the Christian story. "Because I live, you will live also." The paschal mystery, the dying/rising of Jesus, is not simply something that happened one long weekend in the Middle East, a spectacle we mourn and admire. In Paul's pithy phrasing, he "was put to death for our trespasses and raised for. our justification" (Rom 4:25). Today's reading from Romans puts it tersely in the context of life: "The death [Christ] died he died to sin, once for all, but the life he lives he lives to God. So you also must consider yourselves dead to sin and alive to God in Christ Jesus" (Rom 6:10–11).

"Alive to God in Christ Jesus." Only this makes sense of Calvary's wood and the rock of resurrection. That is why water is poured over you, the Holy Spirit poured into you: that you might become Paul's "new creature" (2 Cor 5:17), transformed into the likeness of your risen Lord, alive with the very life of the God-man, believing what you cannot see, hoping against human hope, loving as Jesus loved. That is why oil anoints your forehead—in the shape, significantly, of a cross—the power of the Spirit to live that life with the courage of Christ, to live for God and your sisters and brothers even unto crucifixion. Such is the reason for reconciliation: Should you lose God's life, the risen Christ stands ready to restore it. "I'm sorry, Lord." "And I, dear child, I forgive you." To feed that life—"Give us this day our daily bread"—the Lord of life gives you the Bread of life; for "unless you eat [my] flesh and drink [my] blood, you have no life in you" (Jn 6:53). To pass that life on to another generation, you stand hand in hand before an altar, and husband gives to wife, wife to husband, the wedding gift of grace—a measure more of God's own life. And as the shadows lengthen, and evening comes, and the busy world is hushed, and the fever of life is over, and your work is done, priestly hands anoint the senses that have imperiled that life, to ease your passage, not from life to death, but from life with God in restless time to life with God in endless ecstasy. "Because I live, you will live also."

III

This breathless Christian tradition compels my third question: What might this blessed night say to you now? One answer brings us back full circle to Luke's Gospel. You see, to be "alive to God in Christ Jesus" is not a private party. Once they believed on good authority that Jesus was alive, Joanna and Susanna, Magdalene and the other women did not reserve a banquet room for themselves at the Sheraton Jerusalem with lots of lox and liters of Manischewitz. They hurried back to tell "the Eleven and all the others" (Lk 24:9). They became "apostles" themselves, sent by angels to spread the good news, to share the glad tidings, to bear witness that the Lord Jesus had not only died but had been raised to life again.

And so for you—those newly born in baptism and those grown old in our faith. Baptism is indeed a breath-taking personal gift. Any action that with one swoop of God's hand washes away your every sin, adopts you as God's daughter or son, enrols you in Christ's community, and grants you on earth a title to heaven is something to treasure. But not to clutch stingily to your own Christian skin. Baptism sends you out on mission, commissions you to bear witness, to testify to a whole little world around you that is looking for the living among the dead: "He is not here."

As risen Christians, your life should bear witness that the risen Christ is not in a resurgent rugged individualism, not in economic man or woman in pursuit of private self-interest: Get to the well first before it dries up, look out for *numero uno,* and the devil take the hindmost.[4] He is with "the poor in spirit, for theirs is the kingdom of heaven" (Mt 5:3). Your life should testify that Christ has not rented a condo in TV's "Dallas," that J.R. is not J.C.; it is "the merciful" who are blessed, "those who hunger and thirst for righteousness" (Mt 5:6–7). Your way of living should proclaim that in a culture that canonizes youth and beauty, activity and productivity, power and sexual prowess, the aging too can be "alive to God in Christ Jesus," those who suffer in spirit or flesh, those Paul calls "foolish in the world . . . weak in the world . . . low and despised in the world . . . so that no human being might boast in the presence of God" (1 Cor 1:27–29).

The examples are legion, but time is pressing. Let me leave you with my most recent experience of Easter, of the risen Christ. There I was, last month, sitting restlessly in the office of the Division of Gastroenterology at Georgetown University Hospital, waiting for the nurse to prep me for a feared colonoscopy. And there in front of me, perhaps 12 feet away, sat a little black lady. She must have been all of 80, with no teeth but the most entrancing smile this side of the beatific vision. The smile simply lit up the little room. A few moments went by, and I could no longer restrain myself. "Excuse me," I said. "Do you always smile like that?" She said she did. "But," said I from the deep gloom of my diverticula, "how can you?" Her response I shall never forget. "Ah lives every hour. Some of them are sad . . . but even so, ah lives every hour."

My Easter prayer for each of you risen Christians: Live every hour . . . *every* hour. Live it "to God in Christ Jesus."

Dahlgren Chapel
Georgetown University
March 29, 1986

7

IF YOU HAD LOOKED INTO HIS EYES
Third Sunday of Easter (A)

- Acts 2:14, 22–28
- 1 Peter 1:17–21
- Luke 24:13–35

My homily today is on a verb. A single verb. Why? Because today's Gospel reveals one of the most thrilling, one of the most valuable, verbs in our Christian vocabulary. It is this verb I want to talk about this afternoon. The verb is "recognize." Luke tells us: Two disciples "recognized" the risen Jesus (Lk 24:31). I shall (1) begin with Luke's story, (2) broaden it out to the wider Christian story, and (3) end with a startling story from our own times.

I

First, Luke's story. You have to recapture its rich reality; otherwise it's just another cute story. Get your imagination going. It's a Sunday in old Jerusalem. Not a normal Sunday—Jerusalem is still buzzing about the three criminals crucified the Friday before. Two were undistinguished, hardly worth talking about; but one had been unique. Three years ago he had suddenly appeared out of nowhere—a nowhere named Nazareth; gathered a group of devoted disciples around him; played fast and loose with the Sabbath; worked marvels over blind and deaf, over dead and lame; said he was God's Son in a special sense; taught with an authority no rabbi would have claimed; loved to "hang out" with sinners; dared to attack the rich and the powerful; preached a kingdom "out of this world"; even looked as if he just might rescue God's people from the tyranny of Rome. He was loved by many, hated by some; was accused of crimes civil and religious; refused to defend himself; was

47

condemned to die; ended his earthbound existence in shameful agony on a hill outside the city—not much different in death from the two criminals hanging near his right hand and near his left.

On that Sunday still abuzz about Friday, two of his followers were returning home.[1] Home was Emmaus, a small town about seven miles from Jerusalem. They were disciples whose deepest hopes had been dashed: "We *had* hoped that he was the one to deliver Israel" (Lk 24:21), free it from Roman occupation. So, when a perfect stranger "drew near and began to walk with them" (v. 15), he could see that they were terribly sad. Even when he gave them a cram course in the whole of the Old Testament, even after they discovered that "the Messiah had to suffer all this before entering into his glory" (v. 26), even though their "hearts burned within" them while he "opened the Scriptures" to them (v. 32), they still did not "recognize" him (cf. v. 16). They knew only a brilliant young Jew who gave new meaning to their old books.

Surely the best thing Cleopas and companion ever did was to invite Jesus to "stay with" them, "because it is almost evening, and the day is already far spent" (v. 29). For it was then that he supped with them. "He took the bread, blessed it, broke it, and gave it to them. Then their eyes were opened and they recognized him" (vv. 30–31).

Why didn't they recognize him earlier on, while he was lecturing so brilliantly on biblical theology? Because the risen Jesus was at once the same old Jesus and yet different. The same, because he was still Jesus born of Mary and crucified on Calvary. Different, because the body they now saw was not quite the body they had seen. Well then, what *did* it look like? What kept the two travelers from instantly shouting "Master"? Why did Mary Magdalene think he was the gardener, beg him: "Sir, if you have carried him away, tell me where you have laid him . . . " (Jn 20:15)? Why did the seven disciples out fishing not know that the man calling from the beach was Jesus (Jn 21:4)? How could he pass through the stone-sealed door of the tomb, pass through the shut doors of the disciples' room?

I do not know what the body of Jesus looked like on the first Easter. But this I do know: To recognize the risen Jesus, even his dearest friends needed a God-given gift, a special grace, a beginning of faith. They needed an invitation from the Lord; the initiative had to come from him—as when he murmured to Magdalene "Mary" (Jn 20:16), told the seven where the fish were biting, broke bread in a way that spoke to the hearts of the two disheartened disciples. Only then could they respond; only then could Magdalene say "Teacher" (Jn 20:16), John cry to Peter "It's the Lord!" (Jn 21:7), Cleopas and companion know him "in the breaking of the bread" (Lk 24:35).

II

This leads naturally into my second point: I want to broaden Luke's story out to the wider Christian story. To recognize Jesus is not an act that is open to a neutral or hostile observer.[2] You don't recognize Jesus because you are smart, own a 4.0 or an M.B.A., have a keen eye for the true, the beautiful, and the good.

How, then, *do* you recognize him? Clearly, you recognize him, as the Emmaus disciples did, "in the breaking of the bread."[3] But a few billion folk do not. Why not? I dare not conjecture, for each human heart in its relation to the God-man is a mystery all its own. Judgment I leave to the Judge. But this much I do dare to say. To recognize Jesus as the risen One, as the God-man, you need (1) an invitation from Jesus that comes in all sorts of unexpected packages, and (2) a response that is at once God's gift and your own free yes.

It is a wonderful thing, at times a fearful thing, to encounter the living God. I never cease to be amazed at the different forms it has taken in history. Anti-Christian Saul recognized the Lord when he fell to the ground and heard the shocking words "I am Jesus, whom you are persecuting" (Acts 9:5). Augustine, torn terribly in two, recognized Jesus finally in a Milanese garden, when "a voice from some nearby house" urged him to "Take and read," and he opened the New Testament to read from Romans: "Put on the Lord Jesus Christ, and make no provision for the flesh, to gratify its desires" (Rom 13:14).[4] Novelist Flannery O'Connor relates why a relative was attracted to the Church: "the sermons were so horrible, he knew there must be something else there to make the people come."[5] That remarkable saint of the homeless and hopeless Dorothy Day, long a Communist, long Godless, recognized God and His Christ slowly and painfully, at strange turns in her road. Reading philosopher William James, she fell in love with St. Teresa of Avila. Seeing friends kneeling to pray, she was convinced that "worship, adoration, thanksgiving, supplication" are "the noblest acts" of which we are capable. Looking on her newborn child, she "felt that only faith in Christ" could give this new Teresa a way of life. The only solution to "the long loneliness," she discovered, lay in love, and "love comes with community."[6] Several years ago, a Georgetown student asked me to baptize her. When I asked what had moved her to recognize Christ in his Church, she mentioned two influences: the love of the Dahlgren Chapel community and her experience (humbling to me) that your homilist had been so human.

Each of you has come to recognize the risen Lord; each of you has your own story. But however different your stories, one fact is common to all of you, is beyond dispute: You would not be here if the risen Christ had not taken the initiative, had not somehow, somewhere, sometime shown his face to you. That is why you could recognize him when his word was proclaimed to you; that is why you will recognize him when his body nestles in your palm and his blood moistens your lips.

III

So much for Luke's story; so much for the wider Christian story. One more story remains to be told, to round out our recognition of the risen Christ. One version of the story goes like this:

> One day a young fugitive, trying to hide himself from the enemy, entered a small village. The people were kind to him and offered him a place to stay. But when the soldiers who sought the fugitive asked where he was hiding, everyone became very fearful. The soldiers threatened to burn the village and kill every man in it unless the young man were handed over to them before dawn. The people went to the minister and asked him what to do. The minister, torn between handing over the boy to the enemy or having his people killed, withdrew to his room and read his Bible, hoping to find an answer before dawn. After many hours, in the early morning his eyes fell on these words: "It is better that one man dies than that the whole people be lost."
>
> Then the minister closed the Bible, called the soldiers and told them where the boy was hidden. And after the soldiers led the fugitive away to be killed, there was a feast in the village because the minister had saved the lives of the people. But the minister did not celebrate. Overcome with a deep sadness, he remained in his room. That night an angel came to him and asked: "What have you done?" He said: "I handed over the fugitive to the enemy." Then the angel said: "But don't you know that you have handed over the Messiah?" "How could I know?" the minister replied anxiously. Then the angel said: "If, instead of reading your Bible, you had visited this young man just once and looked into his eyes, you would have known."[7]

If you had looked into his eyes. . . . The novelist and creative apologist C. S. Lewis once gave a sermon titled "The Weight of Glory." He concluded: "Next to the Blessed Sacrament itself, your neighbor is the holiest object presented to your senses. If he is your Christian neighbor, he is holy in almost the same way, for in him Christ . . . Glory Himself, is truly hidden."[8] When you receive Christ in Communion, you will indeed recognize him—but you will not see him. You may remember Thomas Aquinas' "Hymn to the Blessed Sacrament," his poetic prostration before "Godhead here in hiding." In Gerard Manley Hopkins' graceful version, part of it runs like this:

> Seeing, touching, tasting are in thee deceived;
> How says trusty hearing? that shall be believed:
> What God's Son has told me, take for truth I do;
> Truth himself speaks truly or there's nothing true.

> On the cross thy godhead made no sign to men;
> Here thy very manhood steals from human ken:
> Both are my confession, both are my belief,
> And I pray the prayer of the dying thief.

> I am not like Thomas, wounds I cannot see,
> But can plainly call thee Lord and God as he:
> This faith each day deeper be my holding of,
> Daily make me harder hope and dearer love.[9]

In the Eucharist you do not actually see the risen Christ, glorified wounds and all. But like Cleopas and companion, in this modern Emmaus you recognize him; for he has opened the eyes not of your flesh but of your faith. In the power of that faith you can exclaim with the apostle Thomas "My Lord and my God!" (Jn 20:28). In like manner, in your own journeying, you will meet thousands of women and men. The Christian question is not, what will you see with the eyes of your flesh? The Christian question is, what will you recognize with the eyes of your faith? Will it be "Godhead here in hiding"? Or will seeing keep you from recognizing? Will the grime and the grit blind you, AIDS or Alzheimer's, the ugly and the spiteful, the color and the smell—all those very human things that make for difference and indifference, for hostility and hatred?

It's terribly important, you know. Why? Because it is when you recognize your own risen Lord—not only in the broken Bread but in the breaking heart—it is then that Easter dawns for you in all its realism. It is then that you too rise to a fresh and glorious life. Not after death—now! It is then that your hearts too will burn within you—not only when the Scriptures are proclaimed, not only when common bread becomes the body of Christ, but also when you recognize the risen Christ in every creature shaped of a spirit that is willing and a flesh that is weak.

Please, my friends, don't let a single day end when an angel or anyone else has to say to you: "If you had only looked into his eyes, if you had only looked into her eyes. . . . "

Dahlgren Chapel
Georgetown University
and
Holy Trinity Church
Washington, D.C.
May 3, 1987

8

CHRISTIAN SHEEP?
Fourth Sunday of Easter (C)

- Acts 13:14, 43–52
- Revelation 7:9, 14–17
- John 10:27–30

Perhaps I'm nearsighted, but whenever the Sunday Gospel focuses on shepherd and sheep, few of your eyes light up. Here is one of the most enduring of Christian images, the Good Shepherd who lives for his sheep and lays down his life for them, and we yawn or pick our noses. Without turning a homily into a lecture, let me ask three questions. (1) What is it that has kept the shepherd image alive through the Christian ages? (2) Why doesn't this age-old image turn us on? (3) How might this image make contemporary Christian sense, speak to people who have never seen a shepherd, who see sheep only on Christmas cards?

I

First, what is it that has kept the shepherd image alive through the Christian ages? More than anything else, the role it plays in God's own Book. In the Old Testament, Yahweh is Israel's shepherd, leading His people "like a flock" (Ps 80:1). We all know and sing Psalm 23:

> The Lord is my shepherd, I shall not want.
>   He makes me lie down in green pastures.
> He leads me beside still waters;
>   He restores my soul [my life].
>
> (Ps 23:1–3)

53

But Yahweh's shepherding was not sheer poetry; it was embedded in Hebrew history. A dying Jacob spoke of "the God who has shepherded me all my life long to this day" (Gen 48:15). When His people were enslaved in Egypt, the Lord "led" them from exile like a shepherd, "guided them in the wilderness" (Ps 78:52). When Jerusalem was laid waste and thousands of Jews were deported to Babylonia, the Lord promised through the mouth of Ezekiel: "I myself will be the shepherd of my sheep. . . . I will seek the lost, and I will bring back the strayed, and I will bind up the crippled, and I will strengthen the weak . . . ; I will feed them in justice" (Ezek 34:15–16). And this He did: He gathered "the remnant of Israel," set them together "like sheep in a fold" (Mic 2:12), restored Israel "to his pasture" (Jer 50:19). The straying He turned back with compassion, "as a shepherd his flock" (Sir 18:13); but those shepherds, the kings, who fed themselves and not the sheep (Ezek 34), those who exploited the sheep and deserted the flock (Zech 11:15–17), He threatened with His wrath.

In the New Testament, it is Jesus who is pre-eminently shepherd. He sees himself "sent to the lost sheep of the house of Israel" (Mt 15:24), sent by the Father to give the kingdom to his "little flock" (Lk 12:32). In his death he sees the prophecy of Zechariah fulfilled: "I will strike the shepherd, and the sheep will be scattered" (Mk 14:27; cf. Zech 13:7). He is "the good shepherd" who "lays down his life for the sheep" (Jn 10:11).

In the New Testament, too, the community's leaders are seen as shepherds. The risen Jesus commissions Peter to "tend" his sheep, to "feed" them (Jn 21:16, 17). The First Epistle of Peter exhorts church officials: "Tend the flock of God that is your charge, not by constraint but willingly, not for shameful gain but eagerly, not as domineering over those in your charge but being examples to the flock. And when the chief Shepherd is manifested, you will obtain the unfading crown of glory" (1 Pet 5:2–4). Paul urges the "presbyters" of the Church in Ephesus: "Take heed to yourselves and to all the flock, in which the Holy Spirit has made you guardians, to feed the Church of the Lord which he obtained with his own blood" (Acts 20:28). To shepherd the flock of God is to walk in the footsteps of Christ. And those steps are not shaped of glory, they are steeped in blood.

II

No doubt about it, shepherd and sheep stud the pages of Scripture. Which compels my second question: Why doesn't this inspired image turn us on? One answer: our American experience. Shepherds do not loom large in our Eastern existence, and in the West they look more like cowboys. Oh yes, TV resurrects them at Christmas, "keeping watch over their flock by night" (Lk 2:8), racing to Bethlehem to see the Savior sung by angels. But come the New Year, shepherds give way to the three-piece suit, to "Dallas" and "Fantasy Island" and "Miami Vice."[1] And east of the Mississippi there are very few sheep. Not like Australia—8½ sheep for every person; or New Zealand—20.7 for every person.

More importantly, sheep is a symbol that gives off bad vibes. Sheep are mute creatures, save for an occasional baa. Remember the Suffering Servant in Isaiah? "Like a sheep that before its shearers is dumb, so he opened not his mouth" (Isa 53:7). Sheep do what they're told to do; they don't lead, they follow. If they haven't enough sense to follow, a sheep dog will keep them in line. The dictionary calls you a sheep if you are "meek and submissive."

In consequence, sheep is not our favorite image for Christians. We are not dumb animals, we are creatures of reason and freedom and speech. We do not mind following, but we do not care to be led by the nose. We have a healthy respect for authority, but we do not want the sheep dogs yapping and snapping at our heels. And to some Christians with unfortunate experience, the bishop's crosier, in the shape of a shepherd's crook, recalls only the original purpose of the crook: to catch the back leg of a straying sheep.

The point of these remarks? I am not surprised that shepherds and sheep fail to light up your eyes. Symbols do not exist in a vacuum; they symbolize or not, they "grab" you or turn you off, in a real-life context. For the Papuans of New Guinea, it is not the lamb of our Scriptures that is a sacred animal; it is a pig. Women nurse pigs at their breast if no sow is around. For economic reasons: Without the pig, life would be hard to sustain. For the Hebrews, the pig was a scavenger. Remember the parable of the Prodigal? What was the low point, the hopeless stage, of his humiliation? He was feeding pigs. The most wonderful thing a Papuan can do is to feed pigs. To communicate to Papuans what "lamb of God" meant among the Hebrews, what "lamb of God" means to the religious tradition of the West, I would have to say "Christ is the pig of God."[2]

III

So then, the symbol of shepherd and sheep is enshrined for ever in our Scriptures, but it rarely moves us the way it moved the men and women of Israel, the way it moved our early Christian ancestors. In consequence, my third question: How might this inspired image make contemporary Christian sense, speak to people who have never seen a shepherd, who see sheep only on Christmas cards?

I have one strong suggestion, but I must preface it with a stern warning. Don't surrender the symbols of Scripture too swiftly. You see, God has revealed Himself to us, disclosed to us who He is and what we are to be, not primarily through clear, catechetical propositions: "God is three persons," "Jesus is both human and divine," "Marriage is a sacrament of the New Law." No, God has spoken to us most often through symbols. I mean signs I can sense, signs I can see or hear or touch or taste or smell. A special kind of sign. Signs that work mysteriously on my consciousness, signs that suggest more than they can clearly define or describe, signs pregnant with a depth of meaning that is evoked rather than explicitly stated. It might be an artifact: a temple, a crucifix, the bronze serpent Moses raised in the wilderness. It might be a person or an event: Moses leading the Israelites out of Egypt, Christ crucified and risen. It might be a story: the parable of the Prodigal Son.[3]

This is the primary way God speaks to us; such are the special sounds of Scripture. Not a classroom lecture, with Cartesian clarity. Somewhat as painting and poetry, sculpture and architecture, music and dancing, stage and screen speak to us. I mean da Vinci and John Donne, the Vietnam Memorial and Chartres Cathedral, Simon and Garfunkel's "Bridge over Troubled Waters" and Tchaikovsky's *Swan Lake*, Eugene O'Neill's *Long Day's Journey into Night* and Ingmar Bergman's *Virgin Spring*. Each has its own language, too rich to be imprisoned in a single sentence.

So it is with today's symbol—shepherd and sheep. Don't shrug it off because there are no sheep on Healy Lawn or Wisconsin Avenue, in Flatbush or Gary, Indiana. God is still trying to tell you something. The problem indeed remains: How do you hear God's voice from an alien culture? How can you make contemporary sense out of it? I say, take the image out of Palestine. Stir it briskly like a bland yogurt, to get at the fruit on the bottom. Work it over, and let it work on you. For the moment, listen to one homilist's effort, through sweat and tears, through much mulling over Scripture and long looking into the signs of our times.

For me, the shepherd without peer is the Good Shepherd, the Jesus who took our flesh and still wears it before his Father. Oh yes, others are called shepherds—bishops and pastors, counselors and kings. But they are shepherds only in the measure that they resemble him. And why is shepherd so seemly for Jesus? In a word, because he *cares*. Dear God, how he cares! The only Son of the living God could have left us to our hellbent sinfulness. But no. He borrowed our skin, grew in it as we grow, sweated in it as we sweat, faced Satan in it and Judas the way we must, bloodied that skin in an act of love unique in history. And not only for reasonably respectable folk like you and me! He found his supreme joy when he left the 99 docile sheep to search for the single sheep that had strayed. And what does he do when he finds it? Curse it roundly, beat it with the shepherd's staff? No, "he lays it on his shoulders, rejoicing. And when he comes home, he calls together his friends and his neighbors, saying to them: 'Rejoice with me, for I have found my sheep which was lost' " (Lk 15:5–6). *My* sheep.

More than that, this shepherd who cares loves *all* his flock. Not in a shapeless mass. Not like the character who confessed "I love humanity; it's people I can't stand." Jesus cares for you as a unique person, unrepeatable, shaped for ever in his image and likeness, destined to live his life, to live with him, not simply today but days without end. As Jesus himself put it, "he calls his own sheep by name" (Jn 10:3), somewhat as Palestinian shepherds have pet names for favorite sheep, "Long-ears," "White-nose," and so on.[4] "I know my sheep" (v. 14). He knows you more intimately than you know yourself. He knows what makes you tick, what turns you on or off and why. He knows how thrilling and how tough it is to be a creature of flesh and blood, of matter and spirit, of intelligence and freedom; he suffered it himself, joyed in it. And no matter how far you stray from him, he never stops loving you, will ceaselessly search for you, track you down; and when he finds you, please God, you will let him cradle you once again in his arms.

Most astonishing of all, this shepherd who cares for you died for you. Not only for Adam and Eve, for Mary of Nazareth and Mary of Magdala, for Father Damien and Mother Teresa. For you, as if no one else existed on Calvary save you. No need for words of mine; let Calvary, Calvary-for-you, sear your soul, fire your flesh.

Which brings us from the model shepherd to us sheepish

sheep. I admit, to see yourself as following like sheep can bring the bile to your throat, make you gag. But only if woolly sheep make you woolly-headed. Only if you forget whom you are following, and how. This is not a Hitler or a Qaddafi; this is Love enfleshed, Love that gave life itself for you, Love that at this moment is a living prayer for you before the Father. To follow him is not mute slavery, mindless submission. To follow him is the most human, the most sensible thing you can do; for to follow him is to return his love— that love which is actually Jesus' only hold over you, the only bonds with which he draws you.

But to follow Jesus is not for the fragile, the timid, the self-centered. To return his love is to love as he loved: intelligently and passionately, freely and with every fiber of your being. To love as he loved is to care as he cared: not for a misty mass called humanity, but for every sister and brother who crosses your path; not simply those you like and who like you, but those you dislike on sight, those who have no socially redeeming qualities, the weirdos, those who live and think and even sin differently from you. More than anything else, to love as he loved is to care for the sheep that limp: those who hunger for bread or justice or love; those who have no pillow for their head, no shoulder for their troubled heart; those who are imprisoned behind bars or within their tortured selves.

Good friends, I hope with all my heart that the Jesus whom the First Epistle of Peter calls "the shepherd of your souls" (1 Pet 2:25) will spark you with fresh enthusiasm for an inspired image. But in the last analysis, the image is not all-important; you can pass St. Peter's portals in total ignorance of it; you can refuse to be called sheep. What you dare not refuse is to *follow* your shepherd. To be Christian, you must dare to care, let yourself love, open your arms wide to a whole little world that is desperate for your compassion. Do that, and when the Good Shepherd finally calls you by name, you won't have to look . . . sheepish.

> Dahlgren Chapel
> Georgetown University
> and
> Holy Trinity Church
> Washington, D.C.
> April 20, 1986

9
SHAKE THE SPIRIT LOOSE!
Pentecost Sunday

- Acts 2:1–11
- 1 Corinthians 12:3–7, 12–13
- John 20:19–23

If you focus on today's Gospel, Pentecost means peace: "Peace be with you" (Jn 20:19, 21). Or Pentecost means pardon: "If you forgive the sins of any, they are forgiven" (v. 23). But today I want to picture Pentecost not as peace, not as pardon, but as power. To make sense of this, let me entertain you with power on three levels: power in the world, power in the Spirit, power in you.

I

First, power in the world. Power, at its simplest, is the ability to do something, to act, to accomplish. There is sheer physical power, corporeal power: You can rock and roll, jog along the canal, lift a finger or bat an eye, make music or thunder with your voice. There is mental power: You can think, shape an idea, paint pictures in your phantasm, remember (perhaps) where you were last night. There is the power that is free will: You can say yes or no.

There is political power. A Reagan can rain hell on Libya or veto a budget bill, pressure nations to act against terrorism or congressmen for aid to Angola. A Botha can keep millions of blacks voiceless, voteless, homeless, powerless, isolate them from the mainstream of South African life. The Russian Bear can chain 250,000,000 serfs to its all-powerful paw.

There is economic power. If you think it's love that makes the world go round, you've never tried money. America's day doesn't end with love-making; it ends with the Dow Jones average.

59

There is social power. The society that surrounds you can be your salvation: strengthen you when weak, inspire you when leaden, remove the dread loneliness that makes living unlivable. But society can enslave you as well. Peer pressure is beer pressure, drug pressure, sex pressure. This year Valentino will design your cocktail dress, De la Renta your bathing strings. Powerful role models seduce you from screen and music, from TV and tape: a new Madonna and a new Equalizer, J.R. and Joan Rivers, Joe Theismann and the "soaps."

There is computer power. It lifts men to the moon and teenagers into ecstasy. It flies planes and fights wars. It plumbs the planet Uranus and my inflamed ileum. It sends the world's weather to a common network and balances the checkbooks of every bank.

II

So much for power in the world. It excites and entrances me, baffles and dismays me. But more importantly, it reminds me that there is another kind of power, a power that in a sense is "out of this world," a power we bypass at our peril, a power more critical for human existence than politics and economics, society and the computer. I mean . . . power in the Spirit.

This is not pious pap; the New Testament thrills to it. How could a teen-age Jewish virgin clothe God's Son in her flesh? Listen to an angel: "The Holy Spirit will come upon you, the power of the Most High will overshadow you. Therefore the child to be born will be called holy, the Son of God" (Lk 1:35). What did the risen Jesus promise his apostles just prior to his ascension, to make their evangelizing effective? "You shall receive power when the Holy Spirit has come upon you; and you shall be my witnesses in Jerusalem and in all Judea and Samaria and to the end of the earth" (Acts 1:8). How did St. Paul preach to the people of Corinth? "I was with you in weakness and in much fear and trembling; and my speech and my message were not in plausible words of wisdom, but in demonstration of the Spirit of power, that your faith might not rest in the wisdom of men but in the power of God" (1 Cor 2:3–5). How did Paul win obedience to Christ from the Gentiles? In his own words, "by the power of the Spirit" (Rom 15:19). What was Paul's prayer for the Christians of Rome? "May the God of hope fill you with all joy and peace in believing, so that by the power of the Holy Spirit you may abound in hope" (Rom 15:13).

In all these instances the Greek word we translate as "power" is the same: the word we carry into English when we say "dynamic," "dynamism," "dynamo," "dynamite." The Holy Spirit is dynamite. Once again, thumb through your New Testament. What was the dynamo that drove Jesus across the dust of the Holy Land? Listen as he describes his mission:

> The Spirit of the Lord is upon me,
> because He has anointed me
>   to preach good news to the poor.
> He has sent me
>   to proclaim release to the captives
>   and recovering of sight to the blind,
> to set at liberty those who are oppressed.
>   (Lk 4:18)

This is the dynamo Jesus promised the apostles the night before he died: "another Counselor, to be with you for ever, the Spirit of truth. . . . He will teach you all things, bring to your remembrance all I have said to you . . . guide you into all the truth" (Jn 14:16–17; 16:13). This same Spirit the risen Jesus breathed into his disciples for the forgiveness of a whole world's sins: "Receive the Holy Spirit. If you forgive the sins of any, they are forgiven" (Jn 20:22). This is the Spirit that filled the Twelve on the very first Pentecost, when they "began to speak in other tongues" to "devout [Jews] from every nation under heaven" (Acts 2:4, 5). This Pentecost, Peter proclaimed, fulfilled the dynamic prophecy of Joel:

> And in the last days it shall be, God declares,
> that I will pour out my Spirit upon all flesh,
> and your sons and your daughters shall prophesy,
> and your young men shall see visions,
> and your old men shall dream dreams;
> yea, and on my menservants and my maidservants . . .
> I will pour out my Spirit. . . .
> And I will show wonders in the heaven above
> and signs on the earth beneath. . . .
>   (Acts 2:17–19; cf. Joel 2:28–30)

Dynamized by this Spirit, Peter and John, "uneducated, common men," preached Christ crucified and risen with "boldness" (Acts 4:13), defiant of death itself; "for we cannot but speak of what we have seen and heard" (v. 20). Dynamized by this Spirit, the apostles laughed at chains and threats, "left the presence of the council rejoicing that they were counted worthy to suffer dishonor for the Name" (Acts 5:41). In fact, the Acts of the Apostles is from beginning to end a story of the Spirit: the irrepressible power of God's presence in the apostles and their disciples, in converts Jewish and pagan, in martyrs like Stephen and persecutors like Paul.

Read Paul's letters, and the power of the Spirit takes on fresh flesh and flavor. Here is a thrilling theology of the Spirit. The Holy Spirit lives in you as in a shrine, frees you from sin and death, makes you sons and daughters of God, helps you in your weakness, intercedes for you with the Father. Only in the power of the Spirit can you believe the unbelievable, hope for the grace beyond your grasp, the glory beyond the grave, love with God's own love poured into your hearts. If you walk by the Spirit, Paul insists, you will be kind and good, grow gentle and prove faithful, experience incomparable peace, a joy the world cannot give.

III

So then, two powers: power in the world, power in the Spirit. Where do we go from here? A preacher's temptation is to "sock it" to the one and canonize the other. I shall resist that temptation. This world is not the work of the devil, though the devil works within it. For all its flaws, this is still the world God crafted, the world God gazed on in the beginning "and behold, it was very good" (Gen 1:31). Politics and economics, society and the computer are not God's natural enemies, are not the beasts of the Book of Revelation, "allowed to make war on the saints and to conquer them" (Rev 13:7), deceiving "those who dwell on earth" (v. 14). Despite all the sin that can bedevil them, they are born out of the intelligence and freedom God gave us when He commanded us to master the earth.

In this perspective your Christian task is not to sever the two powers but to link them together, unite them in a splendid harmony. This calls for a profoundly Catholic imagination. I mean the thrilling vocation which Vatican II sketched for you in its Decree on the Apostolate of the Laity:

> The redemptive work of Christ has for essential purpose the salvation of man and woman; and still it involves as well the renewal of the whole temporal order. Consequently, the Church's mission is not only to bring to men and women the message of Christ and

his grace, but also to penetrate and perfect the temporal sphere with the spirit of the gospel. In carrying out this mission of the Church, the laity therefore exercise their apostolate in the world as well as in the Church, in the temporal order as well as in the spiritual. These areas, though distinct, are so intimately linked in the single plan of God that God Himself intends, in Christ, to take up the whole world again and make of it a new creation, initially here on earth, consummately on the last day. In both areas the lay person, at once believer and citizen, should be guided ceaselessly by one and the same Christian conscience.[1]

The point is, a "Sunday Christian" is a contradiction. This liturgy is not an escape from a godless world, a private party where the "good guys" huddle together for one blessed hour of forgetfulness. The liturgy, especially this liturgy of the Holy Spirit, sends you back to the world and its powers: back to society and the computer, to politics and economics, to the countless instruments of power great and small that dynamize this universe and your acre therein. Not to despise or destroy them, but to grace them "with the spirit of the gospel." Whatever power you possess—and there is no one among you without power, without the ability to do something, to act, to accomplish—shape that power into a servant, not a tyrant. Wall Street or Congress, Children's Hospital or the Pentagon, Bread for the City or the C.I.A., law firm or lobby, Washington *Post* or NBC, wherever you are and whatever you do, make sure of one thing above all else. Make sure that your power *in* the world is a power *for* the world. Make sure that, the more powerful you are, the more you are men and women for others.

Only one way to assure this, to guarantee that power in the world will not corrupt, will not pervert your hands and the hands you are privileged to touch. Only one way: if your power in the world is shaped by your power in the Spirit; if your every thought and word and gesture reflects the presence of God within you, the presence that is a living, throbbing person, the presence that can be dynamite if you will only let it be.

The proof? Mother Teresa cradling Calcutta's children, offering to take any and every infant unwanted by the world. Father Ritter transforming Times Square into a refuge of the Spirit for thousands of youngsters scarred and scared. Bread for the World mobilizing Congress against the scourge of hunger across the earth. Hundreds of Georgetown students, Dahlgren worshipers, Trinity parishioners ministering to the homeless and the helpless, the battered in body and the seared in soul—lending the powerless the power to believe again, hope afresh, love anew.

The examples are legion, the needs endless. Right now, the need I see beneath all needs is for each of you to simply realize how powerful you are. Rediscover where and how you can make things happen—from a smile on a careworn face, through legislation for the afflicted, to peace in some corner of your world. Link your power in the world to the Power within you, the Spirit of light and of life and of love. Shake that Spirit loose! In a nutshell, let God come alive in you!

Dahlgren Chapel
Georgetown University
and
Holy Trinity Church
Washington, D.C.
May 18, 1986

ORDINARY TIME

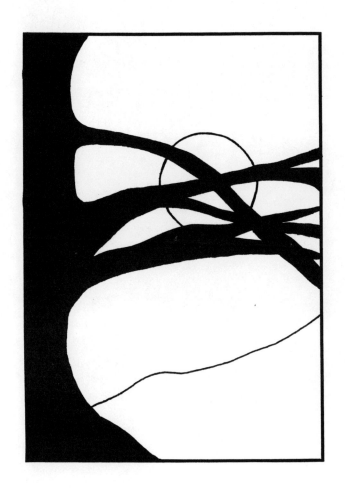

10

IS THERE LIFE AFTER CHRISTMAS?
Second Sunday of the Year (A)

- Isaiah 49:3, 5–6
- 1 Corinthians 1:1–3
- John 1:29–34

It's a funny feeling. Today we come into a house of God that is still lovely but strangely different. The crib is back in storage; the wise men have returned to the East, the shepherds to their flocks; the angels have stopped singing and the star has disappeared into D.C. gray; even the brilliant poinsettias have wilted. Instead of a Gospel about a newborn baby named Jesus, we hear about a gaunt ascetic called John. Christmas is just a memory. We are now in what the Church, ironically, calls "ordinary time." Back to the old routine, the familiar grind. Oh yes, you can cast a long, longing look ahead— to Easter, spring break, Valentine's Day; you can always thank God on Friday. Meanwhile, slug it out, hang in there—chin up, shoulder to the wheel, nose to the grindstone, ear to the ground, eye on the ball! A human pretzel.

Sorry, good friends, it will not wash. Christmas was not an end, only a beginning. Christmas was a high point, but not the highest. Christmas changed our world, but only if you let it be changed. Let me spell this out in three stages, by looking at three persons: Jesus, John, and you.

I

First, a look at Jesus. Christian though Christmas is, no Christian can live on Christmas alone. Jesus is no longer an infant. He did not stay in Bethlehem, make the crib his condo for life. He had to flee from Herod's terrorists, to escape the massacre of every male child two or under in and around Bethlehem. He spent three decades of his life, about 30 of his 33 years, where you and I would never dream of looking for him: a small town never mentioned in the Old Testament, a town about which his naive disciple-to-be Nathanael asked: "Can anything good come out of Nazareth?" (Jn 1:46). Of these three decades we know little save that the child got bigger and wiser, and was loved by God and the people of Nazareth; little save that at 12 he left his parents for three days without a word, without a note, and ever after "was obedient to them" (Lk 2:51). He gave no more than three years publicly to the people he had been born to save. Even then he descended on them not with angels, thunder, power. He began as we would never have begun: He had John baptize him like any other Jew, and the devil tempted him from his mission with bread, with pride, with riches.

He had friends among the well-to-do—Lazarus and his sisters—loved them, but he spent most of his time with those the self-righteous despised, those they called "sinners." He preached a twin message everyone could understand: Love God above all else, love your sisters and brothers as much as you love yourself. He made enemies of the powerful, because he put compassion above tradition, love above law, people above things. He claimed a relationship with the Father so intimate that the scandalized took up stones to cast at him—"for blasphemy, because you, being a man, make yourself God" (Jn 10:33).

Those three years were a journey—a journey to Jerusalem. For Jesus took our flesh from Mary not simply to say something, to tell us truths we could never have suspected about God and about ourselves. He borrowed our flesh to do something. Every word he spoke and every breath he drew, every curse that mocked him and every stone that missed him, was a step on his way to Jerusalem. For there, in surely the most mysterious of God's mystery-laden deeds, our salvation from sin and Satan and self would be consummated in crucifixion. Not our crucifixion; the crucifixion of God's only Son. Yes, one dark day we humans he had created pinned God-in-flesh to crossbeams, and the Son of God closed his eyes in death. For us.

No, my friends, Bethlehem was but a beginning. Bethlehem was prelude to Jerusalem, the crib promise of a cross. But even the cross, thank God, was not an end. If Jesus was born to die, he died to rise again. To take that bruised body of ours, our scarred spirit, and in his own flesh raise it to his Father. To return to his Father in our flesh, the first fruits of human resurrection, of life with God and without end.

II

Now turn from Jesus to John. The Baptist may not be the most attractive character in the Gospels. He is not the type of male who comes to mind when you are shaping up a New Year's social. He comes to us, in Matthew, clad in "a garment of camel's hair" hardly crafted by Calvin Klein, "a leather girdle" Ralph Lauren would laugh at, eating "locusts" not served at the 1789 (Mt 3:4). His beard hasn't been styled since he left home. A reformer, he would crash your party shouting "Repent!" (Mt 3:2). A teetotaler, he would axe your barrels of Bud.

And still Jesus spoke of John to the Jews as he spoke of no other. "What did you go out into the wilderness to behold? A reed shaken by the wind? Why then did you go out? To see a man dressed in soft garments? Look, those who wear soft garments are in kings' houses. Why then did you go out? To see a prophet? Yes, I tell you, and more than a prophet. This is he of whom Scripture says, 'Behold, I send my messenger before your face, who shall prepare your way before you' (cf. Mal 3:1). Truly, I say to you, among those born of women there has risen no one greater than John the Baptist . . . " (Mt 11:7–11).

Forget the wilderness wardrobe, the desert diet. The Baptist was great in God's gaze because he had an uncommon commission, because his whole life had a single focus: John pointed to Jesus. "Look, the Lamb of God, who takes away the sin of the world!" (Jn 1:29). He never pointed to himself. "I am not the Christ," he told the priests and Levites. "Among you stands one whom you do not know, . . . the thong of whose sandal I am not worthy to untie. He must increase, but I must decrease" (Jn 1:26–27; 3:30).

Not only in life but also in death John pointed to Jesus. You remember how King Herod imprisoned John because the Baptist had rebuked him: "It is not lawful for you to have [Herodias,] your brother's wife" (Mk 6:18). How Herodias hated John. How Herodias' daughter pleased Herod with her dancing. How Herod promised her whatever she might ask, even half of his kingdom. How the daughter, at her mother's request, asked not for half of Herod's kingdom but for the head of the Baptist on a platter. How Herod, much as he feared and revered John, could not break his oath, could not be embarrassed before his guests. And so you have that sad sentence in Mark: "A soldier of the guard beheaded [John] in the prison, and brought his head on a platter, and gave it to the girl; and the girl gave it to her mother" (Mk 6:27–28).

But death was not the end of John. Not much later, the Gospels report, Herod was perplexed by the marvels told of a man named Jesus. "John I beheaded," he said; "but who is this about whom I hear such things?" Luke adds: "And he sought to see Jesus" (Lk 9:9). Even in death John pointed to Jesus.

III

Now turn from John to you. Why? Because the Baptist broadcasts down the ages, to your age, what your Christian calling demands. Very simply, you point to Christ. John challenges you to proclaim to the little world on which you walk: "Among you stands one whom you do not know" (Jn 1:26).

We point to Christ in different ways, and we point to Christ in one same way. We point to Christ in different ways, because he calls us to *do* different things. Stephen, first to be martyred, pointed to Christ with his blood; Augustine and Aquinas, gifted minds, pointed to Christ with their theology. Teresa of Avila pointed to Christ as a mystic in action; Thérèse of Lisieux, from Carmelite contemplation. Gerard Manley Hopkins pointed to Christ with his poetry, his sprung rhythm; Michelangelo, with his "Last Judgment" and his "Pietà." A Trappist points to Christ in silence; a Jesuit (poor fellow) is more likely to talk about Christ. People in professions point to Christ by penetrating technology with the gospel; civil servants, by planning passionately for peace. Professors point to Christ by touching young minds to the true, the beautiful, and the good; students, by growing on two levels that are really one: rich experience of reality, and close encounter with its creator God and its redeemer Christ. And perhaps the most unforgettable Christian I have ever met was a lady who for 25 years pointed smilingly to Christ from a bed of all but total paralysis.

Amid all this diversity, we point to Christ in one same way, because Christ calls all of us to *be* one person. Whatever you are called to *do,* you point to Christ ultimately by who you *are;* and in the concrete this means you point to Christ in the measure that you are Christlike. This is not pious pap; this is what Bethlehem was all about, what the Son of God took our flesh to enable us to be: to be like him.

The critical question: Where does Christ our Lord rank on your admiration list, your imitation list? Is he your model on what it means to be human, to be alive? Is it around him that your living revolves? How tall does Christ stand over against Rambo or Moses Malone, Tina Turner or Cory Aquino, Bruce Springsteen or George Burns, Mother Teresa or Joan Collins?

What our post-Christmas liturgy trumpets is this: To imitate Christ is not to settle down in a cozy crib. To be Christlike is not to look like him; it's not a make-up job, facial cosmetics. To imitate Christ is to follow him on his journey—his journey to Jerusalem. I don't mean reproducing him, copying his every action. After all, there is ever so much that Jesus never experienced. He was a man, not a woman; he was a teacher, but not a scholar; he did not experience old age or Alzheimer's disease; he had no chance to become a Jesuit!

But if your journeying to Jerusalem does not mean copying Christ slavishly, dotting his every i and crossing his every t, what does it mean? At bottom it means that, whoever you are, whatever your work, the root principle that motivates you from morning to night is the principle that powered our God-in-flesh: "I seek not my own will but the will of Him who sent me" (Jn 5:30). In point of fact, you profess that principle day after day; in a quarter hour you will profess it together, pray it publicly: "Thy will be done on earth as it is in heaven." For your comfort, I confess to you that this is the single most troublesome phrase in my thick packet of prayers. Most of the Our Father falls trippingly from my tongue: "Hallowed be thy name. Thy kingdom come. Give us our daily bread. Forgive us our trespasses. Lead us not into temptation. Deliver us from evil." Through these I dance, I trip the light fantastic. But "Thy will be done," "Whatever you want, Lord"?

Why is that prayer so troublesome? Two good reasons. First, at times I do not know what God's will is; nor at times do you. In bedroom or board room, in cloakroom or courtroom, in nuclear room or operating room—almost anywhere you think and live and breathe—difficult, agonizing questions surge, and the answers are often murky, shrouded in mist. At times, too, two trumpets sound loud but dissonant notes: the conscience God gave me when He shaped me from nothing, and the Church Christ gave me when he bought me with his blood.

Second, and perhaps more troublesome still, you may know

well what God wants of you, but your whole being rebels against it. Don't feel guilty. Christ himself experienced it in Gethsemane. His prayer reads so poetically on the printed page: "Father, if thou art willing, remove this cup from me; nevertheless, not my will but thine be done" (Lk 22:42). But take that prayer out of the Book back to the garden and you will see why "his sweat became like great drops of blood falling down upon the ground" (v. 44). With the incomparable clarity of his intelligence, he knew what his Father wanted; he knew God's will. And still his very blood and bones, his spirit and every facet of his flesh cried out in chilling protest: "Dear God, good Father, don't let me die!"

Christian life after Christmas? A swift summary. Like John the Baptist, you point to Christ. Not with a wave of your hand; not by pious prattle; not simply through a Sunday obligation. You point to Christ by a wondrous wedding of what you do and who you are. Whatever your work, you do it in such Christlike fashion that the Father can say of you as well "This is my beloved son, my beloved daughter, with whom I am well pleased" (cf. Mt 3:17). And wherever you are, you never cease searching for what our Lord would have you do—today, tomorrow, for life. If it's the same journey *you* have in mind, rejoice and be glad! If it's not, fall on your knees and sweat it out with Christ in the garden.

Obviously, life after Christmas is not "a piece of cake." Perhaps not as obviously, it can be fascinating, a journey of joy. Why? Two quick reasons. First, if your life points to Christ, you will experience what the Fourth Gospel relates. "The next day again John was standing with two of his disciples; and he looked at Jesus as he walked, and said: 'Look! The Lamb of God!' The two disciples heard him say this, and they followed Jesus" (Jn 1:35–37). Point to Jesus with your life, and others will follow—follow not you but Jesus. Second, in pointing like John to Jesus, paradoxically you are pointing to the Christ within you, the Christ you are becoming, the Christ you are. There is no greater joy than this—especially when your garden is a gethsemane, when all you love has been stripped from you—all save the Christ within you.

Dahlgren Chapel
Georgetown University
and
Holy Trinity Church
Washington, D.C.
January 18, 1987

11
DO WHATEVER HE TELLS YOU
Second Sunday of the Year (C)

- Isaiah 62:1–5
- 1 Corinthians 12:1–11
- John 2:1–11

Today's readings are remarkably rich. Each is extraordinarily enticing to a preacher. There is the Old Testament prophet promising God's people, so long in exile, a new name: "You shall be called 'My delight is in her' "; for "as bridegroom rejoices over bride, so shall your God rejoice over you" (Isa 62:4–5). There is the powerful passage from Paul on charisms, particularly pertinent because it is at once a comfort and a challenge, at once a reminder of gifts beyond compare and a divine dare to use them for the salvation of a world. There is the Gospel, with the first of Jesus' "signs"—an unexpected pointer to God's presence in him: about 150 gallons of water turned into "good wine" (Jn 2:10) to the amazement of Cana's expert cellarer.

But I have yielded to a strange temptation. I shall indeed preach on the Gospel; at least the Gospel will be my springboard. But I shall not talk about the leading man in the episode; I shall focus on the best supporting actress. I know I am treading thin ice. The Catholics among you may squirm in embarrassment, my Protestant brothers and sisters think: Here we go again—from immaculate conception through perpetual virginity to glorious assumption. How gauche can a visiting Roman be?

The point is, I am not concerned today with privileges, with prerogatives. My concern is far more radical: How can you and I live a Christian existence in a world that constantly challenges our values? After seven decades, I can think of no one, save for Jesus, who has answered the question, lived the answer, more simply and more profoundly than his mother. To make sense of this, my sce-

73

nario has three acts: (1) Mary, (2) another Madonna, (3) you and
me.

I

Act I: Mary. Here I ask you to pretend, make believe. Pretend
you have never heard of her. Clear your mind of all you know or
think or believe about her, and let me tell you a story. Listen to it as
if for the very first time.

Long centuries ago, in a town nestled among the hills of Galilee,
there lived a teen-age girl. She was perhaps 15, engaged but not yet
married, when a message came to her from God. If you are a
scholar, you may argue: Was it an interior, spiritual experience, or
did an angel from heaven actually descend on Nazareth? It matters
little. The point is, God spoke to this girl. He told her that she would
conceive a child; this child would be not only a Davidic Messiah but
God's own Son.[1] He would not be conceived the way the rest of us
are, of human intercourse; the Holy Spirit would effect this in her.
As far as we know, the message told her little else. It did not sketch
a theology of Trinity, did not say that only the Second Person would
take flesh, said nothing about daily life with him whom she would
call Jesus. Nothing about Bethlehem or Calvary, nothing about
death and resurrection. We are not even sure how deeply the teen-
age girl understood the message. What she did understand was the
all-important thing: It was God who was speaking, God who was
asking something of her, God who wanted her to mother His Son.
And at so critical a moment in the story of salvation this teen-ager
responded simply: "I am the Lord's handmaid. Let it be with me as
you say" (Lk 1:38).

Nine months later, teen-age Mary gave birth to a boy, the long-
awaited Messiah. But not where you might expect God's Son to be
born: in a capital city, in a palace, in purple and silk. No, in a small
town five miles from Jerusalem, in a feeding trough for animals, in
ordinary swaddling clothes. Not because Mary liked it that way; only
because this was apparently the way the Lord wanted it: "Let it be
with me as you say."

Not many months later, this teen-age mother was a refugee. A
mighty king was afraid of her child, afraid of a threat to his
throne—so fearful that "in a furious rage" he massacred all the male
children in and around Bethlehem two years and under (Mt 2:16).
Mary and Joseph fled with the child, spirited him to Egypt. Not be-

cause she liked to travel; only because the Lord had told her husband: "Rise, take the child and his mother, and flee to Egypt" (Mt 2:13). "Let it be with me as you say."

For almost 30 years this mother lived with her son back in backwater Nazareth. It was a paradoxical period for Mary; for at one and the same time she was shaping him as child, as adolescent, as young man, *and* discovering slowly who he really was. Slowly indeed, and painfully. Especially slow and painful when Mary and Joseph lost their 12-year-old son, searched for him frantically for three days, found him in the temple asking questions about the Torah, answering the teachers with Duke-like distinction.[2] Mary asked him how he could possibly treat his parents so thoughtlessly. His reply? "Didn't you know that I had to be in my father's house?" (Lk 2:49). Luke tells us "they did not understand what he was saying to them" (v. 50). To understand her runaway child's disobedience, Mary had to learn a good deal more about him. As Simeon had predicted in the same temple 12 years before, "a sword" would "pierce" her (v. 35). She too would have to learn through sorrow and anguish just who this Jesus was, would have to discover that he was destined to be a source of division. Not only in the Israel around her; his obedience to God's word would set him against his very own parents, against her.[3] She would have to learn through the scandal of a continuous cross what it means to murmur "Let it be with me as you say."

Once Jesus left her, the cross weighed more heavily each day. It was difficult enough to have him leave, to lose him once and for all to his mission, to the people of Israel. It was doubly difficult, heartbreaking, to see him come back to Nazareth, hear him preach in Nazareth's synagogue,[4] then watch in shock as their own townspeople "filled with fury . . . took him to the edge of the cliff on which the town was built, to throw him over it" (Lk 4:28–29). It was doubly difficult to sit at home or stand on the outskirts of the crowd, not only when he fed thousands with "five barley loaves and two fish" (Jn 6:9) or raised a dead Lazarus he loved, but when his enemies shouted he had a devil, when his friends and relatives insisted he was mad. How helpless she must have felt when one of his dear Twelve betrayed him with a kiss and the rest "forsook him and fled" (Mt 26:56), when soldiers whipped him like a dog and pinned him to a tree, when she stood beneath those twin beams and heard him cry to heaven as if forsaken by his Father, when she watched his eyes close mercifully in death, when she cradled him on a bloody hill as once she had rocked him in a lonely stable. How difficult it must have been to really believe that this lifeless flesh would shatter the rock that entombed it and her son would stand before her in resurrectional life. How agonizing it must have been, soul pierced with Calvary's sword, to whisper again what she had first exclaimed in quiet ecstasy: "Let it be with me as you say."

And yet she did. If you read Luke with care, you know she did. For Luke, the disciples of Jesus are those men and women "who hear the word of God and do it" (Lk 8:21; cf. 11:28). Such, in peerless fashion, was the mother of Jesus. In Luke's accounts, Mary was the first of disciples, the perfect disciple, the model of discipleship. She was the first to hear the gospel, heard it before the birth of Jesus, heard it and said yes. All through Jesus' ministry Luke praises her as one of those who hear the word of God and do it. After Jesus' resurrection Luke places her with the Eleven, with the whole believing community he left behind. "All these with one accord devoted themselves to prayer, together with the women and Mary the mother of Jesus, and with his brothers" (Acts 1:14). With them Mary waited and listened, waited for the Holy Spirit to descend at the first fiery Pentecost, waited for the Spirit to speak, so that once again and for ever she might repeat the wondrous words that transformed our world: "Let it be with me as you say."

II

So much for Act I. For anyone who has ears to hear, a remarkable story. Little wonder that Roman Catholicism's Second Vatican Council termed the mother of Jesus type or model of the Church, insisted that where "faith, love, and perfect union with Christ" are concerned,[5] she is what the Church ought to be, what our good Lord expects every Christian to be. But that is Act III. Before we raise that curtain, a short Second Act must intervene.

You see, another comet has flashed across the American sky. Except for professional astronomers, this phenomenon is far more fascinating, ever more enticing, than Halley's Comet. I mean the latest Madonna. *Advertising Age* calls her "Our Lady of MTV."[6] She is not only a capitalist success story; this Madonna is little short of a religious object, a sacred image, an icon. *Spin* Magazine purred over her: "She's a shiny heavenly body, a seductive look and a sexy voice. She's sleazy, trashy, cheap and completely out of your price range. Fans dress like her, confide in her, pray to her. She's our lady of rock and roll."

If that doesn't turn you on, our lady of rock and roll likes crucifixes. They dangle from her ears, hang down from her neck onto her waistline. Why? Listen to her very own confession: "Crucifixes are sexy." Why? "Because there's a naked man on them. Crucifixes are something left over from my childhood, like a security blanket. I liked the way they looked and what they symbolized, even before they were fashionable."

This Madonna has a book ready for your bedside table. Its title? *The Spirit of the Flesh.* It tells you all sorts of basic truths indispensable for a nuclear age: how to dress like Madonna, how to act like Madonna, how to make it in New York like Madonna.

Don't misunderstand me. This is not an assault on contemporary fashions, a Jesuit's jeremiad against lace gloves, fluorescent socks, Madonna buttons. Fads and vogues and crazes we always have with us—and they are not limited to the young, the bad, and the beautiful. What triggers my hiatus hernia, what inflames my esophagus, is not something sheerly external, what you can buy at Neiman-Marcus or the Dope Shop. My distress runs deeper; it has to do with values, with the ideals we hold dear, the convictions we live by. Precisely here is a perennial crisis of civilized societies. Not simply the abstract question, what values do we cherish? More concretely, who models our values? In whom do they take flesh so as to inspire the millions? Mother Teresa or Alexis Colby[7]? South Africa's Botha or Martin Luther King? J.C. or J.R.[8]? Lady Diana or our lady of rock and roll? Who models, who should model, your values and mine?

III

All of which raises the curtain on Act III. Here the characters up front are not quite Madonna I and Madonna II; the action shifts to you and me. Behind us, however, is the neuralgic, nerve-tingling question: How serious am I in suggesting that the mother of Jesus should be the model for us sophisticated Christians of the 80s—not only papists but Wesleyans as well?

How serious am I? Dead serious. Simply because the pith and marrow of your Christian existence and mine is summed up in the single sentence of Mary to the servants at Cana: "Do whatever he tells you" (Jn 2:5). This, we have seen, was the secret, the driving force, of Mary's existence, from Nazareth to Calvary and beyond. She listened to God's word and did it.

You see, Mary is not your model because she tells you how to bring a child into the world without obstetrician or midwife. She does not show you how to escape from tyrannical kings and terrorists. She does not instruct you in "the joy of cooking,"[9] does not replace Dr. Spock, has no word for you on domestic dialogue, neat hints on teen-age drug abuse. In fact, if you carry that sort of detailed, minute modeling far enough, Mary will end up the perfect model only for the mother of a single child, and that without benefit of husband!

When I say that what Mary is, the Church and every Christian should be, I am reflecting a rich tradition: By God's providence and with God's grace, the mother of Jesus lived to human perfection what God intends for each of us and for the whole Christian community—what God demands of each and all, under peril of being unchristian. And what is that? Simply, that when we hear the word of the Lord, we say yes; that we listen with ears aquiver to Jesus' every whisper—listen and then "do whatever he tells" us.

A simple set of monosyllables, right? Hear the word of God and do it. Simple in sound, terribly difficult in brute reality. Oh, it's easy enough when God's word is your word, when you hear what you hoped to hear, when what God wants is what you would have chosen anyway. It's relatively easy when things are going your way: when academic life is a fantastic 4.0, the Blue Devils have humbled the Tarheels,[10] and the Michelob is flowing freely; when there is sap in your veins and a spring in your step; when your love life is sheer romance and your Honda is purring; when your job is joy, wife or husband a daily miracle, your children shaped by angels, and money grows on trees; when death has taken a holiday.

The problem is, no human life remains quite that idyllic. And so, Christian existence calls for the faith of Mary, her trust, her love. What complicates matters, what makes faith crucial early on, is that, with you as with the mother of Jesus, God does not greet you with a *curriculum vitae*, with a life script, at birth, or when you turn into a teen, or when you shake the dust of Duke from your feet.

Let me turn uncommonly personal. When God called me to be a Jesuit priest (at least I think I can blame it on God), He did not unfold a full scenario for my century, did not detail the bittersweet of priestly existence. He did not assure me that for decades I would delight in dusting off the early Church Fathers, editing a respected theological journal, teaching in seminary and university, lecturing across the country, preaching to appreciative audiences such as you. He did not tell me that the unbending Church of my baptism would be shaken to its roots in the 60s; that thousands of its ordained, many of them dear friends of mine, would discover their priesthood too difficult to endure; that many fellow Jesuits would feel alienated from the Society they had embraced in their teens; that, as the world around me grew and changed, I would experience confusion and uncertainty, surprises and crosses, anger and fear and resentment. No angel announced to me in advance that basic presuppositions of my youth would have to be agonizingly reappraised—on authority in the Church and the ministry of Protestants, on contraception and natural law, on loyalty to Rome and the freedom of the Christian conscience, on "one true Church." When He called, God told me only enough for me to say yes, only enough for me to put my hand in His and murmur with the mother of His Son "Let it be with me as you say."

And so must it be with you—if your living is to be genuinely Christian. For some of you, what the Lord would like from your life is reasonably clear; for others, His word is still to be spoken. In either case you need the loving faith of a teen-age virgin of ancient Nazareth. For, wherever the years take you, whithersoever God calls you, you had better begin with the one indispensable Christian response, the response that transcends denominations, links Catholic and Protestant in a unique unity: "Let it be with me, Lord, as you say." With those giant monosyllables on your lips and in your heart, you will have built your house on the Gospel rock. The rains will fall and the floods come, the winds will blow and beat upon your house, but it will not fall. Building on the rock that is Christ, you will always, by his gracious giving, "do whatever he tells you." Do that and I can promise you one thing without the slightest Roman reservation. "Do whatever he tells you" and you will experience the joy which, Jesus promised, "no one will take from you" (Jn 16:22). In the midst of sin and war, of disease and death, you will echo and re-echo the infectious invitation of Eugene O'Neill's Lazarus summoned from the grave:

> Laugh with me!
> Death is dead!
> Fear is no more!
> There is only life!
> There is only laughter![11]

Duke University Chapel
Durham, North Carolina
January 19, 1986

12
I HAVE NO NEED OF YOU?
Third Sunday of the Year (C)

- Nehemiah 8:2–6, 8–10
- 1 Corinthians 12:12–30 or 12:12–14, 27
- Luke 1:1–4; 4:14–21

You know, St. Paul never ceases to amaze me. This bald, bearded, bowlegged little fellow[1] with nine lives, this anti-Christian terrorist turned lover of Christ, this explosive missionary to the nations in darkness, this earliest theologian of Christian freedom—Paul is constantly confronting us with fresh insights that challenge our smallness, dare us to be bigger than we are.

So it is again this Sunday. If you want to know what it means to be a Christian, to be baptized, if you would grasp what all of us have in common besides neuroses and the common cold, take to heart this 12th chapter of Paul's first letter to the community in Corinth. It is a startling wedding of theology and life, of theory and practice; it flings the first century into the twentieth. To suggest how contemporary that chapter is, let me treat you to a supersaver round trip: back in time to Paul's Corinth, then a return journey to Georgetown.

I

First, a quick shuttle to Corinth. When Paul wrote to this community he had himself founded, his pen was quivering. The community of his birthing, the church he loved so dearly, was torn within. Four factions were at odds, four Christian cliques, each with its special hero, its idol. Some were mesmerized by Apollos, eloquent expert on the Hebrew Bible. Others were pledged to Peter, "top dog" in their religion. The poor and the slaves clung pretty

80

much to good old Paul. A proud elite fixed on Christ, but claimed an inside track to Christ not open to the "great unwashed." Bad enough, such unchristian catfights; but there was more: schism and incest, lawsuits and food from pagan sacrifices, disorderly conduct in church and abuses in the Lord's Supper. Some even denied the resurrection of the body.

It is in this context—doctrinal division, moral misconduct, personality problems—that you must read chapter 12 of Paul's letter. In this atmosphere Paul propounds a theology basic to Christian believing, essential to Christian living. It is a theology of church—what the community of Christ is basically about. It has for springboard a living, breathing, pulsing reality: our own bodies. This body of ours, Paul argues, this incredible invention of an infinitely imaginative God, casts light on a body still more unbelievable: the body of Christ. Not his bone and blood; we, we Christians, we are the body of Christ.

How does Paul work out the analogy, move from physical to spiritual? Four fascinating facets. First, the one and the many. As with this structured body I inhabit, so with the Christian community: It is a single reality, but shaped of many members. "We were all baptized into one body—Jews or Greeks, slaves or free . . . " (1 Cor 12:13). In the language of Vatican II, "all those justified by faith through baptism are incorporated into Christ."[2] One body yes, but not a monolith, a monster: all head or hands, all liver or lungs, all heart. On this, Paul is pointed. Not only do Christians not look the same; our "gifts" are different, our "service" varies, our "activities" move in many directions (vv. 4–6). "Are all apostles? Are all prophets? Are all teachers? Do all work miracles? Do all possess gifts of healing? Do all speak with tongues?" (vv. 29–30). No indeed! The Christian community, like the human body, is a work of art precisely because it is a mosaic; it is a thing of beauty when the varicolored fragments fit together, play their interlocking roles. Each body, my own and Christ's, is God's creation at its best when it is at once one and many.

Second facet: Who is responsible for the one and the many? Again Paul is pellucid, limpid, crystal-clear. My own body? "God arranged the organs in the body, each one of them, as He chose" (v. 18). The body of Christ? "Varieties of gifts, but the same Spirit; varieties of service, but the same Lord; varieties of activities, but the same God who inspires them all in every one. . . . All these are inspired by one and the same Spirit, who apportions to each one individually as He wills" (vv. 4–6, 11). Each body is God's handiwork.

Third facet: Why this wondrous variety, in the body of Christ as in my own body? Paul's response: "for the common good" (v. 7), for the welfare of the whole. At this very moment, I stay alive, I look out at you, I can mouth syllables that make some sense to you, only because hundreds of God's gifts inside of me are working as one, are engaged in a silent conspiracy that makes each moment a new creation. And so it is for the body of Christ. At any given moment, the community called Christian is alive and reasonably well only because uncounted believers of all ages and conditions activate an awesome array of God-given gifts, great and small, to the glory of God and the health of His people.

Which summons up Paul's fourth facet: In the Church, as in the human body, no single part is insignificant, without worth or value. Now Paul is not playing professional physician; he is not suggesting that each organ in your body is as important as any other, that without your appendix or spleen, without your big toe or little finger, you would be dead. He is simply saying that in a well-ordered body different parts perform different functions; each has its own contribution to make. The head is not the whole of the body; you may indeed "walk on your head," but the head is not made for walking; for that the head needs feet. Your baby-blue eyes may be more beautiful than your jug ears, but they will never hear Haydn's *Creation*. So too for Corinth's church. At a given moment, Paul may prove more necessary to the church he fathered than a fresh convert. Paul does not deny this, but it is not the point he is making. In his theology of the Church, God has so blended the people of His new covenant that each member of the body is linked in Christ to every other. No more sensitive a nervous system has ever been devised: "If one member suffers, all suffer together; if one member is honored, all rejoice together" (v. 26).[3]

Live this theology, Paul implies, and a measure of peace will return to Christian Corinth. Live this theology, and joy will once more flood its founder's heart.

II

Enough of Corinth; let's fly back to Georgetown. Our local church, this Archdiocese of Washington, is the universal Church in miniature; and our little community, I suspect, is not terribly different from Paul's Corinth. Not the same details: I'm not accusing anyone of incest or eating Pizzas offered to idols. But we do compare with Corinth in our conflicts and our confusions, in our contrasting convictions on the way Catholics should think, should act, should worship. To some extent, at times frightening, we are torn by our differences—from papal authority to the rights of conscience, from intercommunion to Communion in the hand, from absolutes in moral theology to sacraments for the divorced-and-remarried, from contraception to female priests, from sterilization to that ultimate "Here I stand" in Catholic identity ... the kiss of peace! The list is long but, at the risk of disappointing you, I shall reserve my infallible answers to a later date. With our conflicts no more than context, I shall stress for Georgetown in the winter of '86 what Paul preached to Corinth in the spring of 57.

You see, for all our differences, we form a single body. Not primarily because we are struggling together to reach a single goal— God from here to eternity. We are so intimately linked to the risen Christ that we can call ourselves his body. Not only were you and I plunged into it one glorious baptismal day; in Paul's words, "Because there is one bread, we, many as we are, are one body, for we all share the one bread" (1 Cor 10:17). Not that dogma and morality, how we think and what we do, are unimportant. Only that, even more importantly, God's water and God's bread transform our deepest selves, change us from isolated individuals on a hostile earth to a single body that our Lord Christ claims as his very own.

But within that wondrous oneness which is Christ, you and I are not simply the same; all of us have been graced in divinely different ways. Whatever your inferiority complex, however little you think of yourself, you are splendidly gifted. You need not envy the ordained. In this one body of Christ, the Holy Spirit has so artfully blended all of us that each of us is indispensable. In this body as God has crafted it, we need Pope John Paul II. But a miracle of Christ's body is that this head cannot say to us feet "I have no need of you." If you squander your gifts or let them lie fallow, the whole body suffers. For the Spirit has inspired these gifts in you—your faith and your love, your strengths and your very weaknesses—not simply for your personal salvation, so that you can clutch them in your hot little hands and return them unchanged to the Master like the servant in the Gospel parable: "Here I am, Lord. And here is what you gave me. You're a hard master, and I knew it. I was afraid; so I hid what you gave me in the ground. Here it is, unused, untouched, just as you gave it to me" (cf. Mt 25:24–25). No. Whoever you are—pope or peasant, wealthy or impoverished, healthy or ailing, brilliant or modestly endowed—whatever God has given you, He has given you "for the common good," for your sisters and brothers, for others.

Let me lay it frankly on the Christian line. All of you here before me have a tough task for which the oils of ordination do not qualify me. When Vatican II insisted that your mission is "to penetrate and perfect the temporal sphere with the spirit of the gospel,"[4] the Council was not spouting abstractions into the Roman breeze. It was specifying your irreplaceable role in the body of Christ. Not some special, high-powered, privileged in-group among you; each and all of you baptized into Christ. Not temporary substitutes for a decimated clergy; now and always, by God-given right and duty. For, with rare exceptions, only you can carry Christ, can wing the Catholic vision, to an American culture some experts claim is 19th-century rugged individualism reborn. It does not take a doleful Jeremiah to cry out in pain from the midst of a paradoxical nation—where we weep (rightfully) over hundreds of Marines massacred in Lebanon while millions of the unborn perish unmourned; where the marvels of technology conquer space and time, yet we cannot subdue our own cities; where the Dow Jones average skyrockets and business ethics plummets to a new low; where the powerful, like Luke's Dives, feast "sumptuously every day," while the homeless hungry beg for what they throw away (Lk 16:19–20); where we glory in being all born equal, yet nearly half our black children are being raised in stultifying poverty.

In many ways a frightening specter, but it should not paralyze you. Quite the opposite. It should summon you back to St. Paul, to recognize who you are and to what you are called: a single body, the body of Christ, variously gifted by the Spirit "for the common good," agonizingly aware that what the Lord Jesus proclaimed in the synagogue at Nazareth is true of each of you. The Spirit of the Lord is upon *you*. It is *you* the Holy Spirit has anointed. *You* are to "preach good news" to all who are in any way impoverished, open the eyes of so many who walk blind, "set at liberty" men and women dreadfully "oppressed" in flesh or spirit (Lk 4:18).

But to do this in more than piddling ways, to recapture this anointing as a full-time vocation, we Catholics have to raise our sights, lift our eyes from our own small navels. We can no longer waste our energy in guerilla warfare, slashing our own sisters and brothers without mercy, excommunicating the Right or the Left, refusing to be fed with the flesh of Christ because the liturgy bores us, offends us, clashes with our sacred memories. We cannot simply be swallowed whole by today's culture, from an amoral responsibility to myself alone, through the lust for megabucks, to a seduction by a new Madonna with a crucifix that spells sex. Above all, we have to love God not with half of our heart but with every fiber of our being, get to know and live intimately with this Jesus who lives inside of us.

Good friends in Christ: I trust that over the years you have come to sense my affection for you, my admiration for all you are and all you do. If I appear impatient this afternoon, dissatisfied, chalk it up to an intense realization that increasingly tears at my bowels: Christ is being crucified out there, and all too many Christians, all too many Catholics, are running away, or passing him by, or just looking on from a safe distance. We must—all of us—come closer to each cross that beckons us, stand with Mary right under it, look up . . . and meet the eyes of today's Christ.

Dahlgren Chapel
Georgetown University
and
Holy Trinity Church
Washington, D.C.
January 26, 1986

13
NOT HIDE YOURSELF FROM YOUR OWN FLESH
Fifth Sunday of the Year (A)

- Isaiah 58:7–10
- 1 Corinthians 2:1–5
- Matthew 5:13–16

Today I find Jesus and Isaiah challenging. Uncomfortably challenging. Both are strong, blunt, uncompromising. Each tells me something I really would rather not hear. Jesus, because he tells me what I should *be* and usually am not; Isaiah, because he tells me what I should *do* and usually don't. Let me describe my discomfort through three stages. I shall move from (1) a bit of Jewish history to (2) a sense of Christian mystery to (3) a bitter dose of 20th-century realism.

I

First, a bit of history—two domestic items from early Israel.[1] Why did Jesus choose these two metaphors, salt and light? Because in Palestine each item would have caught an Israelite's eye like an imaginative commercial. As if I were to flash on your TV screen a Hefty Trash Bag from Jonathan Winters or a Double Blush from Estée Lauder—obviously indispensable for human living. In Palestine salt was a must, irreplaceable. As with "water and fire and iron," Sirach proclaims, salt "is basic" to our needs (Sir 39:26). Not yet for margaritas, but to improve the taste, say, of meat and fish. "Can that which is tasteless," Job asked amid his ashes, "be eaten without salt?" (Job 6:6). Even more importantly, to simply preserve your food. A small thing indeed, a pinch of salt, compared to the meat and fish, even to the vegetables—yet incomparably important. Salt changed what it touched, kept it from spoiling, rotting, corrupting; salt even purified. That is why, in Old Testament times, salt was used to season every sacrifice. "With all your offerings," God told His people through Moses, "you shall offer salt" (Lev 2:13).

And what can I say of the light? In the one-room cottage of the Oriental peasant, the small dish-like devices in which oil was burned were essential. Not a particularly bright light; hardly our 3-way Sylvania; but without it life would have been dark indeed. I could not have seen you once the sun went down, could not have read the Torah, could not have walked with sure foot and light heart. So much of life would have stopped at dusk—like the evening in Manhattan in the 60s, when I watched all the lights of the city gradually go out, and millions of men and women sat in darkness or by candlelight, afraid to move.

II

All well and good—a neat footnote to ancient history. But the Jesus of today's Gospel is not playing the historian, reminding you how fortunate you are with a "frig" for your cold cuts and PEPCO for your light bulbs. He is making an astounding affirmation—directly to his first followers, indirectly to every disciple since he came down from the Mount: "You are the salt of the earth; you are the light of the world" (Mt 5:13, 14). Me? Are you being serious, Lord? Or is this one of your deliberate exaggerations, like "If you don't hate your father and mother, your kid sister and big brother, you cannot be a disciple of mine"? Or, "If you have faith the size of a tiny mustard seed, you can face up to Mount Everest and tell it to 'get lost' "?

Sorry, good friends, no hyperbole here. Imagination indeed, but not fantasy. You *are* the salt of the earth. Jesus is insisting that, for its moral well-being, for its ethical good, this world depends in large measure on the Christian disciple. Not simply apostles like Andrew and Peter, fervent followers like Mary of Nazareth and Mary of Magdala. Not just Francis of Assisi and Francis Xavier; not just Teresa of Avila, Thérèse of Lisieux, Mother Teresa of Calcutta. No. For genuine human existence, if we are ever to move from war to peace, from starvation to satiety, from hating to loving, this earth of ours rests on your shoulders and mine.

Oh, not on our shoulders alone; not simply on Christians. Shiites and Sunnites, South African blacks and whites, believers and unbelievers alike, all who are alive, are involved here. And still, you and I have a clear call from Christ. Not a gentle suggestion; a loud trumpet sound. We may seem small in our own eyes, insignificant; we cannot claim the power of a Khomeini or a Qaddafi, a Tutu or a Thatcher. Nevertheless, our task, like salt, is to improve the quality of human living, change what we touch, preserve from devastation this God-shaped, dreadfully scarred earth, this paradox of beauty and the beast. If we disciples turn flat, lifeless, tasteless, if like salt from the Dead Sea we give off a stale, acrid, alkaline taste, some of our sisters and brothers will suffer, spoil, corrupt—will starve for bread or justice or love. And we? Listen not to me but to the harsh judgment of Jesus: You will be worthless, useless, fit for the garbage heap, deserve to be thrown into the street with the rest of the rubbish.

And you *are* the light of the world. Meaning what? Jesus is insisting that we who believe he is Savior of humankind, we who have risen with him and live in his presence, we who eat his flesh and drink his blood, have no right to hide our gifts in a sort of flour bin, have no right to clutch them in hot little hands for ourselves or our groupies. The gifts we have—of nature and grace—should stand out, shine like neon lights or glow lamps, should make people pause, force them to stop and look and listen. Our faith should lend fidelity to the faithless, our hope raise the hopeless from the gutter, our love assuage the cancer of hate that rages through all too many hearts. Why? Not to make others like us, admire us, envy us. In Jesus' words, that those who cross our path may "give praise to [our] heavenly Father" (Mt 5:16), that in His human images *God* may be glorified.

Here, in four Gospel verses, is what I dare to call your "Christian mystery." Mystery in the sense that a tremendous truth hidden in God has been disclosed to you by His very own Son. Your task as Christians is not to mimic the culture that encompasses you. Your task, like mine, is to furnish a fresh flavor to the world you walk, to shine like Bethlehem's star for such as are searching—searching for something, for someone, to make life more human, to make each day worth waking up to.

III

Hard to argue with that—but perhaps because it's so terribly vague. How do you move from metaphor and mystery to 20th-cen-

tury realism? How do you get the salt out of the cellar, how shine
your light so that men and women can be dazzled by the Christ
glowing within you? Isaiah 58 thunders one way. Not the only way,
but a way that is as imperative in 1987 as it was five centuries before
Christ was born. Listen once again to the Old Testament prophet[2]
as he challenges the first Jews returning to Jerusalem from exile in
Babylon. But as you listen, don't picture these returnees as a group
of slaphappy hostages coming back to a homeland high in hope and
bursting with joy. What met the exiles' eyes was a Jerusalem des-
perately in need of reform. The temple, center of Sion, was far from
finished, and foreign gods mocked Yahweh. The law had to be re-
established, the Sabbath restored. The leaders had to be purified,
the faithless among the people refashioned to fidelity. Exiles em-
bittered by Babylon had somehow to be reconciled with fellow Jews
who had never known banishment.[3] In this context, where so much
was needed, from physical labor to radical reconversion, the
prophet hits hard at a practice dear to the Lord and His people:

> Fasting like yours this day
>   will not make your voice to be heard on high.
> Is such the fast that I choose,
>   a day for a man to humble himself?
> Is it to bow down his head like a rush,
>   and to spread sackcloth and ashes under him?
> Will you call this a fast,
>   and a day acceptable to the Lord?
> Is not this the fast that I choose:
>   to loose the bonds of wickedness,
>   to undo the thongs of the yoke,
> to let the oppressed go free,
>   and to break every yoke?
> Is it not to share your bread with the hungry,
>   and bring the homeless poor into your house;
> when you see the naked, to cover him,
>   and not to hide yourself from your own flesh?
> Then shall your light break forth like the dawn,
>   and your healing shall spring up speedily;
> your righteousness shall go before you,
>   the glory of the Lord shall be your rear guard.
> Then you shall call, and the Lord will answer;
>   you shall cry, and he will say, Here I am.
> If you take away from the midst of you the yoke,
>   the pointing of the finger, and speaking
>   wickedness,

> if you pour yourself out for the hungry
> and satisfy the desire of the afflicted,
> then shall your light rise in the darkness
> and your gloom be as the noonday.
>
> (Isa 58:4b–10)

Are you surprised that, in God's sight, this is when "*your* light shall break forth like the dawn" (v. 8), this when "*your* light shall rise in the darkness" (v. 10)? It shouldn't surprise you. It was in such Isaian syllables that Jesus summed up his own mission in the Nazareth synagogue: "The Spirit of the Lord is upon me, because He has anointed me to preach good news to the poor. He has sent me to proclaim release to the captives and recovering of sight to the blind, to set at liberty those who are oppressed" (Lk 4:18; cf. Isa 61:1–2).

You see, whether it's Jewish exiles returning to Jerusalem, or Jesus returning to Nazareth, or you returning from this serene sanctuary to your hopped-up or downbeat scene, the Lord has some of His troubled people waiting. Waiting for exiled relatives or fellow Nazarene, good reason indeed. But why should an acre of God's world be waiting for *you*? Because, like the exiles from Babylon and Jesus of Nazareth, you are uncommonly gifted. Not that all of you have "the smarts," have power to manipulate people like pawns, rate a "10" for sexuality. St. Paul had to remind the Christians of Corinth: "Not many of you were wise according to worldly standards, not many were powerful, not many were of noble birth" (1 Cor 1:26). To *all* of them—foolish to the world and weak, low and despised—he made one poignant point: "Consider your calling."

Yes, my sisters and brothers, consider your calling. You are graced with what Paul called "the fruit of the Spirit: love, joy, peace, patience, kindness, goodness, faithfulness, gentleness, self-control" (Gal 5:22–23). But not simply for yourselves—to contentedly contemplate your spiritual navel with a Bud Light. You leave here to hook up with as many oppressions as ever Isaiah and even Jesus conceived, a campus or city where Paul's nine fruits of the Spirit clash constantly with nine fruits of Satan: love with hate, joy with bitterness, peace with war, patience with intolerance, kindness with cruelty, goodness with evil, faithfulness with infidelity, gentleness with savagery, self-control with unbridled license.

I cannot pronounce to any single one of you precisely what fruit of the Spirit you ought to plant, precisely where, precisely how. A session with Jesus will be far more fruitful than a bout with Burghardt. And I assure you, word of honor, Hoyas past and present, Holy Trinity and Dahlgren, amaze me, thrill me, humble me with the oppressions you oppose, from exiled children through battered women to men without work or bread or dignity. I dare make but three suggestions, from seven decades of people-watching and a frank examination of my own conscience.

First, despite all we actually do, many of us can do more; and unless we do much more, our Christianity will be tasteless, our world continue to corrupt, many salted Christians fit only for the rubbish heap. Second, while lighting the world with wonderfully visible beams—So Others May Eat, Bread for the City, Sarah House, Mother Teresa's hospice for AIDS—look more closely, more lovingly, into the eyes you meet each day. Oppression is not in exile from our pews and our dorms, is not confined to 14th and U. The oppressed rub shoulders with us. Third, I am not suggesting that you should "loose the bonds of wickedness, break every yoke" (Isa 58:6) because you are utterly free yourselves, unoppressed, filled to the brim with the fruits of the Spirit. No, you are still wonderfully and fearfully human; and so your own flesh and spirit will be burdened with yokes at times barely bearable. But this, strangely, can be all to the good; in fact, it seems indispensable for "the salt of the earth" and "the light of the world." For, as the exiles from Babylon and the Christ of Calvary both reveal, the most effective servant is the suffering servant, the servant whose experience makes for com-passion, the servant who "suffers with." It is especially "then" that "you shall call, and the Lord will answer; you shall cry, and he will say 'Here I am' " (Isa 58:9).

Dahlgren Chapel
Georgetown University
and
Holy Trinity Church
Washington, D.C.
February 8, 1987

14
A KINGDOM FOR THE SHREWD
Twenty-fifth Sunday of the Year (C)

- Amos 8:4–7
- 1 Timothy 2:1–8
- Luke 16:1–13

I trust that today's Gospel disturbed you, even shocked you, at least puzzled you. An employee who cheats on his employer, a manager who manipulates his master's money to make friends for his forced retirement. And a master, with Jesus' approval, praising the dishonest manager "because he had acted shrewdly" (Lk 16:8a)![1] What brand of business ethics is this? Is this the morality with which Vatican II sent the laity into the world "to penetrate and perfect the temporal sphere with the spirit of the gospel"?[2] Clever operators, wheeler-dealers?

Decades ago, we priests were lucky. This Gospel used to be read in high summertime, and we, your devoted servants, could plead the heat and vacation, skip the sermon, and send you forth swiftly to beach or bar, to pool or fairway, without any of us being the wiser for the parable of the Dishonest Manager.

No longer can we avoid it. Summer is over, and the parable is now. A tough parable, difficult to decipher. And still, it comes from the mouth of God's Son, and it says something terribly important for your life and mine. But to grasp that, you must address three issues: (1) What did the parable mean in Jesus' own mind? (2) What applications did the early Christians draw from the parable? (3) What might the parable say to you and me today? Briefly, Jesus . . . first-century disciples . . . 20th-century Christians.

I

First, what did the parable mean in Jesus' own mind? Here New Testament scholars have been splendidly helpful, especially on economic realities in Jesus' time. But a homily is not a lecture. So, rather than bore you with my biblical brilliance, let me simply retell the parable as we can now reconstruct it.[3]

Here is a rich man who owns quite a bit of property. This plutocrat has a manager. The manager's job? To handle the finances of the estate. He has broad powers, much leeway for discretion, comes off as a combination of CPA and loan shark. He keeps his master's accounts, can contract loans in the owner's name, may even liquidate debts.

But one day our manager gets his comeuppance. He is accused of dishonesty. Who accuses him? We are not told. Of what is he accused? Squandering his master's property. How exactly? We don't know: neglect? swindling? poor judgment? At any rate, the owner summons him, stat. No discussion; the case is open-and-shut. "You're fired. But before you pack up, prepare an inventory; tell me who owes me and how much."

Exit the manager. Outside the office he sits himself down, chin in hand, brow wrinkled. "What shall I do? I'm not strong enough for physical labor; my hands are too soft; I'm a white-collar man. I won't panhandle; that's beneath my dignity. . . . Aha! I've got it! A super idea. If this works out, people will put the welcome mat out for me when I leave here."

Quickly he summons his master's debtors, all those with whom he has made deals. "You. Your IOU reads a thousand gallons of olive oil, correct? Write a new IOU. Cut your debt in half. Put down only the 500 gallons you owe my master as your original loan; take out the interest, the 500 gallons I charged you as *my* interest." "You. Your IOU reads a thousand bushels of wheat, correct? Write a new IOU. Forget my 25% interest; simply write 800 bushels, exactly what you owe my master." No dishonesty here; this is not the squandering for which the owner fired him. The manager is playing within the economic rules; he is giving up not his master's rightful return, only the interest he himself charged, *his* interest.

Somehow the owner gets wind of the deal. His reaction? Anger? No, sir! He shakes his head in admiration: "Clever little fellow. I fire him and he trades on disaster to ensure his future." But notice. The master does not praise the manager for squandering his property; that was something different, and for that he had dismissed him. Nor does the master praise the manager for lending out money at interest; that was against Jewish law, though commonly practiced. He praises him for making a clever ethical deal, doing what he was entitled to do. The manager is renouncing his own profit, renouncing usury, releasing the debts of fellow Jews. For this, the scribes, the Jewish lawyers, would have given him a standing ovation, "high fives" in the end zone.

And Jesus: What precisely is *he* approving? And what has this parable to do with the kingdom of God? Simply this. The dishonest manager, at a critical moment in his life, when his entire future was at stake, acted decisively to cope with the crisis, planned shrewdly to secure his future. Similarly for Christians. Jesus' preaching of the kingdom brings a crisis into our lives; we have to act decisively, plan shrewdly, to ensure a place in God's kingdom. That is where the parable proper ends: "And the master praised that dishonest manager because he had acted shrewdly" (v. 8a).

II

Terribly abstract, isn't it? I see no neon lights flashing in your eyes. For your consolation, the early Christians apparently felt the same way. After the death of Jesus, the parable was told and retold, at times in places where Christians were puzzled about its meaning—and didn't have a Jesuit to explain it! The result? Much moralizing over Manischewitz. That's how you have the last part of today's Gospel (vv. 8b–13): three applications, three lessons, three concrete directives for living which the generation after Jesus drew from a puzzling parable.

Application 1: Make wise use of material possessions—what Luke calls "the mammon of dishonesty" (v. 19)—dishonest not because material things are evil in themselves, but because they can seduce you, lead you to dishonesty. Here we are faced with a gem of wisdom that should trouble any follower of Christ: "The children of this world are shrewder in dealing with their own generation than are the children of light" (v. 8b). Meaning what? Meaning this: Men and women whose outlook on life is totally conditioned, solely shaped, by this world, men and women who have no interest whatever in the godly aspects of human existence, are shrewder in dealing with their own kind than are the disciples of Christ in making their way to the goal that is God. Unbelievers put us to shame. Imitate their shrewdness!

Application 2 focuses on day-to-day fidelity. If you cannot be trusted with something quite small, say a Miller Lite or a Colt 45, who will trust you with a whole brewery? If you cannot take care of ordinary things like my car keys, why should I trust you with something really valuable like a volume of my homilies? If you are irresponsible in handling my secondhand jalopy, I'm not at all sure that you'll do better by your own new Saab.

Application 3 is a general attitude toward wealth: "You cannot serve both God and mammon" (v. 13b). Not that you cannot *have* both; simply that you cannot make both your master. Which of the two will you serve? If gold is your god, the God of Jesus Christ is not. Choose!

III

So much for the parable as Jesus intended it; so much for what the early Christians drew from it. Now, what of you? What will *you* draw out of it? What might it say to *you?* I say "you" deliberately, because no preacher, not even a Jesuit, has the right to tell you what the parable must say to you. Oh yes, I can discourse brilliantly, with impressive footnotes, on what the parable of the Dishonest Manager meant 20 centuries ago: what it meant on the lips of Jesus, what it meant to first-century Christians. And that is highly important. But even more important is what the same Christ is saying to you through the same parable *today*. For that, you have to listen, not so much to me as to him. You have to say, with the boy Samuel in the temple: "Speak, Lord, for your servant is listening" (1 Sam 3:9). What can *I* do? Trigger your thinking, stimulate your sensitivity, lob over to you a link or two between the first century and 1986.

The basic link is what Jesus intimates at the close of the parable. Each of you has been put in a crisis situation. Not from terrorist bombs; not from nuclear threat; not from midterms on the horizon; not because an employer has decreed that you can be his manager no longer. Each Christian, rich or poor, frightened or slaphappy, has to face up to a crisis. Perhaps once, perhaps often. How come? Because the kingdom of God has been preached not only to first-century Jews but to you. So what? So this. The kingdom of God is not a place, like Sweden or Great Britain or the old Kingdom of the Two Sicilies. The kingdom of God, the pith of Jesus' preaching, the ground of the Gospels, is the rule of Christ over the human heart. Not political power; he is king of hearts. Of *your* heart. "You are not your own," St. Paul insists to the Christians of Corinth; "you were bought with a price" (1 Cor 6:20). What price? "The precious blood of Christ" (1 Pet 1:19). That is why Paul writes bluntly and unconditionally to the Christians of Rome: "None of us lives to himself, and none of us dies to herself. If we live, we live to the Lord, and if we die, we die to the Lord. So then, whether we live or die, we are the Lord's. For to this end Christ died and lived again, that he might be Lord both of the dead and of the living" (Rom 14:7–9).

A lovely sentiment, "None of us lives to himself," but how true is it? I pick up the September 8 issue of *Time;* I read the cover story on Harvard at age 350.[4] Harvard's president, not too happily, reports on the stated goals of incoming freshmen: (1) money, (2) power, (3) reputation.[5] "None of us lives to himself"? And I wonder within myself: Are the streets of Cambridge unique, or do the red-brick walks of Georgetown resound to the same beat?

Am I saying that, to Christian eyes, money, power, reputation are evil? No, no, and again no! Joseph of Arimathea, who boldly buried the body of Jesus, had money to burn; John Paul II possesses incomparable power; Mother Teresa has a world-wide reputation. But like the "mammon of dishonesty" in today's Gospel, these are perilous possessions. Why perilous? Because they can *lead* to evil: to dishonesty, injustice, self-love, devastation of the human spirit. When? Whenever goal number one is not God; whenever your primary purpose is not the age-old catechism response, "God made me to praise, reverence, and serve Him"; whenever to be alive does not mean, in the first instance, life in Christ; whenever money, power, reputation become gods, your masters instead of your servants.

The parable of the Dishonest Manager is a challenge to every Christian, more especially if you are gifted with the good things of earth, or hold in your hands the living or dying of others, or your ears ring with the *Sieg Heil* of your subjects, with the applause of appreciative audiences, with the screeching and howling of frenzied fans. It is then especially that you have to confront the wisdom of the world with the foolishness of God, with the folly of the Beatitudes: Blessed are the poor in spirit and those persecuted for Christ, the meek and those who mourn, the merciful and the makers of peace, the pure in heart and those who thirst for righteousness (cf. Mt 5:3–12).

So then, look into your heart this Sunday of crisis. Discover what towers atop your list of goals. See where God stands on the list, where money, power, fame, whatever. Then, like our manager friend but even more shrewdly, take the IOU you have with God, rip it up, write a new one—this time not less but more, this time in tune with the command of Old Testament and New: "I shall love the Lord my God with all my heart, all my soul, all my mind, all my strength." And while you're at it, you might as well add: "And I shall love others, all others, as I love myself" (cf. Deut 6:5; Lev 19:18; Mt 22:37, 39; Mk 12:30–31).

Is this what God is asking of you? *I* cannot say for sure; but the same Jesus who spoke the parable can. Remember the lines with which St. Augustine closed his *Confessions:* "What man will give another man the understanding of this . . . ? Of you [God] we must ask, in you we must seek, at you we must knock. Thus only shall we receive, thus shall we find, thus will it be opened to us."[6]

> Dahlgren Chapel
> Georgetown University
> and
> Holy Trinity Church
> Washington, D.C.
> September 21, 1986

15
CUT IT OFF?
Twenty-sixth Sunday of the Year (B)

- Numbers 11:25–29
- James 5:1–6
- Mark 9:38–48

If you were listening with both ears to James and Mark, you might well have concluded: To be a Christian is a tough proposition. Are you well off financially? Do you gad about in Gucci garments, dine deliciously at Dominique's, whip through Washington in a Volvo? Then, it seems, you had better "weep and howl for the miseries that are coming upon you" (Jas 5:1). And if you take our Lord literally, following him is absurd, out-and-out nonsense. Pluck your eye out? Cut your hand off, your foot—not to mention other unmentionables? Would not Christian ethics call this "mutilation" and castigate it as immoral?

To redeem the time, suppose we let James go for today; you can read all about riches and the Christian in my book of homilies *Still Proclaiming Your Wonders,* modestly priced at $9.95.[1] I want to concentrate on Jesus, on that astounding text in Mark. Three stages to my development, three questions: (1) What did the passage mean back then? (2) How does this fit into the Christian scheme of things? (3) What might it say to you and me right now?

I

First, what did the passage from Mark mean back then, when it fell from the lips of Jesus?[2] One issue we can settle speedily: Jesus was not recommending mutilation. Not because mutilation is always and everywhere immoral. After all, we may remove a cancerous eye, a mangled hand, a gangrenous foot; we do so when the health of the whole body demands it. So I suspect it's not simply impossible for Jesus to insist that I sacrifice a lustful blue eye for the health of my whole person before God.

But that is not the point in our passage. If you fasten too firmly on the physical in certain phrases of Jesus, you run into absurdities. Jesus did indeed say, "If you have faith as a grain of mustard seed, you will say to this mountain, 'Move hence to yonder place,' and it will move" (Mt 17:20). But he was not urging us to rap the majestic Rockies and command them, "Get lost!" It's a typically Semitic way of speaking—graphic, vivid, even exaggerated. Jesus was assuring us that, if we really believe, we can manufacture miracles of grace, what we cannot do with our nakedly human powers, what is impossible save to God.

So in the passage from Mark. It is graphically Semitic. The stress is not on a particular organ of the human body. After all, if I excise one lecherous eye, I can still "scope" with the other.[3] Focus on the physical and you risk missing the message. And what is that? It is a violent way of saying: In your journeying to God, you have to be ruthless against obstacles. Jesus said the same thing in different language when he warned the multitudes: "If anyone comes to me and does not hate his own father and mother and wife and children and brothers and sisters, yes, and even his own life, he cannot be my disciple" (Lk 14:26). *Hate* father and mother? Hardly. Not when Jesus' whole life, from Bethlehem to Calvary, was one long command to love—to love even our enemies, even those who hate us. The meaning of that text in Luke is provided by the parallel passage in Matthew: "He who loves father or mother more than me is not worthy of me; and he who loves son or daughter more than me is not worthy of me" (Mt 10:37). Nothing comes before Christ.

Similarly in today's reading from Mark. Whatever causes you to sin, Jesus told his disciples, whatever supplants God in your life, get rid of it! Whatever the cost—even life itself—let it go! "It is better for you to enter [eternal] life, to enter the kingdom of God, [without that possession] than to be thrown into hell [with it]" (Mk 9:43–47). If you want to be alive with God's life, now and for ever, let no love so possess you that God and His Christ take second place in your life.

II

Such is Jesus' message, such his meaning. The imagery ("cut it off") is rough indeed, but the imagery is justified by the issue: heaven or hell? My second question: How does this fit into the Christian scheme of things? Admirably. Our spirituality reflects the intent of Jesus, if not his imagery; for it echoes the first of the Ten Commandments in Exodus and Deuteronomy: "You shall have no other gods before me" (Exod 20:3; Deut 5:7); and it echoes what Jesus called "the great commandment" in the law: "You shall love the Lord your God with all your heart, and with all your soul, and with all your mind, and with all your strength" (Mt 22:37; Mk 12:30). This basic spirituality was summed up four and a half centuries ago by one of the more believable Jesuits, St. Ignatius Loyola. His Spiritual Exercises open on two affirmations fundamental for Christian living. (1) You and I, all of us humans, are created to praise, reverence, and serve God, and by so doing to grasp our destiny, life with God days without end. (2) Everything else on this earth is intended by God to help us achieve this end. Ignatius' ironclad conclusion? Therefore we are to use the things of earth in so far as they help towards that end, rid ourselves of them in so far as they obstruct it.[4] Less colorful than Jesus' "cut it off," but in substance the exact same imperative.

I trust you noticed: For Ignatius, as for Jesus, Christianity is not in the first instance negation, rejection, refusal, "cut it off." Why not? Because the earth on which we dance and sweat is not the creation of some evil genius, the work of Darth Vadar; it stems from a God who lent it to us to shape as His good servants, to mold with intelligence and freedom and imagination. The ideas we struggle with, the tools we work with—microscopes and formulas, atoms and spacecraft, laws and scalpels, diplomacy and politics, computer chips and basketballs—these are not Satanic instruments forged by Faust; they represent our response to God's own urging that we extract from His creation its inmost secrets and lay them before our sisters and brothers for their life and growth, their health and wealth, their delight and their salvation.

Of course they can be misused: atoms for peace, atoms for conquest; laws that civilize, laws that enslave; scalpels that heal, scalpels that kill. That is why the Second Vatican Council flung out to the laity a critical challenge. The Council insisted that you have a distinctive role in the Church, distinctive because it is a role you alone can fully play. It is your task to "penetrate and perfect the temporal sphere with the spirit of the gospel," to co-operate with a God who "intends, in Christ, to take up the whole world again and make of it a new creation. . . . "[5]

III

Terribly vague, you say—abstract, idealistic, impractical—the kind of ivory-tower stuff you expect of a theologian. That's why we have a third point, a down-to-earth question: What might all this say to you and me right now? Jesus' incisive "cut it off" and Vatican II's "penetrate [your world] with the spirit of the gospel," how ought these twin commands of Christ and Church shape your concrete existence, your 24-hour day?

First, "cut it off." Forty-four years of priestly ministry have brought me profound joy and painful sadness. Joy because I have experienced thousands of you struggling day after day to live like Christ, to love God with all your heart, soul, mind, and strength. Sadness because I have seen so many—dear friends and casual acquaintances—set up false gods, idols that controlled their lives, forced the living and true God into the background, ruined human relationships.

The strange gods have been several and seductive: pride or passion, work or play, lust for power or the lure of beauty, another human person. Today, sociologists suggest, the strangest and strongest god may be myself, looking out for Number One, the god of "yuppie love"[6] incarnate in megabucks. This is not just a green-eyed Jesuit envying your greenbacked future. Four years ago, a survey in *Psychology Today* revealed that, from their own responses, a central passion of men and women between 18 and 25 is money. In consequence, they are in disturbing measure sexually unsatisfied, in worsening health, worried and anxious, discontented with their jobs, and lonely as hell.[7] And, I'm afraid, at odds with the God who alone can give meaning to their lives. Not all, by any means; but enough to cause me deep distress.

An all-important question for each of us, including your homilist: What claims top priority in my case? What tops my Top Ten? Not as abstract principle, but in day-to-day practice, in the way I live. Who or what rules my life? What sits up on that throne, commanding me "Go!" and I go, "Move!" and I move, "Do this!" and I do it? If it is not in some way the God who made me, the God for whom I am made, I am in desperate straits; I had better get my Christian act together. There is no surer way to start than the simple question St. Paul asked after Jesus knocked him from his horse: "What shall I do, Lord?" (Acts 22:10).

But cutting an unchristian cancer out of your life is only one side of the Christian coin, the negative side. It makes possible the positive, the priestly—the sublime burden your baptism laid on you. Water was poured on you not only to wash Satan right out of your hair. At that same instant you were commissioned by Christ to carry him wherever you go, especially where the ordained rarely set foot: E. F. Hutton and IBM, Capitol Hill and the Oval Office, Hollywood and Broadway, public classroom or private board room, CBS or the C.I.A., Children's Hospital or the Washington *Post*, the Redskins' dressing room and the 19th Hole. Here, and in a thousand other places, here is your apostolic turf. Not by papal or episcopal permission; not by patronage of your pastor; not filling in till we can buy more Roman collars. Here *you* are the Church, by God's gracious calling and the power of your baptism.

I say "carry Christ." Not by mounting a soapbox and spouting Scripture. You carry Christ by *being* Christ. I mean, fully human and, by God's grace, more than human. Fully human, therefore attractive; more than human, therefore a challenge. Concretely, a man or woman of flesh and blood, but of spirit and imagination as well. Liking who you are, but loving others as much as you love yourself. Open to all that is alive and life-giving, closed only to what deals out death. Sensuous and sensual and sexual, but always with reverence—sex indeed play but never a plaything. Absorbed in your work, but even more preoccupied with people. Eager to get ahead, but not at the expense of Christ's "little ones," at the cost of community. Shrewd and sharp-witted perhaps, but without walking an ethical tightrope. Content to live in comfort, but uncomfortable as long as your sisters and brothers hunger for bread or justice or love. Proud to have "made it," but prouder still to help the less fortunate "make it." In love with God's creation—persons and things— but more deeply in love with God Himself. Critical of the Church and her sins, but poignantly aware that the Church is you, that the prophet Nathan can face you as he did adulterous David: "You are the man" (2 Sam 12:7).

Good friends in Christ: Across the centuries we Catholics have been accused of a nauseously negative approach to life on this side of the grave. And many of us lend warrant to such a charge; in religion we are "sad sacks." Mass is an obligation, and the faith is an endless "don't." Lent means "give up," and holiness says "cut it off."

For ages we have prayed to Mary: "To thee do we send up our sighs, mourning and weeping in this valley of tears."

Of course the cross is a constant in our lives; death in some form haunts us each day. But you are less than Catholic if you fail to see that "cut it off" is not mutilation but liberation: It frees you to love God with every fiber of your being. You are missing the depth and the thrill and the joy in Catholic living if you carry Christ only *into* church, if you fail to carry him from Communion to the concrete and glass outside, to the condo and the slum, to your desk and your bed—in a word, to the men and women who people your days.

Love God above all else and you won't have to calculate just how you carry Christ to your turf; it will be second nature, as easy as breathing. All you will need is to be yourself; for that self will be Christ. It may not be all fun—Christ himself did not laugh on Calvary. But I can promise you a delight in human living that will only grow richer as you grow grayer, a fascination with your creation that will rival the breathless day when God looked on what He had shaped "and behold, it was very good" (Gen 1:31).

Dahlgren Chapel
Georgetown University
and
Holy Trinity Church
Washington, D.C.
September 29, 1985

16

HOLD A BABY TO YOUR EAR

Twenty-seventh Sunday of the Year (B)

- Genesis 2:18–24
- Hebrews 2:9–11
- Mark 10:2–16

Whoever the powers be that link liturgy to life, they have betrayed me today. With seminarians for my congregation,[1] I am confronted with the miracle of marriage—its origin in Eden, its permanence in God. Not mine to make wedlock too winsome for you; not mine this day to sell celibacy to you.

Fortunately, the minor functionary whose task it was to divide the Sunday Gospel into a "longer form" and a "shorter form" has come to my rescue. He allows me four additional verses: the exciting episode where children are brought to Jesus "that he might touch them." The disciples rebuke the parents; Jesus rebukes the disciples. He takes the little ones into his arms, blesses them, and issues a stern warning to his closest friends: "If you do not receive the kingdom of God like a child, you will not enter it" (Mk 10:13–16; cf. Mt 19:13–15; Lk 18:15–17). For all its brevity, the episode is crucial for every Christian, suggestive for every seminarian. Two questions for your reflection: (1) What was Jesus saying to his disciples then? (2) What might Jesus be saying to his disciples now?

I

First, what was Jesus saying to his disciples then? Two words from the incident rise above the rest, two mysterious realities: kingdom and children. Kingdom rings hollowly in our ears, gives off bad vibes: bloody kings like Herod who butchered all those children, mad kings like Ludwig who built all those castles. And still,

104

like it or not, kingdom is critical for a Christian. Not simply because the Synoptics use "kingdom" 107 times; more importantly because it is the gospel in a nutshell, it sums up why the Son of God took flesh. What did Jesus proclaim when he "came into Galilee preaching the gospel of God"? "The time is fulfilled, and the kingdom of God is at hand" (Mk 1:15). And what did Jesus answer when the people of Capernaum wanted to keep him to themselves? "To the other towns as well must I preach the good news of God's kingdom, because it is for this that I was sent" (Lk 4:43).

How did Jesus understand this kingdom? Not easy to say. He never favored us with a definition; he preferred to speak of it in parables; he revealed it not to the wise of this world but to the childlike, the innocent, those unspoiled by learning (cf. Mt 11:25); and, to prove his point, we the wise have for centuries spilt oceans of ink over it. For our purposes, see God's kingdom not spatially, some super-Arthurian empire covering the globe; see it rather as God's kingship or lordship, His ruling or reigning. But not lordship as an abstract concept, the eternal rule of the Creator. Jesus eyed the kingdom after the fashion of the prophets and psalmists: God personally, graciously, lovingly breaking into history to make His will prevail among us and to destroy the sovereignty of Satan. To "enter" God's kingdom (Mk 10:15) is to bow to His will without condition, without reservation. Somewhat simplistically perhaps, to enter the kingdom is to be "saved."[2]

What stuns us in the Synoptics, what takes our breath away, is that Jesus not only *announces* God's latest intervention in human history; he *is* that intervention. God now breaks into our story not through a patriarch like Abraham, a liberator like Moses, a prophet like Isaiah, an angel like Raphael. He enters our history through His very own Son, born like us of a woman, the Divine in the skin of David. And Jesus not only proclaims God's kingship; he brings it about—by preaching it yes, but in the last analysis by fixing it to a cross. And one day, Paul promises, at the culmination of history, humankind and all it possesses, "the whole creation" that "has been groaning in travail together until now" (Rom 8:22), even death itself, will be subjected to Christ, "when he delivers the kingdom to God the Father after destroying every rule and every authority and power" (1 Cor 15:24).

A breath-taking panorama, from the powerless *poverello* in Bethlehem, through the thorn-crowned "King of the Jews" (Jn 19:19), to the Lord trailing clouds of glory. But to whom does his kingdom belong? Who enter it? Who, in a word, are "saved"? Jesus' answer is astonishing: "Let the children come to me, do not hinder them; for to such belongs the kingdom of God" (Mk 9:14). Astonishing for two reasons. Astonishing, first, because literally to little children Jesus promised a share in his kingdom. To the "minors in human society."[3] To those not old enough to say yes or no to the kingdom. To those whom the Hebrew people would hardly have thought of when imagining the kingdom promised them. To those whom the disciples kept away from Jesus, kept from bothering their busy Teacher, kept from interfering with his "real" ministry. "Let the children come to me. . . . "

More astonishing still, little children are not only members of Jesus' kingdom; they are "models for all adults who would like to accept it."[4] What did Jesus see in children that might commend them as paradigms? What childlike qualities should characterize candidates for the kingdom? Well, little children are refreshingly fresh, not faded and jaded by the years. They are open rather than cynical, delighted to be surprised. They are rarely if ever suspicious. And—very pertinent here—the little ones can only receive, can only respond spontaneously to love and affection. They have no claim to achievement, nothing can they claim proudly as their own.

Oh yes, if you want to turn analytic, you can counter all this with the other side of the coin. Children can churn out all the bad qualities opposed to St. Paul's paean to love in 1 Corinthians 13. They can be *im*patient and *un*kind, jealous and boastful, arrogant and rude, irritable and resentful; they can love little and endure nothing; they can be noisy gongs and clanging cymbals. But if you play child psychologist, you will miss the point of the comparison. To enter the kingdom, to accept the dominion of Jesus, is not to lapse into second childhood, to mewl and squall, to grouch and grouse, to reproduce the baby and the adolescent. It is to recapture—but now in adult fashion and in the face of God—the openness and nakedness, the sheer receptivity and utter dependence, that called out to a compassionate Christ, that made him see in children what he wants to see in all his disciples.

II

Which leads into my second question: What might Jesus be saying to his disciples now? The disciples I have in mind at the moment are not *all* who follow Christ, not the whole Church, not the total community of disciples. I mean specifically this select group in front of me. Select not because you are destined to ride high in the Christian saddle, above your fellow disciples. You will indeed be ordained; but sacramental ordination will simply expand what sacramental baptism initiated: You will be disciples of the Lord with fresh responsibilities. You are indeed chosen by the community to be its official representatives, to act in the name of Christ and the Church; but not representatives in lordship, only in service. Service in proclaiming the word, in forming community, in presiding at worship, in serving that for which your priesthood exists: the human person.

In this context, 44 years of priesting have finally convinced me: Jesus was right on target! For your ministry and mine, one quality is indispensable: We have to become like children before God. My service to God's people is not primarily psychological—the stunning effect of my powerful personality on the motley mob. I may be incomparably keen of mind and strong of will, a workaholic and wondrous weaver of words. I may, as Paul put it, "have prophetic powers, understand all mysteries and all knowledge, have all faith, so as to remove mountains" (1 Cor 13:2). But if I am not naked before my God, if I do not live my ministry totally dependent on His power and mercy, I run two radical risks: My people may not be fed with Christ, and I may become a castaway.

This is not ivory-tower speculation or pious pap. Such has been my experience—at times devastating. My low moments in ministry? When *I* took first place, and Christ retreated to second. When I imagined that *I* was changing minds and hearts, and forgot Jesus' pungent affirmation: "Apart from me you can do nothing" (Jn 15:5). When I prided myself that my homily had turned a sinner from his hellish ways, and did not heed Augustine's insight: "If we but turn to God, that itself is a gift of God." When I ceased formal prayer or espoused an ambiguous "To work is to pray." When I was no longer honest with God, but played games with Him, with myself, pretended to a holiness I did not possess. When my response to the urgings of the Spirit echoed the Athenians' reaction to Paul: "I'll listen to you some other time" (cf. Acts 17:32).

No, good friends. Whether at an altar with the God-man in your hands or in a pulpit with his word on your lips, whether shaping a whole community or fashioning a single disciple, whether feeding faith or struggling for justice, the most important aspect of your ministry is a childlike receptivity. If it is always God who takes the initiative in salvation, it is perilous for a priest to act the "adult," the rugged individualist, the man who "has it made," has the world by the tail.

Of this I can assure you: You will experience your deepest satisfaction and profoundest influence as a priest when you let God lead you like a child, take you wherever *He* wants to, take you even where you may be reluctant to go—a Jerusalem, a Gethsemane, a Calvary not of your choosing. Remember Jesus' prediction to Peter: " . . . when you are old, you will stretch out your hands, and another will gird you and carry you where you do not wish to go" (Jn 21:18). It is a Christian image that holds for all ages, not just for old age.

Let the Lord lead you. To a thriving cathedral or St. Martin-on-the-Rocks. To a people who pour libations to your gifts of nature and of grace, or a people happy to tune you out. To a pastor open to your wisdom on word and sacrament, or an autocrat who knows exactly what Jesus had in mind for his parish. To glowing good health that improves your preaching as well as your golf, or a cancer that cripples your service and your spirit. To changes in the Church that charm you or chill you, challenge you or crucify you. All of this, and so much more, can be grist to your ministry—especially the passion in your priesting—if you are persuaded with St. Paul that you are strongest when you are weakest, because then you are letting God do the work of God. Not an unchristian quietism; simply that all your activity is rooted in Christ, your every gesture enfolded in the hand of God.

Last Tuesday, October 1st, a supreme stylist died at 86 of Alzheimer's disease. For half a century E. B. White had profoundly influenced the writing of American English. Not only by pieces in the *New Yorker* and children's books that are classics, but by a deathless best seller on style that a homilist disregards only at peril to his preaching. As a *Times* obituary put it, White "never wrote a . . . careless sentence."[5] As we close this day for seminarians, I commend to you two gifts from E. B. White. Specifically for your preaching, his *Elements of Style.* More generally for your priesthood, in harmony with today's Gospel, his short poem "Conch":

> Hold a baby to your ear
> As you would a shell:
> Sounds of centuries you hear
> New centuries foretell.

Who can break a baby's code?
And which is the older—
The listener or his small load?
The held or the holder?[6]

Yes, dear priests-to-be, if you would enter the kingdom of God and help others enter, if you want passionately to play priest and not God, disciple and not master, "hold a baby to your ear."

Seminary of the Immaculate Conception
Huntington, N.Y.
October 6, 1985

17
TELL THE NEXT GENERATION
Twenty-seventh Sunday of the Year (C)

- Habakkuk 1:2–3; 2:2–4
- 2 Timothy 1:6–8, 13–14
- Luke 17:5–10

Quite some years ago, a Catholic bishop felt it appropriate to question some youngsters about to receive Communion for the first time. The bishop had precious little experience with boys and girls of that unpredictable age; so he thought it best, for them and for him, to run down a few pages from Baltimore Catechism One. The interrogation went like this:

Q. Tommy, who made the world?
A. God made the world.
Q. Barbara, who is God?
A. God is a pure spirit.
Q. Johnny, where is God [expecting, of course, "God is everywhere"]?
A. God's in the bathroom.
Q. What did you say?
A. God's in the bathroom.
Q. In the bathroom? Why on earth would you say that?
A. Because every morning I hear my daddy shouting out, "My God, aren't you ever going to come out of that bathroom?"

My fellow educators: I begin with Johnny and the bishop not to harass the hierarchy. I begin this way because the story suggests a counterpoint to this Sunday's Gospel, because Gospel and counterpoint together shape a Catholic harmony that may well be the song you sing to the next generation.[1] Concretely, I shall say (1) that the Gospel is a call to divine faith, (2) that a counterpoint to divine faith is human experience, (3) that your task as Catholic educators is to blend, to harmonize, faith and experience into a single, singular song, for yourselves and for your young disciples. Three movements, therefore, to my own song: (1) faith, (2) experience, (3) you.

I

First, faith. We hear of it this afternoon in a snippet from one Gospel. The Twelve beg their Lord, "Increase our faith." Jesus does not respond directly to their request. What he does, as so often, is to put the apostles on the spot. The point of importance, he says, is not how *much* faith you have, its size, its amount. What is important is the *kind* of faith you have: It has to be genuine. If it were no bigger than a grain of mustard, but were genuine, real, its power would be enormous. With such faith "you would say to this mulberry tree, 'Be uprooted and planted in the sea,' and it would obey you" (Lk 17:5–6). Or, as Matthew's Gospel has it, "you will say to this mountain, 'Move from here over there,' and it will move" (Mt 17:20).[2] With genuine faith you can do things utterly unexpected, things impossible to naked nature. "Nothing will be impossible to you" (Mt 17:21).

The problem is, what is genuine faith? Building on Scripture and tradition, Catholicism put together succinctly the Act of Faith with which I grew up, the Act of Faith enshrined in many a catechism and prayer book: "O my God, I firmly believe that thou art one God in three divine Persons, Father, Son, and Holy Ghost. I believe that thy divine Son became man and died for our sins. I believe these and all the truths which the holy Catholic Church teaches, because thou hast revealed them, who canst neither deceive nor be deceived."

This is indeed genuine faith: I submit my intellect to a revealing God. With my mind I accept as true certain propositions that come to me from the word that is Scripture, from the Word that is Christ, from the word the Church speaks in Christ's name. This is genuine faith, but it is not the whole of genuine faith. By itself, it is not the faith that saves. The New Testament Letter of James puts it pungently: "You believe that God is one; you do well. [But] even the demons believe—and shudder" (Jas 2:19). The faith that saves, the faith that moves mountains and mulberry trees, is not simply a matter of propositions—precious as propositions are within a faith that is Catholic. My act of faith must be love-laden, a yes in the first in-stance not to some specific proposition, not to a determinate set of truths, but to a person: to our Lord himself, to God in Christ. More than that, it is a yes that engages my whole person—not only un-derstanding but heart and will as well. It is a total self-giving: "I my-self, I in my entirety, surrender myself to you." The peak of saving faith is the sort of selfless love that once inspired a famous piece of poetry long attributed to St. Francis Xavier. The Spanish sonnet loses something in translation, but I believe the basic idea breaks through:

> It is not your promised heaven
> That moves me, Lord, to love you.
> It is not the fear of hell
> That forces me to fear you.
>
> What moves me, Lord, is you, Lord,
> Fixed to a cross and mocked.
> What moves me is your wounded body,
> The insults and your death.
>
> What moves me really is your love, so that
> Were there no heaven, I would love you still,
> Were there no hell, I would fear you still.
> For me to love you, you need nothing give,
> For even if I did not hope as indeed I hope,
> Even so I would love you as indeed I love.[3]

II

Such is the loving faith a loving God holds out to us. It is a gift of God, and it is expected to grow, from small beginnings to the height of Xavier's faith, from intellectual acceptance of truths to surrender of the complete person to God in Christ. I cross now to the counterpoint: experience. You see, though faith is a response, a yes, drawn from us by unmerited grace, by God's gracious giving, that faith is inseparably tied to experience. We do not live our faith on a fantasy island, isolated from the blood and guts of contem-porary living. Our personal commitment to God in Christ is incred-ibly indebted to a community, to the Church, for its birth and its growth, for its origin and its evolution.

Its origin. Whether baptized in infancy or converted later, you have been able to say yes to Christ's self-disclosure, to his self-giving, because in a context where you could hear it the Church has proclaimed the lordship of the risen Christ, the hour of the kingdom, the good news of God's love, the forgiveness of sins; because the preached gospel was accompanied by signs as powerful for you as the miracle of Christ's rising was for the apostles; because the Spirit of Christ's Church gave you heart and tongue to murmur "Jesus is Lord" (1 Cor 12:3).

Its growth. In the first place, the Church as a prophetic institution introduces you progressively into the mystery of Christ. Not as a professor of academic religion, but as a charismatic teacher that bears wondering witness to God's word. From magisterial affirmations, through theological research and religious education, to the child at its mother's knee, the Church is one breathless, ceaseless effort to "know the only true God and Jesus Christ whom [He] has sent" (Jn 17:3). It is through the Church that Scripture becomes for you the dynamizing word of God, through the Church that you find the face of the God-man on the printed page.

Second, the Church as a worshiping community focuses your faith on the very heart of the Christian reality. At the Eucharistic celebration two intertwined processes are constantly at work: Faith forms community, and community feeds faith. If you are to deepen progressively your basic commitment to Christ, your original unreserved yes, I see no substitute for the liturgical community, for the body of Christ feeding together on the body of Christ.

Third, faith, like a child, matures best within a community of love. Like it or not, I am part of you, and you are part of me. And I will grow in faith, or shrink in faith, in large measure as your love supports me, or your love deserts me. St. Paul was so terribly on target: No Christian can say to any other Christian "I have no need of you" (1 Cor 12:21). With any failure to love, *I* am diminished. In Paul's striking image, no living member of a living body is insensitive to, unaffected by, what happens in the rest of the body. We are incredibly one, all of us who eat of the same body.

III

An absorbing vision of Catholic Christianity, isn't it? But it raises a disturbing issue: your role as Catholic educators. You see, the faith of your young charges, like your own faith, is strengthened or shivered by their experience of Catholicism, their experience of the Church as a prophetic institution, as a worshiping community, as a community of love. But their experience, unlike yours, is perilously limited. They do not take the long view of the Church, the scholar's view, the episcopal view, the view that comes with wisdom. In large measure, *you* are their experience of church.

The Church as prophet? For them, the prophet is not some Platonic Idea suspended in midair. The prophet is this priest in this pulpit, proclaiming exciting Good News or parroting pious platitudes or mumbling nonsense syllables. The prophet is this teacher in this classroom, revealing how "the world is charged with the grandeur of God"[4] or dulling their minds with pedantry or a sour, crotchety, satirical jerk. The prophet is this administrator in this office, caring and compassionate or lusting for power or in love with his own image. The prophets are these parents in this home, imaging the fatherhood and motherhood of God or sousing themselves with alcohol while damning the drug generation.

The Church as locus and focus of worship? For them, worship is this celebrant, actually celebrating with joy in his heart and eyes or seemingly going through the motions. Worship is this Mass, people in love with the Sacrifice of Christ and their own sacrifice or eyes on their Timex to clock another obligation. Worship is this gathered community, at peace one with another or dreading the hand of still another stranger, one in its openness to the new and unknown or severed into two camps—Latin or English, Communion in the hand or on the tongue, a stately Bach or those dreadful St. Louis Jesuits.

The Church as community of love? For them, love is not a word in Scripture or in a Roman document. Love is this parish, if it is open to the homeless and does not leave them to the warmth of a sidewalk grille. Love is this school, if the mind is important but takes second place to the person. Love is you, if you care as much for the dullard as for the talented, as much for the unattractive as for the "tens" of this world. Love is someone to whom they can talk, who will listen, who refuses to condemn but, like Christ, helps them to "go in peace."

Good friends: The theme of your conference, "Tell the Next Generation," is splendidly suggestive and painfully provocative. It leaves unspoken, it has deliberately left to your deliberations, *what* you are to tell the next generation and *how* you are to tell it. By focusing on faith, I have suggested that *what* you tell the next generation is summed up in the Psalm from which your theme is borrowed: "Tell the next generation that this is God, our God for ever and ever" (Ps 48:13–14). *This* is God—a God of creation and cross; and in loving faith He is ours days without end. By focusing on experience, I have intimated that *how* you tell the next generation that this is our God is not so much in words as in deeds, less through abstract doctrine than through concrete living; that for the next generation *you* are the Church—each one of you individually, and all of you in your corporate existence. A privilege indeed, but also a burden. For unless you are the Church of which Christ dreamed, many a Johnny will have to look for his God in a bathroom.

Convention Center
Niagara Falls, N.Y.
October 4, 1986

18

GROW INTO YOUR FEATHERS
Twenty-eighth Sunday of the Year (B)

- Wisdom 7:7–11
- Hebrews 4:12–13
- Mark 10:17–30

Reading today's Gospel, a preacher's temptation is to come down hard on riches—especially if he doesn't have any. "It is easier for a camel to go through the eye of a needle than for a rich man to enter the kingdom of God" (Mk 10:25). I shall resist the temptation. Not only because I discoursed on camels and needles from this very pulpit on October 10, 1982, and those of you who heard me have surely not forgotten.[1] More importantly because our first reading, from the Wisdom of Solomon, is less negative, more constructive. Without deploring possessions, Solomon puts riches in a richer perspective. "I called upon God, and the spirit of wisdom came to me . . . and I accounted wealth as nothing *in comparison with her*" (Wis 7:7–8). A striking sentence, essential for human and Christian existence. To fathom its riches, let me play my piece in three movements: (1) a brief overture on the wisdom and folly of Solomon; (2) a central section that touches biblical wisdom to you; (3) a concluding aria from a wise woman of today.

I

First, Solomon. To flesh out the passage proclaimed to you (Wis 7:7–11), you should go back to the First Book of Kings, a dream of Solomon (1 Kgs 3:5–15). The Lord appears to Solomon: "Ask what I shall give you." The king's reply is a minor classic, woven in equal parts of humility and realism. In summary: Lord my God, you have made me king in place of David my father. But,

116

Lord, I am terribly young [he was about 20], inexperienced; I hardly know what to do, how a king acts. And here I am charged with the care of a people, a huge people, your people. Give me, therefore, "an understanding mind to govern your people, that I may discern between good and evil . . . " (v. 9). Pleased with Solomon's plea, the Lord responds (vv. 11–12):

> Because you have asked this, and have not asked for yourself long life or riches or the life of your enemies, but have asked for yourself understanding to discern what is right, behold, I now do according to your word. Behold, I give you a wise and discerning mind, so that none like you has been before you and none like you shall arise after you.

As bonuses, the Lord loads Solomon with riches and honor as well, and promises him long life if he will walk in God's ways.

Solomon's wisdom has become proverbial. You remember the two women who stood before him in bitter dispute (1 Kgs 3:16–28). Each has given birth to a son; one infant has died; each claims the surviving son is hers. Solomon calls for a sword: "Divide the living child in two, give half to the one, half to the other." At that, one mother cries: "Oh, my lord, don't kill the child; give it to her." Not so the other: "Neither mine nor thine; divide it." "No," said Solomon in his wisdom. "Do not kill the child; give him to the first; she is his mother."

Solomon's wisdom is indeed proverbial; but as he grew old amid 700 concubines and 300 wives, his wisdom lost its edge. "His wives," Scripture tells us, "turned away his heart after other gods, and his heart was not wholly true to the Lord his God" (1 Kgs 11:4).

II

So much for Solomon. But Solomon's wisdom is rather remote from you and me. What precisely is the biblical wisdom that should grace pauper as well as prince, the wisdom beside which "gold is but a little sand" and "silver accounted as clay" (Wis 7:9)? To get uncomfortably concrete, I shall clothe *you* in the garments of Scripture's wise man/wise woman, hold the mirror up to you, let you judge if the suit or skirt fits.[2]

Biblical wisdom has two facets: the kind of person you are and the kind of thing you do. Who are you? You are experts in an art:

how to live well. I don't mean "high off the hog"; you can eat in McDonald's or New South and still be reasonably wise. It is rather a matter of mind and spirit. Knowledge may fill your head: music or medicine, law or linguistics, Shakespeare or Sartre, American history or religious mystery, social or physical science, accounting or anatomy, First World or Third. It fills your head but never puffs it up; sheer knowledge sits securely upon you, but lightly. Technical competence you have aplenty, but this you complement with artistic feel—with da Vinci and Helen Hayes, with Michelangelo and Michael Jackson, with *Giselle* and the *Kiss of the Spider Woman*. You muse and mull over life's meaning, perhaps its absurdity, but not in abstruse abstraction, on the head of a pin or the pink of a cloud; you have a sixth sense of where you sit in this world, how you relate to it. Pious you are, but never syrupy or saccharine. Pious in its pristine sense: faithful, dutiful, reverent. Aware that, for all its mystery and madness, God still rules the world, you have a salutary fear of the Lord. Not slavish but salutary: healthy, the fear that leads to salvation, the fear that is kin to love.

What is it you do that is so wise? In harmony with the Hebrews, your wisdom is practical: You have a goal in view, and a technique for reaching it—through the pitfalls that peril the human passage. You are intimately interested in others—not only in "the people" but primarily in persons. And so your priority in an increasingly me-first culture is the other: to serve the growing and the aging, the crippled in flesh and the broken in heart, the battered and the bruised. You know the human heart, its agony and its ecstasy. You sense our grandeur and our wretchedness, our loneliness, our fear in face of pain and death, our unease and disquiet before a God so often hidden from us. With all and each you yearn to share your wisdom.

Marvel of marvels, you know how to enjoy life: the dawning of a day or an idea, the love of man and maid, Redskins football and a foaming Pub. Oh yes, you sense how imperfect and passing is the world that surrounds you, how sinful and selfish the human heart, how hostile the earth on which you dance, the air you breathe; but none of this shatters you. Through all of this you walk with sympathy and serenity; you enjoy being alive.

Where do you, like the wise of Scripture, get your wisdom? From three sources. (1) There is the accumulated wisdom of the past, the "tradition of the fathers." (2) There is your own experience. From openness to all that is real, you have grown in wisdom, never cease to grow. (3) It is, at bottom, a gift of God. Ultimately, for you the master of wisdom is Jesus. He is the Wisdom of God, in whom the sapiential texts of Scripture find their definitive meaning. He it is who, as Wisdom in flesh, communicates wisdom not to the wise in the ways of the world but to his little ones—those who, like young Mary of Nazareth, listen to the word of God and say yes.

Is this what your Washington mirror reflects back to you? If it is, you may well join Solomon and sing: "I preferred [wisdom] to scepters and thrones, and I accounted wealth as nothing in comparison with her. . . . I loved her more than health and beauty. . . . All good things came to me along with her. . . . I rejoiced in them all, because wisdom leads them; but I did not know that she was their mother" (Wis 7:8, 10–12).

III

All of which leads into my third movement: a concluding aria from a wise woman of today. It is not so much an aria as a dance; for the wise woman is "the most extraordinary ballerina this country has produced."[3] Now 40, Suzanne Farrell has been dancing since she was eight. "Balanchine's ballerina" she has been called; for the master "made more ballets for her than any other dancer—23 in all, most of them masterpieces."[4] A *Washington Post* interview with her, published two Sundays ago, revealed a woman after the heart of both Solomon and Jesus. To enflesh still further the biblical wisdom I have sketched, let me pluck four insights from that interview—insights I can guarantee are genuinely Suzanne, because I am privileged to know her.

First insight: "I prefer to come to a score fresh . . . because I feel otherwise I might be painting the choreographer into a corner. Music inspires me to move. If I know the music too well beforehand, I might tend to move in a certain way, and the choreographer would then have to tear down that barrier."[5] An insight, a wisdom, invaluable even beyond the dance. If you want to come alive in God, if you want to dance to God's music, don't paint God into a corner. As a wise Jesuit once advised me when I asked him what to avoid in an invocation, "Don't tell God what He has to do." Let God choreograph your dance, write the score for your living. It does not mean you'll be passive—simply pliant, flexible, in the hands of a creative Master who loves you.

Second insight: "What I do is listen to the music, and dance to the music. Every note you hear, whether you're dancing that moment or not, is building toward what you hope to achieve in your dancing. Every note is a stepping stone. I can't start a ballet thinking of the level I'm going to reach—that would rob that moment of its quality. So I'm never sure what's going to happen once I get out there. Because I haven't heard the music yet—as it's going to be played then."[6] A wonderfully wise twin principle for life in the Spirit. On the one hand, everything, everything decent you do, can be a stepping stone to what you hope to achieve as a man or woman and as a Christian. On the other hand, live each moment of the Spirit's music, the Spirit's inspiration, as and when it plays. Don't try to live tomorrow at this moment, and don't try to program the Spirit in your personal computer. Let the Spirit surprise you . . . and then dance to the Spirit's tune, dance like fury, for all you are worth!

Third insight: "I'm not intimidated by having to struggle. I can be embarrassed. I don't always have to look great. Nothing is born with all its plumage—you grow into your feathers. A rose can be pretty at different stages of its development."[7] The wise word here is "grow." If Jesus himself, as Luke tells us, "grew in wisdom . . . and in favor with God and man" (Lk 2:52), I too should be patient with my imperfections, not dismayed by my defects, not embarrassed to grow into my feathers, always aware that the task and the thrill of loving God and my sisters and brothers with my whole heart is a lifelong process with its unpredictable way of the cross, a process that will only be consummated on my own final Calvary.

Fourth insight: "I give myself as fully to [other choreographers] as I did to Mr. B. . . . You either believe or not—you can't semibelieve. Balanchine always gave himself completely to every ballet he worked on, always one-hundred percent. If you're given something and you keep it, it's gone when you are. If you give something away, it's forever."[8] Yes, my friends, a profound paradox: If you want your God-given gift to endure, don't clutch it feverishly to your hot skin; give it away, give it to others. It is, in a way, Jesus' own recipe for life without end: "Whoever seeks to gain his/her life will lose it, but whoever loses his/her life will preserve it" (Lk 17:33).

My sisters and brothers in Christ: We have moved from king to ballerina, from book to ballet. But through it all, it is you and I who stand center stage. Solomon and Suzanne can compel our admiration. But in the last analysis the burning question is: How wise am *I*? How wise are *you*?

This shifts our Christian focus, puts today's Gospel in perspective. The heart of the matter is not sheer possessions. Rich or poor or middle-class, can you say, as Solomon did, "I account wealth as nothing in comparison with wisdom, I love wisdom more than health and beauty"? Without the wisdom of the biblically wise, you will always be somewhat screwed up; for your values will be skewed, and in a crisis you too may turn from the Lord "sorrowful" (Mk 10:22). But if you value wisdom above wealth, if you rate who you are over what you have, then you need not worry whether you can squeeze through the eye of a needle. For in you there will be no tension between wealth and wisdom, between having and being. You will be open to whatever God might ask of you: Give it all up, like the apostles; give half of it up, like little Zacchaeus; or use it wisely for the little ones of Christ, as so many have done through the ages.

Like Solomon, call upon God for "the spirit of wisdom" (Wis 7:7). Like Jesus, keep growing in wisdom. Grow into your feathers and one day you may echo Suzanne's final words in the interview: "I can't imagine anything as wonderful as what I've been doing."[9]

Dahlgren Chapel
Georgetown University
and
Holy Trinity Church
Washington, D.C.
October 13, 1985

19

THE CASE OF THE INVINCIBLE WIDOW
Twenty-ninth Sunday of the Year (C)

- Exodus 17:8–13
- 2 Timothy 3:14—4:2
- Luke 18:1–8

Luke's Gospel just might make this preacher paranoid. When I preached to you last month, Luke's parable ran "Once there was a dishonest manager."[1] Today Luke's parable runs "Once there was a dishonest judge." If Luke had lived long enough, next month's parable might have run "Once there was a dishonest Jesuit." Once? At any rate, we have a provocative parable; the parable raises a perplexing question; and the question suggests something over and above the point of the parable.

I

First, the parable itself. Jesus confronts us with two intriguing characters: a powerful judge and a powerless widow. Only a single sentence tells us what the judge was like, but that sentence is terribly revealing—hardly a character reference for a Nobel prize: He "neither feared God nor cared about humans" (Lk 18:2). What's left? Only himself: lots of shekels for a short day's work, a six-pack of Manischewitz with his rack of lamb, maybe a little sex between sessions. "Execute justice" with Jeremiah (Jer 7:5)? With Micah, "do justice, love kindness, walk humbly with your God" (Mic 6:8)? With Isaiah, "correct oppression, defend the fatherless, plead for the widow" (Isa 1:17)? Forget it! That's for bleeding hearts, weak minds, thin skins. No, sir! You want me to rub your back? You rub mine. Justice you get if you can buy it.

And the widow? A plaintiff in some lawsuit. She fits an Old Testament picture: the widow to whom justice was so often denied, who was associated with disgrace,[2] who was cheated by lawyers appointed to take care of her estate[3]—one of the outcasts for whom Jesus was concerned on his journey to Jerusalem. It is the widow in the Book of Sirach: "Do not the tears of the widow run down her cheek as she cries out against him who has caused them to fall?" (Sir 35:15).

Our widow here has a tough time getting justice from the judge, no matter how long and how tearfully she pleads. So what does she do? Get a lawyer? You out of your cottonpickin' mind? She plays it much smarter than that: She makes a nuisance of herself. Luke gives no details, but if you use your imagination, you can see her tossing stones at the judge's bedroom window at midnight, hounding him on the streets, crashing his party, putting a dead mouse in his mailbox.

Finally the judge has had it; he caves in. Not because the widow has put the fear of God into him; not because he now cares for "bag ladies." She is simply wearing him out. He's developed insomnia; gourmet food gives him heartburn; he gets no joy out of the comics in the Jerusalem *Post;* he has to sneak out of his own house, turn the lights out when he's in. "All right," he says. "You win. Whatever you want, you've got. Just leave me alone . . . please?"

The lesson of the parable? The Gospel makes it clear beyond misunderstanding. If sheer persistence can prevail on a dishonest judge to do justice, how much more will an upright God harken to the persistent prayer of His own, "His chosen ones who cry out to Him day and night" (Lk 18:7)![4]

II

So much for the parable. But the parable raises a perplexing question: Isn't Jesus being naive? On the one hand, you have his absolute assurance that persistence in prayer will prevail. It fits in beautifully with his other encouraging directives: "Ask, and it will be given you; seek, and you will find; knock, and it will be opened to you" (Mt 7:7). "Whatever you ask in prayer, believe that you receive it, and you will" (Mk 11:24). "Whatever you ask in my name, I will do it" (Jn 14:13). If you have faith no bigger than a mustard seed, "you will say to this mountain, 'Move from here over there,' and it will move" (Mt 17:20).

On the other hand, you have in apparent contradiction a whole history of everyday experience. I see an innocent infant perish of cancer despite the profound faith, the persistent prayer, the tears day and night of his parents. I read of 45,000 Guatemalans killed in an earthquake—many of them pious peasants. Six million Jews perished in Nazi horror chambers—the vast majority surely believing children of Abraham. Sixteen million of the military died in World War II—not all atheists or foxhole Christians. Two prizefighters make the same sign of the cross; the best God can do is arrange for a draw. And I'm told that even on the Hilltop prayer does not have a 100% record in exams.

The litany is endless, sorrow-laden, in your experience and mine. It raises a tearful question: What about Jesus' solemn promise? He did not simply say "Ask, and I'll think about it." He said "Ask, and it will be given you." He did not qualify his promise: "Ask for spiritual gifts, and I'll be Johnny-on-the-spot." He said "Whatever you ask in my name, I will do it."

Believe me, good friends, I have agonized over this issue far more years than most of you. I agonized over it when my father, only 53, and my one brother, only 27, lay cancer-riddled in different hospitals at the same time, and died within three weeks of each other. I agonize over it each day I skim the newspapers—from Len Bias[5] to Beirut, from AIDS to Afghanistan. I agonize over it each time I walk through a pediatrics ward or a Washington slum, through St. Elizabeth's or the District jail. I am not asking God to move mountains, to remove Mount Rainier to Rockville; I am only asking Him to honor the promise of His Son, "Whatever you ask in prayer, believe that you receive it, and you will."

Frankly, we have no solution that totally satisfies; even your Georgetown Jesuits bow low before this mystery. Oh yes, there are all sorts of partial answers. "Sometimes we do not request what is good for us or for another." Granted, but at times we do, by God we do! "God knows best." Indeed He does, but that doesn't help our human understanding, our need to see God as good. "Whenever we pray, that itself is a good thing for us." Gladly do I admit it, but that doesn't help the poor unfortunates for whom we are praying.

As for myself, I have been aided most by the experience of Job in the Old Testament.[6] Here is a man utterly blameless, inflexibly God-fearing. Suddenly all he has is destroyed: cattle, house, servants, sons and daughters. A disease gives him ceaseless pain, keeps him sleepless, makes him ugly to the eye. He is barred from human society, lives in a community dump. People spit when they see him. His wife's advice? "Curse God, and die" (Job 2:9).

Job is terribly bewildered. Why is this happening to him? He loves God, wants only to please Him. Then why has God turned on him, turned hostile, oppressive? Close to despair, he curses the day he was born, begs God to just leave him alone.

Job's friends are no help at all. Clearly Job is suffering for his sins. Their logic is impeccable: If Job is not a sinner, then God is unjust. But Job cannot confess what is false. He denies deceit or adultery; he has respected the God-given rights of his slaves, shared his possessions with the poor; gold or any creature has never been his god; his door has swung open to every wayfarer.

In Job's wrestling with God I find two splendid moments. The first is Job's act of faith, of trust. God only seems to have changed; He still cares. If Job's sufferings make no sense, God has His own reasons. And still, though faith dissolves Job's doubts, it does not diminish his desolation. The sharpest torment of all is still there: a dark night of the soul. He cannot "get through" to God. He used to experience God's presence; now he experiences only God's absence.

The second splendid moment? At last God speaks to Job. He shows Himself to this anguished believer, this rebellious lover, who has raged against his situation, has demanded that God justify His ways. But notice: God says nothing to Job about his guilt or innocence, nothing about suffering and its meaning; He does not explain. And Job does not say: "Ah yes, now I understand. Thank you." The real experience is simply the encounter: God lets Job find Him. And in the encounter Job is happy to disown his speculations, his complaints; he even discards his ultimate support, his cherished integrity, his innocence.

Like you and me, Job had to face the problem of evil: Why do the innocent suffer, the wicked prosper? Why does not God "vindicate His chosen ones who cry out to Him day and night"? Why does He "delay long over them" (Lk 18:7)? In the face of evil, Job found human wisdom bankrupt. His anguished questioning ended in a theophany: God appeared to him—not to defend His wisdom but to stress His mystery. Job trusted God not because he could prove that God merited his trust, but because he had experienced God. Only trust makes evil endurable—trust not because God has offered proof, but because God has shown His face.

III

God has shown His face. This suggests my third point—something over and above the point of the parable, but not impertinent to the parable. You see, for all its reverence for reason, in the last analysis Catholicism is not a religion of reason. You sit here on your haunches not because you can demonstrate by a syllogism or in a test tube that Christ is God's unique Son and this is his true Church. You sit here because God has gifted you with an incredible power: the power to believe, on His word, that God has shown His face in Christ, that the same Christ who died and rose for you is here among you, here within you, hidden here in what looks like bread and tastes like wine.

This you believe. But your belief risks turning sterile unless the God who once showed His face so awesomely in Christ shows His face to you. I do not mean a vision, an apparition, a mystical experience such as lifted St. Paul to "the third heaven" (2 Cor 12:2). I mean the kind of experience God offers to each and all of you. I mean a God who is as real to you as the man or woman sitting next to you. I mean a relationship where you not only know truths *about* God; you know God. I mean a relationship of love—a love for God so intense that it rivals the love Christ bled for you on the cross.

This is the kind of relationship God wants with you. Why else would He have given His only Son to a feeding trough in Bethlehem, to crossed beams on Calvary? This is the kind of relationship God promises you when Luke's Jesus says to you: "If you, evil as you are, know how to give your children good gifts, how much more surely will the heavenly Father give the Holy Spirit to those who ask Him" (Lk 11:13).[7] With the Holy Spirit within you, you too can love as our Lord has loved, love God "with all your heart, and with all your soul, and with all your mind, and with all your strength" (Mk 12:30).

This is the kind of relationship, the kind of love, you must have if you are to live Christianly with that eternal why: "Why, dear God, did you let *this* happen? How could you and still be God?" You will not answer it with Aristotelian logic; you can live through it with crucified love.

Good friends, one final caution. Despite the unresolved questions to which it gives rise, we have much to learn from "the case of the invincible widow." Whatever your sad experience with prayer, with the prayer of petition, God still wants you to "hang in there." Like Moses against Amalek, hold your hands high, however weary your arms, till the sun goes down—and after (cf. Exod 17:8–13). Like the powerless widow, make a nuisance of yourself. Storm heaven like crazy; don't let the Lord rest even on the Sabbath. You just might prove enough of a nuisance to get what you want—especially if what you want is woven of love.

Dahlgren Chapel
Georgetown University
and
Holy Trinity Church
Washington, D.C.
October 19, 1986

20
DO THIS AND YOU SHALL LIVE
Thirty-first Sunday of the Year (B)

- Deuteronomy 6:2–6
- Hebrews 7:23–28
- Mark 12:28–34

One evening last month, I visited an ailing friend in George Washington Hospital. Before I left, she took me down the hall to another room. On one of the beds lay a black lady somewhere in her seventies. On her face, all through my visit, was a radiant smile of genuine joy; her strikingly blue eyes seemed to sparkle. She spoke of God as of someone closer to her bedside than I was, spoke of current events as if she were right there in the midst of them.

Since age 13, I learned, she had spent much of her life as a live-in servant. Against all the odds, she mentioned two little boys, blood brothers, she had helped bring up in Baltimore a half century ago. She related how she used to scrub the face of the younger boy, Francis, saying the while: "Tad looks good with a dirty face, but you don't." The two lads, she said, grew up to be priests, Jesuit priests; and to her delight I realized, and told her, that I had taught both of them in the seminary at Woodstock.

This is not a commercial for vocations. That bedridden black lady, merry in God, in love with people, aglow with life, was totally blind, and both her legs had been amputated. When I left her, I blessed her; but I knew that in reality she had blessed me. And ever since that evening, all these days that I've been wrestling with Deuteronomy and Mark on loving God and my neighbor, the face of Mary Evans has haunted me. She has ripped love out of romantic outer space, brought it down to a grim earth, made me look at it through her sightless eyes, walk it on her helpless stumps. With apologies to Mary, let me stumble a while, feel my way blindly, stammer a bit about a monosyllable that has taken on fresh meaning for me. First, love before Christ came. Second, love when Christ came. Third, love after Christ, love here and now.

I

First, love before Christ came. The reading from Deuteronomy does us a distinct service. All too many Christians see the Old Testament as a book of fear; the Hebrew God is a vengeful God, a divine despot, a terrorist; the people are not His children but His slaves. Nonsense! Listen to the commandment that transcends all other commandments:

> Hear, O Israel! The Lord is our God, the Lord alone! Therefore, you shall love the Lord, your God, with all your heart, and with all your soul, and with all your strength. Take to heart these words which I enjoin on you today. Drill them into your children. Speak of them at home and abroad, whether you are busy or at rest. Bind them at your wrist as a sign and let them be as a pendant on your forehead. Write them on the doorposts of your houses and on your gates.
>
> (Deut 6:4–9)

On your doorposts and on your city gates: Live the commandment of love in your private lives and in your public lives.

If you turn from Deuteronomy to Leviticus, what do you find? The climax of all the ethical injunctions: "You shall love your neighbor [fellow Israelites] as yourself" (Lev 19:18). But not only fellow Israelites: "When a stranger sojourns with you in your land, you shall not do him wrong. The stranger who sojourns with you shall be to you as the native among you, and you shall love him as yourself; for you were strangers in the land of Egypt" (Lev 19:33–34).

Against this background, you can read the Old Testament as a ceaseless tension between the ideal and the real. The ideal hangs ever before the eyes of Israel: Love God above all else, love your neighbor as you love yourself. But the real is shaped by all the smallness and selfishness that plague earthy existence. Rescued from bondage in Egypt, the Israelites swing like a pendulum between the God of their covenant and all manner of foreign gods. They believe and they doubt; they hope and they despair; they submit and they rebel. Convinced that the Lord is leading them to a land of milk and honey, they are unbelievably blind in reading His signs.

In the Promised Land they do what is "evil in the sight of the

Lord" (Judg 6:1), and the Lord gives them over to Midian nomads. They ask Samuel for a king, to govern them as the Gentiles govern. God gives them their king, but He makes it clear to Samuel: " . . . they have not rejected you, they have rejected me from being king over them" (1 Sam 8:7). Exiles in Babylon, they keep their faith alive, their law, their identity—more alive than do their brothers and sisters back home in Jerusalem. And still they need an Isaiah to indict them for their infidelity, to reproach them when they are blind and deaf, to lift them when their spirits sag, to assure them that their God still cares, that their iniquity is pardoned, that their exile is all but over.

Love your neighbor? Here, too, Israel's ideals constantly clashed with grim reality. They know full well what God wants of them: "Do justice" (Mic 6:8). And yet—one example only—the prophet Amos savages Samaria's wealthy. They "sell the righteous for silver, and the needy for a pair of shoes"; they "trample the head of the poor into the dust of the earth" (Amos 2:6–7); they "store up violence and robbery" (3:10), take bribes (5:12), "lie upon beds of ivory" and "anoint themselves with the finest oils" (6:4, 6). " 'They do not know how to do right,' says the Lord" (3:10).

Despite all this, the Old Testament is studded with men and women who loved God with their whole heart, loved their brothers and sisters as much as they loved themselves. Abraham leaves country and kin, leaves all he has been, in response to God's "Go" (Gen 12:1), is even ready to sacrifice his only son if God so asks. Moses speaks for God to an all-powerful Pharaoh, leads the enslaved Israelites out of Egypt, through sea and wilderness, hustles them heroically to the banks of the Promised Land, though he himself cannot enter it. Jeremiah never ceases to preach the word of the Lord to a stiff-necked people, though he is beaten and put in the stocks, is repeatedly persecuted, risks death itself. Rather than worship man-made gods, three young Hebrews brave a fiery furnace.

Nor do the men of the Old Testament overshadow the women. Gentle Ruth, a Moabite, embraces Israel's God and its destiny, says to her mother-in-law: "Your people shall be my people, and your God my God" (Ruth 1:16), becomes the great-grandmother of David. Esther dares death to save her people from annihilation by the Persians: "I will go to the king, though it is against the law; and if I perish, I perish" (Esth 4:16). A mother watches her seven sons tortured and killed on a single day because they refuse to be faithless to God; she bears it "with good courage because of her hope in the Lord" (2 Macc 7:20); she encourages her youngest against the king: "Do not fear this butcher, but prove worthy of your brothers" (v. 29). The list is long, the love is endless.

II

My second point: love when Christ came. Here, as elsewhere, our Lord does not destroy the law, does not ridicule it; he repeats it with reverence, means by it what his Jewish ancestors meant. How must you love your God? With your whole "heart": Respond to God with all the fire, all the passion, that can possibly sear you. With your whole "soul": Respond to God with all the vitality, all the awareness, that mark a person into whom a loving Lord has breathed His life. With all your "strength": Respond to God with that deep inner drive you can scarcely suppress. To these three faculties Jesus added a fourth: Love God with all your "mind." Love God not mindlessly, not scatterbrained; love Him intelligently, with common sense that plans and looks ahead. Together, the four fashion a total person, a man or woman fully alive, fully in love.[1]

And your neighbor? Jesus echoes Leviticus: You have to love your neighbor like another self. The parable of the Good Samaritan does not contradict the Torah. Jesus reminds the Jews of their own rich tradition: You don't define neighbor by race or religion. Neighbor is a four-letter word: n-e-e-d. The fellow who fell among robbers was hurting; he needed help, someone to bind his wounds. The Samaritan simply did what any Jew was bound to do: He "was moved to pity" by a man who hurt and he "did mercy with him" (Lk 10:33, 37). That Samaritans had no use for Jews was beside the point; a creature of flesh and blood was in need. To respond to that need is to love your neighbor as if you were loving yourself.[2]

And yet, in two instances Jesus took his compatriots a step beyond their traditions. First, in the Sermon on the Mount: "You have heard [the conventional wisdom], 'You shall love your neighbor and hate your enemy.' But I say to you, 'Love your enemies and pray for those who persecute you' " (Mt 5:43–44). Second, at the Last Supper, Jesus' own commandment: "Love one another as I have loved you" (Jn 15:12). Not as before, "Love others as you love yourself." No, love the way I have loved you. And how is that? For love of us, God's eternal Son wrapped Himself in our skin, came out of a woman's body as you and I come out, learned to think and talk as you and I learn, grew as hungry as we and just as weary, sweated blood because afraid to die, was lashed with a whip and showered with spit, was fixed to a criminal's cross and died whispering forgiveness on all of us. He was born to die—for love of us. A love that identified with us, a love that forgave us, a love that was crucified for us.

III

All of which climaxes in my third point: love after Christ, love here and now. You see, what Jesus called the first and second commandments in the law are not pious suggestions: If you can spare the time from RCA or IBM, from Schlitz and sex, please try to love God with your whole heart. If your neighbors are your kind of people—not blacks or Baptists, not poor whites or Puerto Ricans, not Russians or Jews—invite them over for margaritas. No, my friends, here is Christianity at its most critical. Of these two commandments Jesus promised: "Do this and you shall live" (Lk 10:28). Put these precepts into practice and you share God's life now and for ever. The implication? Disregard these commands and you're dead.

The problem is, how can you realistically give your whole heart and soul and mind and strength to a God you've never seen? You have to . . . but how? For your encouragement, countless folk have done it, millions of mortals, since Adam bit into the bitter apple. And most of them did not have a college education, knew less about God than you do.

Precisely there is the heart of the matter: You can know *about* God without knowing God; many a philosopher and theologian is proof positive thereof. And if you only know *about* God—God is, God is good, God is infinite, God knows all things, God rewards the good and punishes the wicked—you have no guarantee that you will love God. He may indeed be important to you—a problem to be solved, a judge you have to face, a last resort in macroeconomics—but you are hardly likely to lay your heart in His hands, to murmur "I love you passionately, above all else."

But how do you ever get to know God? One sure way: Experience God. Not necessarily, or usually, visions or voices. I mean simply that a living, loving God can and does make His presence felt, can and does speak to you in the silence of your soul, can and does warm and thrill you till you no longer doubt that He is near, that He is here. Such experience you cannot force from God; He gives it freely. But He does give it, has given it to such as Moses and Thomas Merton, to such as Mother Mary and Mother Teresa, to Mary Evans. In fact, there is no one to whom God refuses it.[3] But you have to ask . . . and ask . . . and ask. And you know, in the very asking you are already loving.

Besides asking, act! If you want to love God, love God's image; love the men and women who people your everyday life. The Irish satirist Jonathan Swift was at his biting best here: "We have just enough religion to make us hate, but not enough to make us love one another."[4]

If you would refute Mr. Swift, don't try to imprison love in a definition. To love others as God expected the Jew to do, to love others as Christ has loved us, calls for imagination far more than sheer reason. What cries out to me is not a personality but a need—frequently a need that expands my human horizons. When I look at Mary, sightless and legless in a hospital bed, it is blind of me to love simply her sparkling smile, this one black woman who loves so lavishly and is so easy to love. In her I glimpse a people—a vast people who touched our shores not as immigrants but as slaves, in chains; a proud people who were cut off from their culture, stripped of their identity, made to feel inferior, ignorant, unclean; a wounded people still struggling to persuade me that black is indeed beautiful; an angry people to whom John Paul II said bluntly in Cameroon this August: "And now we ask our African brothers and sisters, who have suffered so much because of the slave trade, for forgiveness."[5] From Mary Evans, who has her act together, my love must move out to every black image of God who strains mutely to catch my eye. For it is I who am blind; it is my love that is lame.

The examples are legion, the needs beyond counting. I have chosen a black image because the eyes of sightless Mary bore into mine. But the color is irrelevant, immaterial. God's word, Old Testament and New, is utterly lucid on love of neighbor. Love is where need is—where someone, anyone, is hurting, is vulnerable, is lonely, is afraid. Reach out and you will love; reach out and you will live.

Dear friends, in my stammering about love, I have said little about hate. For one terribly good reason: The opposite of love is not hate; the opposite of love is indifference. I simply don't care.

> Dahlgren Chapel
> Georgetown University
> and
> Holy Trinity Church
> Washington, D.C.
> November 3, 1985

21
END IN FIRE, END IN ICE?
Thirty-third Sunday of the Year (C)

- Malachi 3:19–20 (4:1–2)
- 2 Thessalonians 3:7–12
- Luke 21:5–19

Today's Gospel has never been pure pleasure for a preacher. The destruction of Jerusalem and the end of the world—don't you have to stretch a bit to fit these under "good news," the glad tidings the word "gospel" literally means?[1] A brave man but not a hero, let me set limits to what I can accomplish today. Much as I weep for the holocaust that was Jerusalem in the year 70—six thousand refugees perishing in the flames of the temple, over a million Jews put to the sword, almost a hundred thousand hustled in chains to Rome—I shall not dwell on this.[2] I shall focus on the last days not of the Holy City but of the whole world. To make gospel sense of this, I must ask three questions. First, the word you have heard: Why this Gospel on this day? Second, the relation of that word to the real world: What is the Church trying to tell us? Third, the meaning of that word for day-to-day Christian living: How should you and I react?

I

First, the word you have heard. Why this somber word today? Why not something cheerful, genuinely good news, like Jesus multiplying five loaves of enriched Jewish rye a thousand times, or turning six jars of water into 150 gallons of savory Manischewitz?[3] Why not? Because the Eucharistic liturgy is not a helter-skelter, haphazard selection of readings. The liturgy ritualizes the story of our salvation. We began the story on the First Sunday of Advent; we shall end it next Sunday with the Feast of Christ the King. Throughout this church year we have re-presented in symbol and story God's wonderful works, have tried to relive them, make them a reality in our lives.

In Advent, through a prophet, a precursor, and a pregnant teen-ager—through Isaiah, John the Baptist, and Mary of Nazareth—we shared Israel's burning yearning for its Savior. We sang "Glory" with angels when he came, enfolded him no longer in straw but in our hearts. We grew with him in wisdom as through three silent decades he played and planed in Nazareth. We scuffed the dust of Judea to hear him preach that God's kingdom is here, is within us. We ate of his flesh at the Supper, groaned with him in Gethsemane, ached helplessly with his mother beneath a cross, saw his head crumple in death. We rose with him one roseate dawn, breakfasted on a beach off his bread and fish. In him we too ascended to the Father; his Spirit descended on us as well as on the Twelve. In the months since Pentecost we have caught with our ears and experienced in our lives the mission of the Church, shared its pain and its joy as it struggled to grow into Christ, while we waited in hope for the coming of the Lord, this time not in swaddling bands but in the glorious freedom of his Father.

Now the final act of the liturgical drama is upon us. Next Sunday the curtain will fall: We shall crown Christ king of hearts. But not quite yet. Today we ritualize, we celebrate in anticipation, the second last scene, what precedes the kingship of Christ in its fulness. I mean the end of this world as we know it.

II

This summons up my second point: the relation of the word you have heard to the world you inhabit. What is the Church trying to tell us? Here you must be careful—careful to separate the message from the props, the essential message of Jesus from the stage props he uses. What stage props? "There will be signs in sun and moon and stars, and upon the earth nations in distress, anxious over the roaring and surging of the sea, men and women fainting with fear and foreboding of what is coming upon the world; for the forces of heaven will be shaken loose" (Lk 21:25–26). You find much the same props in the Old Testament, to describe the great Day of the Lord: "I will give portents in the heavens and on the earth, blood and fire and columns of smoke. The sun shall be turned to darkness, and the moon to blood . . . " (Joel 2:30–31).

Now the Gospel is not a lesson in astronomy or oceanography. Luke's Jesus is not really telling us what will happen to the sun that heats and lights our earth, to the moon on which we first walked in 1969, to 200 billion billion stars, to the seas that cover more than 70 percent of the earth's surface. This is Steven Spielberg. These are apocalyptic props, the imaginative setting for a twin truth: This world as we know it will come to some sort of "end," and that end will come when "the Son of Man [comes] with power and great glory" (Lk 21:27).

I find the same sort of imagination at play, but in a modern mode, when I read Archibald MacLeish's sonnet "The End of the World," set in a circus tent:

> Quite unexpectedly as Vasserot
> The armless ambidextrian was lighting
> A match between his great and second toe
> And Ralph the lion was engaged in biting
> The neck of Madame Sossman while the drum
> Pointed, and Teeny was about to cough
> In waltz-time swinging Jocko by the thumb—
> Quite unexpectedly the top blew off:
> And there, there overhead, there, there, hung over
> Those thousands of white faces, those dazed eyes,
> There in the starless dark the poise, the hover,
> There with vast wings across the canceled skies,
> There in the sudden blackness the black pall
> Of nothing, nothing, nothing—nothing at all.[4]

Only one deep difference between MacLeish and Luke: MacLeish's "nothing at all" is filled in Luke with the power and glory of Christ. Precisely there is the Christian message as we near the end of the Church's year. The world we humans know is not the last stage of salvation's story. At some point—I know not when—this paradoxical planet on which God's images dance in delight and perish in pain, where a billion grow fat and a billion fall asleep hungry, where crucified love walks hand in hand with crucifying hate, hope with despair—this kind of existence you and I experience will not endure for ever. It is destined, if not to die altogether, at least to change radically. And the most radical change? Christ our Lord, with the glorious wounds of his redeeming passion, will establish his loving rule at long last over all that is, will (in the powerful prophecy of Paul) "deliver the kingdom to God the Father after destroying every rule and every authority and power . . . [even] the last enemy, death . . . that God may be everything in everyone" (1 Cor 15:24, 26, 28). Such is the faith you will proclaim after bread is transformed into Christ's body, wine into his blood, when you sing "Christ has died, Christ is risen, Christ will come again!"

III

This leads, in my own brand of rigorous logic, to a third point: the meaning of the word you have heard for day-to-day Christian living. How should you and I react? You can, of course, have recourse to our second reading and imitate the Christians of Thessalonica. Convinced that the Second Coming was just around the corner, they quit their jobs, settled their potbellies near a potbellied stove, let others feed them, and just waited for that pink cloud carrying Christ to the general store. The trouble is, you would still have to hear St. Paul's reaction: "If anyone will not work, let him not eat" (2 Thess 3:10).

No, Christians dare not wait idly for the coming of Christ. Even if persuaded that the human race is soon to be nuked, I must still prepare my acre of God's earth to fit into Christ's kingdom—and his kingdom is a kingdom of peace, of justice, of love. I am reminded of that remarkable poem by Robert Frost:

> Some say the world will end in fire,
> Some say in ice.
> From what I've tasted of desire
> I hold with those who favor fire.
> But if it had to perish twice,
> I think I know enough of hate
> To say that for destruction ice
> Is also great
> And would suffice.[5]

Frost is so right. Two passions can destroy our earth from within. One is the fire of desire. Not just any desire; without deep desire you're a wimp. Frost means a disordered desire to get, to amass, to possess, a grasping greed—from Soviet lust for world domination, through J.R.'s latest flimflam to corner the oil market,[6] to any of our all-consuming needs for riches, for power, for fame. The other is the ice of hate—from an anti-Semitism that gassed six million Jews, through black and white bloodshed in South Africa, to the terrorisms that chill airspace and streets.

The end that Jesus foretold—of that end, Jesus told us, "you know neither the day nor the hour" (Mt 25:13). You cannot hasten it; you cannot delay it. It will come in God's own time. But the end as Frost imagined it, the end as coming not from without but from within, this you can do something about. And in so doing (glory be to God!) you will be readying the earth for the final coming of Christ.

How? Temper the fire of disordered desire and melt the ice of hate. Terribly abstract—just what you'd expect of a theologian! So, down to the grime and the grit. Christ *has* come and he *will* come again. But don't live your life at a crib that is past or on a cloud still to arrive. Christ our Lord is here *now*. Not only in the word you have heard; not only in the Bread that will be broken. He comes to you in every human person who crosses your path, haunts your eye, beats your ear. He warms himself in winter on the grates of M Street, begs for shelter at a spot called Calvary, cries for your compassion from behind D.C. bars. In slum and condo he grows old unwanted and unwept. He bleeds not only in Belfast but in every brutal rape, in every sneer or shoulder shrugged, in every student lonely amid campus laughter. He lies alone and afraid on each hospital bed, dies again in each mother bereaved. And, dear God, the children. From the bloated bellies of Ethiopia's skin-and-bones, through the 12,000 battered bodies and shriveled souls that swarm each year into Covenant House at Times Square, to the uncounted "coked" and "crashed" on our own streets, there echoes in my ears Elizabeth Barrett Browning's "The Cry of the Children":

> Do ye hear the children weeping, O my brothers,
>   Ere the sorrow comes with years?
> They are leaning their young heads against their mothers,
>   And *that* cannot stop their tears.
> The young lambs are bleating in the meadows,
>   The young birds are chirping in the nest,
> The young fawns are playing with the shadows,
>   The young flowers are blowing toward the west—
> But the young, young children, O my brothers,
>   They are weeping bitterly!
> They are weeping in the playtime of the others,
>   In the country of the free.[7]

Good friends: Today's liturgy is not a parish pool—put a dollar in the basket and guess when Christ is coming again. Today's liturgy commits you to act as if Christ were already here—because he is.

And you clearly find him *here*. You have heard him in his word, will soon cradle him in your hands or pillow him on your tongue. Today's question is: Do you find him *out there?* Or must you weep with Magdalene at the tomb: "They have taken away my Lord, and I do not know where they have laid him" (Jn 20:13)?

If you have already discovered Christ out there—or when you discover him—what must you do? No homilist can tell you that—not even that high and mighty creature, a theologian-in-residence. With Saul knocked to the ground, ask "What shall I do, Lord?" (Acts 22:10). And the Lord will say in his own way what he said to Saul: "Rise and go into the city, and you will be told what you are to do" (Acts 9:6). "Go into the city." Not necessarily 14th Street or Luther Place or Lafayette Park. Simply go where people are, especially people who hurt; look into someone's eyes; listen a little; and the Lord will tell you what you are to do. When he does, he will have come again . . . to you.

Dahlgren Chapel
Georgetown University
and
Holy Trinity Church
Washington, D.C.
November 16, 1986

MEDLEY

22
I AND THOU, NOT MINE AND THINE
Baccalaureate Sermon 1

- Proverbs 8:22–31
- Romans 5:1–5
- John 16:12–15

Today's liturgy can baffle a baccalaureate homilist. It challenges him to relate two unrelated realities: graduation and the Trinity. Three Persons who never had a beginning, and 1415 persons who are just "commencing." Are there no limits to a theologian's ivory tower? With Qaddafi in your travel bags and antiapartheid on your lawns,[1] with computers jockeying for your bodies and TV evangelists for your souls, with one fourth of the human race hungry and half the world at war hot or cold—dare I preach on three Persons in one God? How jesuitical can a Jesuit get?

Never convicted of being shy, I shall try. Why? Because I am convinced that the most practical reality for your years ahead is a three-letter word: not IBM but GOD. So let me proceed in three stages. I shall move from the Mystery that is God, through the mystery that is you, to the mystery that is your tomorrow. God . . . you . . . tomorrow.

I

First, the Mystery that is God. I do not come to solve it. But when the Son of God borrowed your skin to tell you a bit about it, when one of those "Persons" wrote His scenario for you in blood on the sands of Palestine, it would be impolite, if not chancy, for an educated Hoya to suggest that the Trinity doesn't really matter, that more important for computerized living is the byte in your Apple.[2]

But how do you make sense of a triune God? Begin with God's

own word. God not only loves; "God *is* Love" (1 Jn 4:8). Not in some gossamer, shadowy sense. In the Trinity we discover the perfect realization of perfect love, the model-without-beginning for every love that has ever begun. This we glimpse in two stunning ways: in the secret life of God and in the life God shared with us.[3]

We glimpse it in the secret life of God, the life Father, Son, and Spirit live alone without ever being lonely. Love, you see, is a we: a you and an I. Whether I love God or another human being, I never cease to be myself. Teresa of Avila, caught up in God, never ceased to be Teresa, never became God. Romeo, forsaking his very name for Juliet, did not become Juliet. Love demands "I" and "thou."

But love forbids "mine" and "thine"—what Augustine called "those ice-cold words." The two, remaining two, must somehow be one. But we have long since learned a bitter-sweet lesson: Oneness with someone beloved can be achieved only in terms of self-giving. To love is to give—to give of one's self. To love perfectly is to give till there is nothing left to give. Only then do the two, remaining two, become perfectly one.

The astounding truth about the Trinity is that it is the perfect realization of perfect love. God's secret is this: There is "I and thou" without "mine and thine." The Father is not the Son; the Son is not the Father; the Holy Spirit is neither the Father nor the Son. Each is a real person. And still there is no "mine and thine," no egoism. The Father gives to the Son literally all that He Himself has, all that makes Him God, all that makes Him Love. The Son, perfect image of the Father, loves the Father to selfless perfection. And, marvel beyond comprehension, the love with which Father and Son love each other, that love is a person. That love *is* the Holy Spirit.

But God's love does not hide in outer space. Perfect love has touched our earth; we glimpse it in the life God shared with us. The Father, John declares, "so loved the world that He gave His only Son, that whoever believes in him should not perish but have eternal life" (Jn 3:16). The Son, Paul lyricizes, did not think His glory something to cling to, a prize to clutch. He took our bone and marrow, our skin and sinews. Not because He needed them. He took what is ours only to give us what is His, to let us share God's life, God's glory. And the Holy Spirit? The Spirit is not only the love between Father and Son; the Spirit is God's Gift to you and me. "If I leave you," Jesus said the night before Calvary, "it is only to send you my Spirit, to be with you always, to teach you all truth, to be my Presence among you, my Presence within you" (cf. Jn 16:7–15).

II

All of which moves me from God to you. You see, love does not *stop* with God; it only *begins* with God. The proof is stamped on the second page of Scripture: "God created man in His own image . . . ; male and female He created them" (Gen 1:27). The miracle of your creation is not that you are like one another; the wonder of your being is that you are like God.

How? I cannot count the ways. Like God, you can know. Your four Georgetown years have been a breath-taking sharing: not so much in a professor's notes, rather in God's own knowledge, in the God who *is* Mind. Like God, you can create. From some small beginning like "the dust of the earth" (Gen 2:7) that ended in Adam, you build cities and empires, craft computers and cathedrals, sculpt a "Pietà" and paint a "Mona Lisa," make music that charms the angels, weave words that fire the earth. Like God, you are free. Not "foot-loose and fancy-free." Rather, able to breathe a human yes to all that is good and beautiful and true; able to say no to what is less than human, inhuman, unworthy of God's image.

And all of that—to know, to create, to act in freedom—all of that comes to a peak in this: Like God, you can love. Not a frothy, syrupy, "Love Boat"[4] love. A tough, realistic love. You can face another—an "I" and a "thou"—and say: "There is no 'mine and thine.' " Oh yes, you do own, you possess, you have what others lack. This is not a brief for a Christian communism, not an assault on private property. But private property is not an absolute; it is subordinate to core personal rights: the right to life, to human dignity, to bodily integrity. Paradoxically, in the Christian scheme of things, whatever you have you hold in trust for God's other images. You own not to clutch but to share. Not only your checking account but, more importantly, yourself: your ideas and your discoveries, your insights and your imagination, your freedom and your love. Ultimately, all things are God's: not only divine grace but the world's energy, the fish of the sea and the birds of the air, earth's loam and your life, your time and treasure and talent.

This is not pious rhetoric; this is basic Christianity, the Catholic vision. It is summed up in a thrilling verse from the First Letter of Peter: All Christians should employ (literally, "deacon") the many-splendored charisms they have from God for the advantage of one another, "as good stewards of God's dappled grace" (1 Pet 4:10). As images of a Trinity. You are not Christian unless you reflect a Fa-

ther who cares, the Yahweh who asked a despairing Israel that felt
Godforsaken: "Can a woman forget her sucking child, that she
should have no compassion on the son of her womb? Even these
may forget, yet I will not forget you. Behold, I have graven you on
the palms of my hands" (Isa 49:15–16). You are not Christian unless
you mirror a fleshbound Son who surrendered life itself for you,
not from a pink cloud but from crossed beams as bloody as any you
will ever experience. You are not Christian unless your human
spirit resembles a divine Spirit whose proper name is Gift.

In a word, your vocation is as simple as it is profound. You were
shaped, each one of you, by a Trinity, shaped in love and for love.
Marvel of marvels, the love you must image is not light years away.
The love you must mirror is within you: Father, Son, and Spirit alive
in you this very moment, challenging you to join Their dance, to
come alive with Their life.

III

So much for the mystery that is you. It impels me to the mystery
that is your tomorrow. It is indeed a mystery, hidden from your eyes
and mine. And still I dare not be silent. God's love and your love
are not abstract theses in a blue book, not pretty verses for an Amy
Grant to sing. The Trinity is yours to live, yours to sing.

The problem is, you graduates of '86 are entering a culture
where the Trinity is under terrible threat. Not as a dogma; as a way
of life. Objective sociologists, not biased preachers, insist that we are
experiencing today a resurgence of 19th-century rugged individualism.[5] Listen to Robert Bellah as he describes the new ideal:
economic man/woman, man and woman in pursuit of private self-
interest:

> What is significant here is not the Moral Majority . . . but some-
> thing that comes closer to being amoral and is in fact a majority.
> This new middle class believes in the gospel of success 1980 style.
> It is an ethic of how to get ahead in the corporate bureaucratic
> world while maximizing one's private goodies. In the world of the
> zero-sum society it is important to get to the well first before it
> dries up, to look out for number one, to take responsibility for
> your own life and keep it, while continuing to play the corporate
> game. . . .[6]

Why float this before the class of '86? Because this new ideal finds its strength in the younger generations. Because the dominant theme researchers find in young economic man/woman is autonomy, personal fulfilment; you are responsible only to yourself; in the end you're alone.

The liturgy of the Trinity stands in flat contradiction to the new ideal. From Eve shaped symbolically from the side of a sleeping Adam, through the Church fashioned from the side of a pierced Christ, to the very last human who will be born of woman, no man or woman is alone, responsible only to one's self. The "I" and the "thou" are written into your flesh and spirit.

Here, I submit, is the genius of Georgetown. Yes, you exit these ancient gates into a new world, a world you've read about, touched briefly, but not experienced at its core—its splendid possibilities and its seductive perils. But my hopes for you are high, amazingly high. Why? Because through these four years I have been privileged to see with my own eyes, to hear with my own ears, Trinitarian life and love in you. So many of you whose lives have intersected mine and graced it have proven to me, if proof were needed, that "I and thou" is possible without "mine and thine." From Nicaragua to Peru, from shelters for the homeless to hope for the hopeless, from compassion for Salvadoran refugees to light for the minds of our District's devastated young—in scores of ways you have humbled me with your imaging of a God who *is* Love. Within these very gates I have witnessed a campus ministry from student to student that puts my own to shame. I have seen how, sometimes at great cost, you feed a friend's faith, deliver from near despair, lift love to unexpected heights.

Good friends: An older, moving exhortation in the Catholic marriage ritual had the priest say to bride and groom: "And so, not knowing what lies before you, you take each other for better or worse, for richer or poorer, in sickness and in health, until death." In a sense equally profound, I can murmur similar words to you this grace-filled morning. Not quite knowing the mystery of your tomorrow, you take, in faith and hope and love, this wondrous, perilous world outside—its men and women, its wealth and poverty, its strength and weakness, its politics and its economics and its computers. You take it, not to be seduced by it, dehumanized. You take it to share with it the divine life that throbs within you, to help it live the love to which it too is called.

My prayer for you? May you dance through the Healy gates in sheer delight! Delight in the Mystery that is God: Your God is, first

and foremost, a Trinity of love. Delight in the mystery that is you:
You have been shaped in the image of that love. Delight in the mystery that is tomorrow: Bring to it a unique, irreplaceable "I"; an "I"
dissatisfied with "mine and thine"; an "I" that will find its joy always
and only in a "thou."

Georgetown University
May 25, 1986

23
THE OTHER, THE OTHERS, AND YOU
Baccalaureate Sermon 2

● Jeremiah 9:23–24

It's been a rough year for ethics. A politician, a preacher, an entrepreneur. A politician no longer presidential potential because he is tarred with womanizing. A preacher who can no longer Praise The Lord because he used blackmail to cover adultery. An entrepreneur who gives all Wall Street the shakes when he confesses to illegal inside trading. And all sorts of shenanigans from nursing homes to the basement of the White House.[1]

Now this is not a jeremiad against the modern world. Despite the half century that separates you and me in age, I shall not abuse your Budweiser time by telling you how good things used to be. They weren't; and even if they were, you wouldn't believe me. But this long winter and this strange spring do raise questions, raise them to a pitch of urgency that touches you intimately because tomorrow you replace the Harts and Norths, the Bakkers and Boeskys; you will shape our world after I have joined my ancestors. They raise questions about what it means to be human, to be a man or a woman, to be genuinely religious, to be alive in the Judeo-Christian tradition that helped fashion this singular nation of freedom under law.

Let me, then, speak very directly to you. Allow me to tell you simply what I in the winter of existence expect of you in your spring and summer, what I should like to see in you after four years in Hamilton, what I hope for you, and so for our world, as you begin to dance thereon, as you start shaping it in your image. My hope for you has three dimensions: (1) the Other—capital O; (2) the others—small o; (3) you yourself.

149

I

First, the Other—capital O. To an ancient society that prized three possessions above all else—wisdom, power, wealth—the prophet Jeremiah thundered: "Thus says the Lord: 'Let not the wise man glory in his wisdom, let not the mighty man glory in his might, let not the rich man glory in his wealth; but let him who glories glory in this, that he understands and knows me, that I am the Lord who practice steadfast love, justice, and righteousness in the earth; for in these things I delight, says the Lord' " (Jer 9:23–24).

Now these words are not writ large over your 1400 acres. The Baptists of 1819 surely had them in mind when they established a seminary here; but the movement from ministry to liberal arts and science has meant a movement from tranquil acceptance of God to a search for God, a struggle—to an atmosphere where atheists and agnostics mingle with fundamentalists and liberal believers, where the Quran enjoys equal official favor with the Prior Testament and the New, where the Mahayana Buddhist need not feel uncomfortable. Here is where God is worshiped and denied, prayed to and ridiculed, debated in class and over foaming mugs—or just ignored. The God of Abraham and the God of Jesus Christ makes Himself (or Herself) at home here by human persuasion, not by divine right.

And that can be a good thing. I say "can" because not everyone can "take" it. But for those who can, Colgate should be a liberating experience. For here religion is not the Baltimore Catechism, even No. 3; here religion is not a naked Scripture; here faith seeks understanding. Here you wrestle with revelation, wrestle with ideas, wrestle like Jacob with God. And wrestle you must. For if God is, if you exist only because a loving God fashioned you out of nothing but love, then that God wants you to know Him. This, as Jeremiah exclaimed, this is your glory: that you know the Lord.

But the wrestling is a sweaty job. If you are a Jew, you wrestle with Auschwitz, with mountains of human bones, with six million men, women, and children gassed into oblivion; and you may be tempted to conclude, as some do, that "God died in Auschwitz." If you are a Christian, any brand or breed, you wrestle with a God who gave His own Son to a bloody death, with a God of several hundred sects competing for souls, with a Christ who promises perplexing paradoxes: life through death, losing all to gain all, blessedness on the poor and the hungry and those who weep, woes on the rich and the fat and the merry. If you are a Catholic Christian, you may well wrestle with a Church that claims to know God's mind for you, that breathes down your neck in bedroom and board room, that keeps you from love when your marriage is dead, that seems to keep women in second-class slavery.

I assume you are here, in this house of God, because God has somehow touched you, because you love Him or fear Him or are just plain puzzled by Him. No matter. What I hope for you is that you will never cease wrestling with God, for that in itself is a proof of love: You want to know Him, know what He is like, what makes Him tick, how He can possibly leave His own world the contradiction it is—where we love enough to die for one another, hate enough to kill one another. I hope that by wrestling with God you will discover what I have experienced—discover that your God has never stopped loving you, for in the touching segment from the prophet Isaiah:

> Zion said: "The Lord has forsaken me,
>   my Lord has forgotten me."
> "Can a woman forget her sucking child,
>   that she should have no compassion on the son of her womb?
> Even these may forget,
>   yet I will not forget you.
> Behold, I have graven you on the palms of my hands. . . . "
> (Isa 49:14–16a)

I hope that by wrestling with God you will discover that the Lord not only loves you but lives in you, has compassion on you not from outer space but from within your bone and marrow, is more intimate to you than you are to yourself. I hope that by wrestling with God you will experience the joy, the even sensuous pleasure, that comes from being in love—in love with Him who made you, who is faithful despite our infidelities, cares even in our uncaring.

It's worth getting to know God. After all, you're going to have to live with God . . . for ever.

II

Second, the others—small o. Over two decades ago, a remarkable rabbi, Abraham Joshua Heschel, wrote an article titled "No Religion Is an Island." Two short paragraphs from that article consistently haunt me:

To meet a human being is a major challenge to mind and heart. I must recall what I normally forget. A person is not just a specimen of the species called *homo sapiens*. He is all of humanity in one, and whenever one man is hurt we are all injured. The human is a disclosure of the divine, and all men are one in God's care for man. Many things on earth are precious, some are holy, humanity is holy of holies.

To meet a human being is an opportunity to sense the image of God, *the presence* of God. According to a rabbinical interpretation, the Lord said to Moses: "Wherever you see the trace of man there I stand before you. . . . "[2]

The image of God, the presence of God, in each woman and man—a thrilling thought. The Other comes alive in the other. Regrettably, the traditional thought clashes with contemporary reality. First-rate sociologists insist that what we are experiencing today is a resurgence of late-19th-century rugged individualism, that in today's America what is of supreme importance is for me to get to the well first before it dries up, that in the last analysis the one reality that matters is myself; here is *numero uno,* here my ultimate responsibility.[3] The race is to the swift, the shrewd, the savage; and the devil take the hindmost.

It frightens me, my friends. For religious reasons, to begin with. Both Old Testament and New command us: "You shall love your neighbor as [you love] yourself" (Lev 19:18; Mt 22:39). The God of Abraham demanded that the children of Abraham father the fatherless and feed the stranger, not because the orphan and the sojourner deserved it, but because that was the way God had acted towards *them.* In freeing the oppressed, they were mirroring the loving Lord who had delivered *them* from oppression, had freed them from Pharaoh. The Christ of Christians tells us that when we feed the hungry and welcome the stranger, when we clothe the naked and visit the sick and the shackled, we do it to him.

Heschel is right on target: "humanity is holy of holies." Not humanity as an abstract concept. Heschel's humanity is the flesh and blood seated beside you. Humanity is each person you touch each day. Humanity is the man or woman you work with or compete against. Humanity is the color and smell that makes you gag. Humanity is the down-and-out bum and the "bag lady." Humanity is, yes, the Russian peasant and the Iranian ayatollah. Humanity is,

God forgive us, the Klaus Barbie who sent 41 Jewish children, aged 3 to 13, to the gas chambers of Auschwitz. We are commanded, poor humans, to see in each, somehow, the trace of God. Not to condone what criminals do; only to see, beneath the image of God defiled and desecrated, the God who cannot forget them, the God who has graven even them on the palms of His hands.

Here the religious approach is crucial; for unless you can see the face of God "wherever you see the trace of man [or woman]," you risk limiting justice to an ethical construct: Give to each what is due to each, what each person has a strict right to demand, because he or she is a human being, has rights that can be proven by philosophy or have been written into law.

I am not denigrating philosophy or law. Without philosophers from Aristotle to Whitehead we would be wanting in wisdom; and only in a nation under law can society survive. Nor am I claiming that only if you believe in God can you spend your life for others, lay down your life for the other. History makes a mockery of any such claim; and I suspect that your own Volunteers Colgate has its share of admirable infidels. I do say that if you can add a divine dimension to the purely human, if you can "sense the image of God, the presence of God," in every individual who meets your eye, you will *surely* give to others more than they deserve; you will *surely* not do unto others before they do it unto you; you will *surely* act towards others with the love the Lord God lavished on Israel despite its ceaseless infidelities, the love the Lord God rains on all of us no matter how little deserving of love we prove.

It will not be easy. In medicine you may find it difficult to discern the divine in blood and guts, in meningitis and metastasis. Law may blind you to all save the raw in humankind, all but the rot and the rape in human hearts. Politics has seduced many a good servant with a passion for personal power. And "business as usual" in a computer culture can deafen you to the cries of "the others," those condemned to wallow in the mire of poverty and ignorance. In our age, the age President Reagan has called the era of the entrepreneur, "the other" risks becoming a rival only, a threat, someone who might get to the well before you do.

My hope for you, for your era, is that the human, all that is genuinely human, may increasingly disclose to you the divine, the image of God in every man, woman, and child. It's worth getting to love "the others." After all, you're going to have to live with them . . . for ever.

III

Third, you. I have already said much about you; let me bring it to a focus, get perilously personal. Last year, when Harvard was celebrating its 350th birthday, its president revealed the top three goals the incoming freshmen had declared: (1) money, (2) power, (3) reputation.[4] I suspect, from sociological research, that much the same goals dominate most college scenes today.

Once again, I shall not launch into a lament. Money, power, and reputation are not ethical evils—not in themselves. Like so much else, they take their morality or immorality from a single-syllable question: Why? With Colgate in your résumé, many of you will make megabucks; some of you will wield influence, from rock 'n' roll through E. F. Hutton to the power houses in Washington; and a fair number of you will make headlines or neon lights. Splendid! You have this Jesuit's blessing. But you still have not answered the neuralgic question: Why? Why money, why power, why reputation? To get technical, are these ends for you or means? And if means, means to what?

The robber barons of the 19th century had money to burn, and burned their morals to make it. Hitler and Stalin dominated most of Europe, from the Atlantic Ocean to the Caspian Sea, but they dominated only to enslave. The names in today's news are all too often those who have smashed the tablets on which the Ten Commandments were sculpted.

And what of you? You know, you have been impressively privileged. At Colgate your mind has come to know what is true; your senses, to delight in what is beautiful; your will, to love what is good. Not indeed everything, but a fair beginning. You have struggled with ideas: wrestled with philosophers from ancient Greece to modern Britain; parleyed with politicians from the Soviet State and the Middle East, from China and Central America; marveled at matter through a microscope, at galaxies through a telescope; cruised through cultures and societies other than your own; winged your way back millions of years to the very origins of human living. You have fallen in love with beauty: Sappho and Shakespeare, da Vinci and Michelangelo, the pyramids of Egypt and the Eiffel Tower, Anna Pavlova and Barysnikov, Yoda and *Children of a Lesser God*.[5] You have grappled to grasp what it means to be good: in board room and bedroom, on Capitol Hill and Wall Street, with nuclear warheads and African apartheid.

The task is not finished; it will never be. But I trust that enough of what is true, beautiful, and good has suffused your spirit to instil a threefold conviction. First, money, wealth, however hard-earned, is a gift to you—a gift from the very God who made it all possible by giving you life and breath, talent and toughness; a gift not to be clutched in hot little hands but to be given, to be shared, to lift the less-gifted from the grime and the grit, to slake their hunger for bread or justice, for peace or freedom, for knowledge or under-standing—yes, for God. Second, power is a possession plagued with peril but potent with promise. Not because it satisfies a lust for con-trol, but because it lets you be a servant, lets you minister to your sisters and brothers, lets you imitate the God and Father of us all, whose power is identical with His love, identical with His goodness, identical with His self-giving. Third, reputation, fame, is not yours to ape Narcissus, the mythological youth who fell in love with his own image. Fame allows the other to know you, to know what you are like, and so to lie at your golden gate, like poor Lazarus in the Gospel, and be fed at least with the crumbs from your table (cf. Lk 16:20–21).

Graduates of '87: The more I read about you, the larger is my hope for you. I am thrilled when I read what one of you has written in *The Colgate Scene* about

> the commitment and concern for others that is the driving force behind volunteerism at Colgate. Students have come to realize that reaching out and caring for others is a rewarding experi-ence. They have learned to value an elderly woman's story and the love in the touch of a child's hand. And they have come to appreciate the beauty and dignity inherent in their fellow man. One can but wonder at the learning that goes on in college.[6]

For many of you, this will be the heart, the core, of your lifelong search. For it is "the other" (small o) that will disclose the divine to you, "the Other" (capital O). Disclose the divine where you least ex-pect it: not so much in the palaces of the powerful as in the poverty of the powerless. And it is "the other" (small o) that will reveal your-self to you: who you are, what you ought to be, what you can be. Wed your varied riches—your wealth and power and fame, your truth and beauty and goodness—wed your varied riches to the parti-colored poverty that encircles you, and one day you will know yourself, and you will like what you see. It's worth getting to know and love yourself. After all, you're going to have to live with yourself . . . for ever.

My prayer for you, good friends: May "the Other" show His face to you in love. May "the others" find in you, and you in them, a reflection of "the Other." And may you come to see yourself as an image of "the Other," a delightful mirror of the Lord who looked on "everything that He had made, and behold, it was very good" (Gen 1:31).

University Chapel
Colgate University
May 24, 1987

24
A NEW COKE IN YOUR LIFE?
University Mass of the Holy Spirit

- Isaiah 35:4–7
- James 2:1–5
- Mark 7:31–37

Late Sunday morning . . . the Holy Spirit for brunch . . . solemn opening of the school year—it's handmade for a homilist who wants to play. Seriously, of course, but still . . . play. So, let me do three things. First, I shall treat you to a movie. Second, I shall move from a dark theatre to a bright Hilltop. Third, I shall suggest how screen and school are linked in the Spirit.

I

First, a swift trip to the movies. Last year and this, a mock-heroic film has caught the fancy of America. An engaging title: *The Gods Must Be Crazy*. A small plane is passing over South Africa's Kalahari desert. Quite casually, the pilot tosses out of his window . . . an empty Coke bottle. The bottle lands near some Bushmen, 600 miles from civilization. Gentle folk, unspoiled, they have never known crime or punishment, jealousy or anger. With them there is no "mine and thine"; whatever is there they share. Even their arrows are tipped not with poison but with a soporific; when they must kill to eat, they apologize to the sleeping animal for what they simply have to do.

At first, the Coke bottle is sheer delight. Apart from animals and trees and the earth, they have never touched anything so solid. They blow music over its top, mash fruit with it, dip it in dye to create circular patterns. But soon things change for the worse. For the first time in the Bushmen's existence, a material object sets them at

157

enmity. Why? Because, unlike anything else in their paradise experience, there is only one Coke bottle. And so they argue over it, fight furiously for it, rip it from one another, shed a brother's blood with it. In and through a Coke bottle, Eden faces Babel, primitive innocence discovers the ways of civilization. Ashamed, they rename the object they once thought the gods had dropped; it is now "the evil thing."

Fortunately for the Bushmen, their leader is "a stone age Charlie Chaplin," a man of Eden-like wisdom, a simple wisdom that sets in relief "the craziness of the technologically superior 'gods' around him."[1] Aware that "the evil thing" must go, he decides to walk to "the edge of the world," deposit the Coke bottle, and hope for no return. And this he does, despite the forces of civilization that slow his journey: laws that make no sense, a bullet in his thigh, prison walls that shackle his spirit. As the curtain closes, we see him poised in humble triumph at "the edge of the world," hurling out into space, to whatever gods, "the evil thing" that had come so close to making the innocent inhuman.

II

Second, we move from a dark theatre to a bright Hilltop. Here, be careful. *The Gods Must Be Crazy* is not an allegory; I may not carry each detail from Kalahari to Copley. I shall not claim that your passage to Georgetown is a movement from high-school innocence to college decadence, from paradise to Armageddon, from classic Coke to new Coke. The movie is a parable—fiction with a lesson. I simply submit that this parable can speak powerfully to you—especially to the "fresh" among you—you who find yourselves in the presence of something strange to your experience, you who will surely discover unexpected Cokes with Hoya caps, may even wonder whether your gods have gone crazy. Let me spell out what I have in mind.

We begin with a fact. There is indeed a new Coke in your life. GU is a far cry from prep school—no matter how urban, reputable, sophisticated your secondary school may have been. I do not say you are entering "the real world." There is much that is unreal about a college campus. It's not quite the world of the front page: bloated bellies in Ethiopia, black slavery in South Africa, bombs in Beirut, abortion on demand, panic in the streets, the Dow Jones average. Yours is the world where the highest number is 4.0, human warfare takes place at the Capital Center, the finest of arts is "scoping" on the Healy Lawn, and heaven is the foam on your Michelob.

And still the Hilltop is terribly real. Strangely enough, the "new thing" these four years is not so much what you see around you, what you find outside of you, the Coke bottle in class or on the grass, in the Tombs or on the Hill. Before all else, the "new thing" is you. Psychologists tell us that 17 to 22 is transition, a bridge. You are closing out the adolescent, fashioning the adult. And so there cannot but be a tension within. Be not surprised, then, if at times you feel lost, if you are a mystery to yourself, if you drag and weep, if you spin like a Yo-yo and pogo from manic to depressive, if the new you grows red with rage and green with envy.

But if the "new thing" is largely within, it is still GU that largely shapes it. For here you discover a classroom, a culture, and a chapel. The names are familiar, but you've never found them looking like this. The classroom will challenge your mind as never before. If you touch this "new thing" with reverence and awe, it will liberate you to roam in wonder over all God's incredible creation. You will peer into a microscope and marvel at life the naked eye cannot see.[2] You will speed over oceans more swiftly than the jet and touch human persons from Siberia to South Africa, from Egypt to East Germany. You will flee back into the past and rediscover a universe 15 billion years old, rediscover an America five centuries young. You will slave over economics from Adam Smith through Malthus and Marx to David Stockman, argue from dawn to dusk whether it is economics or love that makes the world go round. You will look into the minds of philosophers from ancient Greece to modern Britain, from Plato's world of ideas to Whitehead's experience and process, to share their tortured search for what is real, for what is true. You will plumb the human psyche to uncover why you act as you do, saunter among sociologists to see how communities communicate. You will explore words as a science, and listen to their music in the prose and poetry of the ages. You will pluck new meaning and fresh feeling from the marble of Michelangelo and of Mestrovic, from Beethoven's *Pastoral Symphony* and Tchaikovsky's *Swan Lake*, from Bruce Springsteen and a Madonna quite different from the original. You will gaze on God as He reveals Himself in creation, on a cross, and in the lines of His own Book; and if He so graces you, you will rhapsodize with John Donne:

> 'Twas much, that man was made like God before,
> But, that God should be made like man, much more.[3]

But the new in GU is not simply the classroom; class is the cutting edge of a culture. What promises to be new is not merely the movement of your mind but a whole way of life. Oh I know, when you scaled the Hilltop you were already shaped, markedly molded through the child and the adolescent. Still, the District's 67 square miles will weigh heavily on who you are and what you become, the values you prize and the attitudes you despise, will sum up the ceaseless struggle between yesterday and today, the classic Coke and the new. Beyond these gates paradoxes rage: power and compassion, black-tie parties and black poverty, the grandeur of democratic government and the machinations of Machiavelli, warm family life and the sleazy sex of center city. Out there da Vinci's "Genevra" vies with Volcker's Federal Reserve, Matisse cutouts with M Street's cutups, Rembrandt's "Self-Portrait" with the media's prophets. On this very campus, ideals rock and roll, men and women touch one another for good and ill, the weak wallow in a scary whirlpool while the strong fashion for themselves a brave new world.

With classroom and culture, chapel too can be wonderfully or fearfully new. Not only a place but your relationship with God. A place indeed, with much that is new: Eucharists long and short, traditional and folksy, mysterious and down to earth; homilies that, believe it or not, are prepared; and you are physically free to go or lie abed, to be hot or cold or lukewarm. More importantly, the role of our Lord in your lives. The "problem of God" is not some academic Nautilus machine jesuitically contrived to confuse you. God is not so much problem as Mystery. Your "new thing" here is to discover, to experience, how a God who cannot be encompassed by your understanding can be enfolded in your love, to realize that, for all you know *about* God, the most perfect way to know God is to be like Him, to share in His holiness.

III

Which leads into my third point. How can you keep this new thing from being the Bushmen's "evil thing"? How do you prevent its dividing you—from one another, from your sisters and brothers outside the gates, from God? How might you integrate all this into your growing, into all that is already true and good and beautiful within you? The Catholic response, century after century, year in and year out, is much the same: " . . . the Spirit of truth . . . will guide you into all the truth" (Jn 16:13).

Not indeed by some miraculous transfusion. Here I resonate to a story told me by the famed Baptist biblicist and preacher Dale Moody. A student in his Spirit course at the Louisville seminary wasn't meeting the professor's expectations. So Dr. Moody called him in and (in a delightful drawl I cannot imitate) said: "Son, you're not doin' all that well in my course on the Holy Spirit. You been studyin'?" "Dr. Moody," the young man replied, "I don't have to *study* about the Spirit; I'm *led* by the Spirit." "Son," Moody asked, "that Spirit ever lead you to the library? If He doesn't soon, you're in deep trouble."

No, the Spirit doesn't supplant Lauinger, is not a cram course in culture, will never replace the Pub. This God we celebrate today operates somewhat as Jesus did in the Gospel just proclaimed to you. All of us are slightly or dreadfully deaf, speak with some impediment.[4] We don't listen as we ought, to man or woman or God; we stammer and stutter to communicate, with man or woman or God. We need the Spirit of Jesus to touch our ears and tongues, our eyes and minds, our hearts and hands, to command our flesh and spirit: "Be opened!" (Mk 7:34). Open not only to what we like, love, agree with; not only what looks good, sounds good, smells good, tastes good, feels good. Open as well to the new and the strange, the painful and the perilous. Open, therefore, to ideas that challenge or affright, teachers who rouse or drowse. Open to ways of living alien to you, life situations that engage hundreds of Hoyas each year—from the shivering homeless on the warm grates of D.C., through countless refugees here and abroad, to the poor mountain folk in Peru. Open to a God who no longer exists in outer space to pass your exams for you; rather a God who shed the glory that was His to wear your flesh, share your sweat, bleed your blood; a God who never forsakes you however faithless you be, pursues you however far you flee, promises you on this earth a dignity and a delight beyond your wildest dreams: nothing less than to be His daughter, His son.

A new thing has indeed fallen among you. But without the Holy Spirit—the Spirit of light and life and love—you risk reacting like the Bushmen of Kalahari. You may misuse it in bizarre ways— cram your Coke bottle with cocaine, lace it with sex, foam it high with bottomless Bud. You can clutch it in hot little hands, keep it neurotically to yourself, let no one else near it; for the competition is keen, there's not enough Coke for all, winning is all that matters, and the race is to the swift, the strong, the selfish. Or you can con-clude that the new thing is an "evil thing," walk away from Healy Lawn to your "edge of the world," fling it far from you with all its works and pomps.

Fortunately, my friends, none of this need be. Surrender to the Spirit—the Spirit of light and life and love—and you can experience what the Lord promised through Isaiah to the dispirited exiles from Jerusalem, experience it for yourselves and in the thousands who surround you:

> Then the eyes of the blind shall be opened,
>   and the ears of the deaf unstopped;
> then shall the lame man leap like a hart,
>   and the tongue of the dumb sing for joy.
> For waters shall break forth in the wilderness,
>   and streams in the desert;
> the burning sand shall become a pool,
>   and the thirsty ground springs of water.
>   (Isa 35:5–7)

So, good friends, may it be with you. Through the Spirit, may the new thing make you new, make the Hilltop new through you.

Gaston Hall
Georgetown University
September 8, 1985

25
HIS LOVE IN TWO MORE WAYS
Wedding Homily 1

- Philippians 2:1–5
- John 15:12–16

Good friends: Three powerful passages have been proclaimed to you today. They stem from three powerful personalities: Christ Jesus, an ancient apostle of his, and a modern disciple.[1] These claim our consideration—not only because their authors were remarkable men, but because they were chosen by Robin and Ken, chosen with exquisite care. This tells us a good deal about *them*— who they are. We may well be what we eat, but more importantly, as philosophers insist, we are what we choose. In the language of theologians, we are what we love. So then, a swift reflection on each passage.

I

First, as is fitting, Christ's own commandment of love. You know, there are various ways in which we humans love, different syllables we shape to express how we love. Many a lover has murmured the lovely sonnet of Elizabeth Barrett Browning: "How do I love thee? Let me count the ways./ I love thee to the depth and height/ My soul can reach. . . . / I love thee to the level of every day's/ Most quiet need. . . . / I love thee freely. . . . / I love thee purely. . . . / I love thee . . . with my childhood's faith./ . . . I love thee with the breath,/ Smiles, tears, of all my life!—and, if God choose,/ I shall but love thee better after death."[2]

Lovely indeed, this confession of love, and I doubt not that Ken and Robin could sing the same song full-throated. Even so, for the pattern of their loving, they have chosen something perhaps less lyrical but surely more stunning, more shocking: "This is my commandment, that you love one another *as I have loved you*" (Jn 15:12). And this sentence of Jesus they select with profound awareness of what it involves.

"As I have loved you." How has Jesus loved us? Try to count the ways; we cannot. We can only stammer and stutter. For us, he stripped himself of everything that would reveal him to be God, exchanged that glory for our flesh, to be all that we are, save for our sin. For us and for our salvation, he was born of a woman, grew up like us, walked and talked like us, learned like us, laughed and cried like us, sweated and slept like us. And finally, he did for us what he was born to do: He died for us. That is why "Love one another as I have loved you" is followed instantly by "Greater love no one has than this: to lay down one's life for one's friends" (Jn 15:13). For Christ our Lord, love and cross were two sides of the same coin. Not simply on Calvary; the cross was erected over his entire life. With every word, in every act and gesture, he gave of his life, died a bit more, till that dark afternoon when all of his loving self-giving was consummated in savage crucifixion.

Too depressing for a wedding? Not really. Only if you ignore two crucial Christian realities: The central symbol of *all* Christian existence is the cross, and the cross is not tragedy but triumph. All Robin and Ken are doing is linking the very heart of Christianity to their love, to their life together. At this altar on which we do what Christ did, at this Sacrifice which replays his Last Supper, Robin repeats to Ken, Ken to Robin, the sentence that redeemed a world: "This is my body given for you" (Lk 22:19). From this day forward, my life and your life are one life. Till time be no more, I shall live for you, as you live for me. I know, it means dying a little, dying daily—but dying only to myself, my isolation, my smallness, so that there may be more room for you, more room for two. Dying, as Jesus did, only to give life. "As I have loved you."

As then, so now, from such dying comes resurrection. From such a cross a new creature is born, thrillingly alive, alive with the life of the risen Christ. Love like this, Robin and Ken, love each other as Jesus has loved you, and I promise you what he promised the night before he died: " . . . your hearts will rejoice, and no one will take your joy from you" (Jn 16:22).

II

A second passage, this from an ancient apostle. St. Paul was writing to the Christians at Philippi in Macedonia, the first community he had established on European soil. It is a touching letter, not only because Paul wears his heart on his pen, but because Paul is writing from prison—and in prison the romantic gives way to the realist. Paul is worried. He has good reason to fear that his dear Christians in Philippi are divided by petty jealousies. And so he urges them: Be "of the same mind," have "the same love. . . . Do nothing from selfishness or conceit, but in humility count others better than yourselves. Let each of you look not only to his own interests, but also to the interests of others" (Phil 2:2–4). And then the sentence that climaxed today's reading: "Have for one another that attitude which you also have in Christ Jesus" (v. 5).[3] Let the thrilling oneness that exists between you and Christ reveal itself in your oneness with one another, in your selflessness, in your freedom from pride and arrogance.

Such is the passage from Paul that appeals to Robin and Ken. It ties in beautifully with their selection from Jesus: "Love one another as I have loved you." Christ our Lord is not only the model, the pattern, the paradigm of their love; he makes it possible for them to love as he did. It is one thing for the Son of God to exhort us: "Love as I love." It is quite another thing for the Son of God to empower us, to enable us to love as he loves. And this he does. The very fact that Ken and Robin are, each of them, linked to Christ in love means that they have the power, the ability, the grace to love each other as Christ has loved them.

A tremendous truth lies hidden here—for all who walk this earth. It is indeed difficult to live alone; "no man is an island." It may be doubly difficult to live together. Tensions threaten all communities, tear some apart. Not only the communal life of husband and wife, but the community of parents and children, religious communities like the Society of Jesus, the community of Christ we call the Church, Democrats and Republicans, NATO, the European Common Market, East and West, the U.S. and the U.S.S.R. Paul's solution is not psychology or political science. Paul proclaims that the closer we live with God, the better chance we stand of living together in love, of loving one another as Christ has loved us.

And so for Robin and Ken. I have high hopes for their life together. Not primarily because they have such engaging personalities, share a delightful sense of humor, eat the same "junk food,"

have Jesuits for friends. Not because they will escape the way of the
cross, rub noses for ever on Cloud Nine. No. Ken and Robin will
walk hand in hand through sorrow and joy, across the deserts and
atop the stars, because the love they lavish on each other is locked
into a love that knows no limits: the God of love who lives within
them. It is His hand that holds their hands together.

III

Third, the modern disciple, Thomas Merton. No hermit he—
much as he wanted to be—but a contemplative who moved from
renunciation to involvement, who made contact with Hindu and
Buddhist and Sufi, wrote about Malcolm X, protested Vietnam and
violence, racial injustice and nuclear war. No passionless poet or
sexless troubadour strumming love songs for others, but a sensitive
man who agonized over love for a woman and the call of God. A
monk convinced that Gethsemani was his monastery, yet he could
write wittily to a troubled friend: "You think I got fun here? Man,
you think more. You think I got no angst? Man, think again. I got
angst up to the eyes."[4] With this in mind, listen once again to that
perceptive paragraph from Merton, as Ken says to Robin, Robin to
Ken:

> Because God's love is in me, it can come to you from a different
> and special direction that would be closed if He did not live in
> me, and because His love is in you, it can come to me from a
> quarter from which it would not otherwise come. And because it
> is in both of us, God has greater glory. His love is expressed in
> two more ways in which it would not otherwise be expressed; that
> is, in two more joys that could not exist without Him.[5]

A profound insight that rounds out, completes, what we have
heard from Jesus and from Paul. Not only is the Christ of Bethlehem and Calvary the *model* for our loving: "Love one another as I
have loved you." Not only is the God who lives within us the *power*
that enables us to love as Christ loved. Beyond all that, beyond
model and power, the fact that God's love is in *you* means that God's
love can come to *me* from still another direction: from and through
you. If you love me, you bring me the love, God's love, that suffuses
you.

Concretely here, the oneness so obvious in Robin and Ken is

unbelievably richer, incomparably fuller, because each brings to the other two loves in one. For in their love each brings to the other all that he or she is. And the "all" that is Robin, the "all" that is Ken, includes their own very human love *and* God's love flaming within them. Such is their total gift each to the other, "two more ways in which [God's love] would not otherwise be expressed." And, as Merton experienced it, such love amounts to "two more joys that could not exist" were not a living God and His Christ so ceaselessly and restlessly part of their deepest selves.

Two more joys. Such has been my personal experience of Ken and Robin; such, I suspect, is yours as well. But not until I mulled over Merton did I sense how profound—not only precious—is the joy they bring me. For they have gifted me not only with their touchingly human love; through that love they have gifted me with God's love. And such, I pray, will be their endless gift to their world—to you and to the thousand others whose lives they are sure to touch.

This triggers a final thought—a wedding gift from Robin and Ken to all of us, a gift that lays a bit of a burden on us. I mean the three texts from Jesus and Paul and Thomas Merton. The passages speak not only to bride and groom; they are addressed to you and me as well. We too are commanded to love one another as Christ has loved us; all of us are so commanded, the single among us and the married as well. We too have the power so to love—as long as God's love has captured our hearts. The ultimate question remains: In our loving, in the way we love, does God's love come through to others? As it does, say, in Mother Teresa? As it does in Robin and Ken?

It may be time for a new beginning. In a few short moments, with the words of their vows, Ken and Robin will begin together a life of loving as Christ has loved them. I suggest that, as the sacred syllables fall from their lips, we too, each of us, murmur in our hearts, not only to husband or wife but to every man, woman, or child whose path will cross our own: "I take you . . . to have and to hold . . . from this day forward . . . for better, for worse . . . for richer, for poorer . . . in sickness and in health . . . until death do us part."

Our Lady of Mt. Carmel Church
Hamden, Conn.
September 14, 1985

26
LET LOVE BE GENUINE
Wedding Homily 2

- Romans 12:4–12
- John 15:1–17

This morning Elise and Bob do me honor. The problem is, they lay on me a heavy burden as well. How do I preach to a man and maid in love? This moment calls not for a preacher but for a poet, a singer of songs. They preach to us, not I to them.

Ah, there's the breakthrough: They preach to us. Not only by the breathless promises they will murmur to each other short minutes from now. They preach to us by the passages they have plucked from Scripture, the readings from Paul and John you have just heard. For with these passages Bob and Elise are telling us something about themselves, about the way they view their lives together, what they value, what they prize. Instead of preaching to them, therefore, let me suggest what they are preaching to us.

One crucial word from God's word sums it up. It is a commonplace, everyday word, a word we strum all too lightly, misuse all too commonly. The word is . . . love. But Bob and Elise have removed it from the commonplace, the trite, the stale, the TV tube. Through Paul and John, they are telling us how genuine love takes flesh—their love and yours. Through Paul and John, they are making three significant statements. (1) Love has taken two different persons and made them wondrously one. (2) To be genuine, this love between them must reach out to others. (3) To stay alive, this love of theirs must be rooted in God. A word on each.

I

First, love has taken two different persons and made them won-drously one. Now Paul is preaching about the Church of Christ. This Church, he claims, is very much like your body and mine. What makes the human body such a miracle of God's artistry? Scores of different parts, hundreds of different functions—all adding up to a single body. We would look strange indeed if our bodies were all head or foot, all arm or buttocks. That is why Paul could write to the Christians of Corinth: "If all were a single organ, where would the body be? As it is, there are many parts, yet one body. The eye cannot say to the hand, 'I have no need of you,' nor again the head to the feet, 'I have no need of you'. . . . God has so adjusted the body . . . that the members may have the same care for one another. If one member suffers, all suffer together; if one member is honored, all rejoice together" (1 Cor 12:19–21, 24–26).

So, too, for the Church: ". . . we [Christians], though many, are one body in Christ, and individually members of one another" (Rom 12:5). We have different gifts, different functions. Not every-one is pope or bishop—thank God! Not every priest is pastor or ad-ministrator—again, thank God! The laity have their own God-given gifts. Some teach, others sing; some are mothers, some fathers; some bring God to hospital beds, others to Wall Street. The marvel is, these differences are not intended to divide us; they make for unity. Without difference there would be no body of Christ, only a monolith, a massive, lifeless block. Our very differences enable the Church to live in love.

Similarly for Elise and Bob. God made each of them in His im-age, made each of them like God. But the ways in which they mirror this infinite God are quite different. Oh yes, both are reasonably human; but within this common humanity each is a distinct person. There is always an "I" and a "thou." Neither will ever become the other; nor should they. Whatever God is—Intelligence and Love, Goodness and Self-Giving, Action and Joy—this God Elise and Bob will reflect in their own individual ways. Male and female; likes and dislikes; different ways of enjoying the days; ways of looking at things and people; different senses of humor (both quite weird, of course); and so on and so forth. But as with the human body, as with the body of Christ, so with Bob and Elise. Because they are differ-ent, they will differ. But if the "I and thou" exclude "mine and thine," what St. Augustine called "those ice-cold words," their very differences will make for oneness. Not sameness; oneness. Here is love: where two, remaining two, become wondrously one. Then it is that St. Paul's exhortation bears fruit: "Let love be genuine . . . be aglow with the Spirit" (Rom 12:9, 11).

II

Which leads to my second point, the second statement Elise and Bob are making to us: To be genuine, the love between them must reach out to others. This is not pious pap; it is gospel truth. This is not a polite suggestion from heaven; it is God's strong command: "This I command you," Jesus told his disciples the first Holy Thursday. "This I command you, to love one another" (Jn 15:17). Love is not a wedding present that bride and groom clutch feverishly to themselves, store in a closet with the Waterford crystal and the fondue dish. Love is a gift to be given, a treasure to be shared.

Fortunately for us, fortunately for a whole little world, this is what Bob and Elise are all about. From the first day my eyes met theirs, I've been captivated not only by their high intelligence and warm personalities, not only because they are perceptive enough to appreciate my sermons and to take me for better or worse. What engages me most is simply that their arms seem ceaselessly outstretched to others. I see Bob tutoring prisoners in maximum-security cell blocks at Lorton Reformatory in Virginia, masterminding a five-course certificate program to prepare them for probation and a human existence in a world that will always greet their release with suspicion. I see Elise tutoring refugee children from El Salvador in depressed areas of D.C.; opening the minds of teen-agers in shelter houses; shaping the writing skills of inner-city minority students at Georgetown University.

Such, I suspect, will their love always be: a love that was born deep inside each of them a quarter century ago; a love that turned them to each other several short years ago; a love that now turns them together to those who experience so much of Christ's crucifixion, so little of his resurrection. Little wonder that I discover in Elise and Bob the specifically Christian love our Lord commanded. Not simply "Love one another," but "Love one another as I have loved you" (Jn 15:12). Love that way, love Christ's way, and sooner or later your love pins you to a cross; you love with arms outstretched in pain. Such is the love we see married today.

III

Which leads to my third point, the third statement Elise and Bob are making to us: To stay alive, this love of theirs must be rooted in God. On this, today's Gospel brooks no contradiction: "Abide in me, and I in you. As the branch cannot bear fruit by itself, unless it abides in the vine, neither can you, unless you abide in me. I am the vine, you are the branches. . . . Apart from me you can do nothing" (Jn 15:4–5).

It is a powerful statement, hurled at us in a culture where most Americans gulp to say "for ever," resist contracts that end "till death do us part." It is not to say that if your love is rooted in God, it will never grow cold. We are strange creatures, and the most religious of our friends have awakened to discover that their love is dead. Elise and Bob are only uttering their conviction that if their love is to last, they cannot depend simply on themselves, on their Brite smiles and good will, on their emotion and their passion, on the high qualities that make them so admirably human. If it takes only two to tango, it takes three to marry till death.

Why? On the one hand, marriage, for all its romance, is a hard-nosed relationship. For one year or 60, day in and day out, two very human, all-too-human creatures must struggle to live together St. Paul's paean to love: "Love is patient and kind, not jealous or boastful, not arrogant or rude. Love does not insist on its own way, is not irritable or resentful, does not rejoice at wrong, but rejoices in the right. Love bears all things, believes all things, hopes all things, endures all things. Love never ends" (1 Cor 13:4–8). For Paul, this level of love is not of our own making. It is possible only because it is "God's love . . . poured into our hearts through the Holy Spirit who has been given to us" (Rom 5:5).

On the other hand, the God who invented marriage and created the married does not leave Elise and Bob at the altar. Today's sacrament is not only a sentimental ceremony calculated to empty your tear ducts. It is God's pledge and promise that He will share these lovers' life till death do them part. Not merely in moments of crisis—the great Miracle Worker in outer space who can be summoned to heal the sick and hire the unemployed, to fix everything from a broken boiler to a ruptured heart. No, at every moment—the incomparable Lover deep within you who keeps your love alive night and day, through ecstasy and monotony, in sickness and in health, in poverty and wealth, in sad times and mad. Elise and Bob, when you leave this lovely house of God, you will take with you not only each other; you will take God with you, the God who is for ever faithful despite our ceaseless infidelities, the God who alone can give lasting joy to your love.

One final word—to all of you who have gathered from near and far because you love Elise or Bob or both. Today's ceremony is not a spectator sport; you are not just witnessing a four-star performance. Remember what I suggested at the beginning: Elise and Bob are preaching to us, telling us how genuine love takes flesh— not only their love but yours as well. When they murmur their self-giving to each other, therefore, I would ask especially the wedded among you, and those who are about to wed, to take to your hearts the inspired ideas they have stolen from Scripture, truths that can grow trite with the passage of the years. First, resolve that the differences between you, your different ways of imitating an infinite God, will not divide you but link you even closer in love, all lost in wonder at the wonder that is the other. Second, make your love still more genuine by extending your intertwined hands to the images of God around you—the starving in the sub-Sahara, of course, but more directly to those who beg for bread or justice or love on your own block, the crucified we pass on the other side of the street. Third, inject fresh life into the branch that is your love by linking it anew to the vine that is Christ, to the vinedresser that is God the Father—newly aware today that, if separated from the Lord of life, your love may very well die.

Do this, my wedded friends—look with new love at each other, at the world around you, at the God within you—do this and you will give to Bob and Elise a wedding gift beyond compare. Do this and their own wedded love will have borne its very first fruits.

St. Patrick's Church
Bedford, N.Y.
June 7, 1986

27
THIS IS MY COMMANDMENT. . . .
Wedding Homily 3

- Genesis 2:18–24
- Colossians 3:12–17
- John 15:9–16

The readings Ellen and Joe have chosen are quite remarkable. Remarkable not only because they are plucked from God's own Book; not only because they are God's word and not mine. Remarkable especially because they reveal a good deal about God one-in-three who invented marriage, reveal a good deal about these two-in-one who this day marry in God.[1]

I

I could focus on the passage from Genesis, because it tells how love *began*. Not God's love but the love of man and maid. It tells of a God so imaginative that He shaped not one image of Himself but two. Creatures at once different from each other and strikingly similar. Similar in shape and spirit, yet not the same. So similar that Scripture, in a flight of high imagination, pictures the Lord God fashioning the woman out of the man's very body. So similar that the man shouts in ecstasy: "This one, at last, this one [not the birds of the air or the beasts of the field], this one is bone of my bones and flesh of my flesh" (Gen 2:23). "That," God announces, "that is why a man leaves father and mother" (v. 24)—leaves for a love where, as in the Trinity, there is indeed "I and thou" but never "mine and thine."

I could focus on the passage from Paul, because it tells how love *grows*. How? "Forgive" one another (Col 3:13). Not only today, when nothing looks impossible to brown eyes and blue, but tomorrow, when you take each other for granted, when your frail humanity breaks out, when only one of you shows up weak. "Let the peace of Christ rule in your hearts" (v. 15), a harmony inside of you, between you, with God; the peace that is Christ at home in you; a peace that is compatible with pain, compatible with a cross. "Be thankful" (v. 15): thankful for the wonder that is the other, for the marvel of your love; thankful for parents who have watered this day with their tears and anointed it with their laughter; thankful to a God who against all the odds has brought Lancaster and D.C. together in another miracle not of coincidence but of providence.

II

I could focus on Genesis and Paul—how love began and how love grows—but I shall not. I shall focus on Jesus, because the passage from John tells how love *peaks*. The text you have chosen takes my breath away: "This is my commandment, that you love one another as I have loved you" (Jn 15:12). Not simply "love one another." That much we expect of you; without love, marriage is hell on wheels. But "love one another as [Jesus has] loved you"? Do you know what you are promising?

How has Jesus loved us? We cannot count the ways. Out of love (Paul sings lyrically), though he was divine, he "did not count equality with God," the glory he had with his Father, "a thing to be clutched, but emptied himself of it" (Phil 2:6–7), borrowed your flesh and mine, borrowed it, as we do, from a woman, became all we are save for our sin. Out of love, he shared our sweat and tasted our hunger, sensed what it feels like to be discouraged and rejected, experienced how lonely we can be, how frightened of death. Out of love, he reached out to all who were heavy-burdened, those bedeviled by demons or paralyzed by pain, all those exiled from the good things of God's earth, exiled from love. Out of love, he gave us not only the music of his voice and the healing of his hand, but his flesh for food, his blood as drink. Out of love, he died a criminal's death, the way a murderer gasps out his life in a gas chamber. Out of love, he came back to life, faithful to his promise: "I will see you again, and your hearts will rejoice, and your joy no one will take from you" (Jn 16:22).

"Love one another as I have loved you." Yes, Ellen and Joe, such is the love you vow this day. Gifts you have from God in abundance: minds alight with intelligence and bodies aglow with health,

jobs that challenge and play that pleasures, families that adore you
or at least endure you, life above the poverty line and a humor a bit
below the bizarre. These gifts you possess not to be clutched in fe-
verish hands but to be shared with arms outstretched. To share with
each other indeed, for here is your first wedding gift: the gift of
your whole self to each other. But not in splendid isolation from the
Lazarus ever at your gates, the less-than-human who begs mutely to
be fed, flesh and spirit, with the crumbs from your table (cf. Lk
16:20). Not that such love is foreign to you; not that you need a Jesuit to exhort you. I simply point out what will now be new to you in
a love already old to each of you. From this day forward such will
be your gift *together*, your gift as one, a gift that moves out from your
love for each other in Christ. Unlike the Pharisee in the temple, you
will delight together not in what makes you different from others;
you will thank God together that, like Jesus, you *are* like the rest of
humankind (cf. Lk 18:9–14), that each man or woman you touch is
brother or sister.

Now such love is not a gentle request from an indulgent Lord:
"Please, if you have time, love one another as I have loved you." No,
"This is my commandment," "This I command you" (Jn 15:12, 17).
But how uncommonly considerate a command! How paradoxical!
Do what I command you and you cease to be servants; you become
my friends. Do what I command and your lives will be for ever fruit-
ful, perennially productive. Do what I command and my joy will be
your joy, and the cup of your joy will be filled to the very brim.

There is "no greater love," our Lord insisted, than to lay down
your life for those you love (Jn 15:30). But if you cannot die for
them, dear Ellen and Joe, the next best gift is to live for them. Live
for the other: for the other who lies beside you, for the other who
lies at your gates, for the Other who lies within you.

III

My final point: a plea to all of you gathered here in joy today.
You see, this vocation that is Ellen's and Joe's, this vocation to love
as Jesus loved, this is a vocation they must live out not on some fantasy island but in the grime and grit of a world where, despite all
our good intentions, we are more likely to kill one another than to
die for one another, where the super slogan is "Take care of *numero
uno*, get to the well first, and 'the devil take the hindmost." In this
context Joe and Ellen cannot fulfil their vocation by themselves, in

a cottage built for two. They need a gift you alone can give. Not so much Waterford crystal or fondue forks, welcome as these may be. Rather, the example of couples who, one year ago or 50, vowed to live the love Ellen and Joe promise today; who, for one year or 50, have tried to love as Jesus loved, have fallen and risen, have failed and tried again, and again, and again.

And so, when Joe and Ellen link their hands a few moments from now, I would ask you not to play a spectator sport, not simply to dab tears of joy from your eyes. I would ask the wedded among you to link your own hands and, with Ellen and Joe, to murmur in your hearts to each other and to a fallen world at your gates: "I promise to be true to you in good times and in bad, in sickness and in health. I will love you and honor you all the days of my life."

Do that and you will have given Ellen and Joe the most practical wedding gift in your power. Do that and a miracle hardly small may touch your own lives: You just might love one another as Jesus has loved you.

Holy Trinity Church
Washington, D.C.
September 6, 1986

28
WITHOUT LOVE I AM NOTHING
Wedding Homily 4

- Genesis 2:18–24
- 1 Corinthians 12:31—13:8
- John 15:9–17

Jeannie and Richard: Much as I love you, it is not easy for me to preach to you. Not that a wedding homily is impossible; I have 13 in my files. Rather because you are singularly special to me, and so a canned homily would be like a wedding gift from Sunny's Surplus.[1]

Fortunately, you've helped me enormously. How? By the passages you've picked from the only book God ever wrote. Those texts tell me something about you: what is important to you, what your priorities are, what may well permeate your life together. In deference to an anxious maître d' at the Congressional Club, I shall take only one of those three texts: the passage from Paul's first letter to the Christians of Corinth. I choose this because we hear it so often that it threatens to turn trite; it washes over us like the proverbial water over a duck's back. I want to recapture three facets of that text; each has to do with love—your love and ours. The first facet is a fearful warning; the second, a profound mystery; the third, a thrilling promise.

I

First, a fearful warning. Without love, Paul declares, I am nothing. Not just less than somebody else; I am out-and-out nothing. On the scale of values in God's eyes, without love I register zero.

Take Paul's examples; imagine them in a modern mode. If I am a superb speaker—the fire of Hitler in a Nuremberg stadium,

the power of Pavarotti reaching for a high C, the richness of Shake-
spearean Olivier musing on the burdens of kings, the charisma of
a Reagan or a John Paul II, the persuasiveness of Gabriel announcing the glad tidings to Mary—if I have all this and have not love, I
am a New Year's Eve foghorn, a cheerleader's megaphone, an ear-
splitting airhorn.

If I am the most learned of men or women—the synthetic genius of Aquinas, the revolutionary reasoning of Einstein, Theodore
Hesburgh's hundred honorary degrees—if I have all this and have
not love, I am a cipher, a nonentity, a bust.

If I have unrivaled faith in God—faith so strong that at my
command the Rockies would move from west to east, faith so strong
that I can exorcise evil spirits from the bedeviled, speak in tongues
I never studied, drink strychnine cocktails, and wrap myself com-
fortably in boa constrictors—if I have such faith but do not love, I
might as well be dead.

If I give away my millions to street people, to "bag ladies," to
the starving in Somalia or the living dead along Luther Place; if, like
Father Maximilian Kolbe, I offer myself to a starvation bunker in
Auschwitz to save a married man and father—if I do all this and do
not love, I am not worth a tinker's dam; I am worse off than a loving
atheist. I am nothing.

II

Pretty rough rhetoric, right? A fearful warning indeed—not
only for bride and groom but for all of us, whoever we are, whatever
our state. It raises a nervous question: What might this love be that
alone can keep me from being a cipher, zero, nothing? What is this
love that, in Paul's paean of praise, is patient and kind, free of envy
and arrogance, unselfish and unresentful, this love that knows no
limits in its trust, in its hope, in its power to endure? Here is our
second facet: a profound mystery. Mystery because it is part and
parcel of a divine plan hidden in God from eternity; but mystery
that has been lovingly disclosed to us in Christ our Lord.

You see, the love Paul is singing is a special kind of love. It is
not the love you spy on prime-time TV, on "Love Boat" or "Fantasy
Island," in "Dallas" or "Miami Vice." Nor is it simply the ordinary,
very human, touchingly lovely love of man and maid that springs
from our inmost being, from the fact that we are fashioned of flesh
and blood. It includes this, but it is more than this. It is the mystery

Paul revealed to the Christians of Rome: "God's love . . . poured into [your] hearts through the Holy Spirit who has been given to [you]" (Rom 5:5).

What precisely is this love? There are two sides to it. On the one hand, it is God's own love for you. I mean the love that was God's when He shaped not one image of His love, but two—male and female, strikingly similar but deeply different; when he said to them and through them to you: "Be fruitful and multiply, and fill the earth . . . " (Gen 1:28). I mean the love that was God's when He gave His own divine Son to a criminal's cross to save you from Satan, from sin, from yourself—the same Son who returned married love to Eden when he declared: "What God has joined together, let no one put asunder" (Mt 19:6). I mean the love that was God's when He did not leave you orphans after His Son's ascension, but sent His Holy Spirit "to be with you for ever" (Jn 14:16).

On the other hand, God's love is not something outside of you, something to admire at a distance or close up. God's love is within you, simply because Father, Son, and Holy Spirit are within you. And God's love within you, God within you, makes it possible for you to love another human person with the kind of love God has for you, the love that was God in our flesh. This is the gist of the Gospel that was proclaimed to you, the stern but love-laden command of Jesus. Not simply "Love one another" (Jn 15:17), but "Love one another as I have loved you" (v. 12). And how did Jesus love you? With his whole heart and soul and mind and strength—even unto crucifixion. "Greater love than this no one has" (v. 13). Such is the love we celebrate today. Such is the love Jeannie and Richard profess to each other, the love they proclaim this afternoon to the world.

III

So far, two facets: a fearful warning and a profound mystery. But this is not the end. God is not content to issue a warning: Without love you are nothing. God is not even satisfied to reveal a mystery: In my love you love as my Son loved. Love's agonizingly human problem is not today; it is tomorrow. Richard and Jeannie are breath-takingly one in 1986. But what of 1996? What of 2006? And so our third facet: a thrilling promise.[2]

What sort of promise? When St. Paul says "Love never ends" (1 Cor 13:8), he is not playing the prognosticator, the way Willard

Scott might forecast tomorrow's weather, Jimmy the Greek set the odds on the Redskins and Packers—or on Dr. Briguglio's next hole-in-one at the Congressional.[3] Paul is contrasting love with faith and hope. When I die and rise unto Christ, faith will pass away, because I shall see in person what I now believe on God's word. Hope too will pass away, because I shall then possess in person what I now expect with confidence. Of these three God-given gifts, love alone will remain for ever—only magnified to the nth degree.

What, then, is Paul promising? Not that it is impossible for love to grow cold. A 50% divorce rate in the United States is a devastating rebuttal to such a promise—and not all those who separate are unbelievers. What, then, do Paul's epistles promise? Simply this: Your love, Jeannie and Richard, the love you declare today, has a splendid chance to stay alive, to grow almost like Topsy, to last till death do you part . . . if. If what? If it shares in "God's love poured into [your] hearts through the Holy Spirit who has been given to [you]."

You see, you will not live your love in desert-island isolation. You will live your love squarely in the midst of a paradoxical world. On our city streets love and hate go hand in hand, some grow fat and others starve. In Belfast brothers and sisters of Christ clobber one another, kill one another. In South Africa humans shaped by God in His image go for the black or white jugular. Life in the fast lane can destroy the strongest of loves. So much of business is not only competitive but cutthroat, survival of the fittest, devil take the hindmost. Religions of love divide ferociously; sex-on-the-side is winked at; and a way-out outfit, people otherwise indistinguishable from you and me, claim to have proved that the beast in the book of Revelation, the number 666 (Rev 13:18), is Ronald Reagan (it used to be the pope).

Now love just might conquer all. But if it does, it will not be the romantic love of Romeo and Juliet, not simply the human love you can manufacture unaided, by yourselves. Such love is indeed a wondrous, glorious, touching thing that must summon a smile or a tear from the angels. But your love has its finest potential for never ending if there are *three* of you in love: you Jeannie, you Richard, and . . . God. This is not a Jesuit in outer space spouting pious pap; this is as real as you can get. Just think of it! An infinite God as intimate part of your life together. A God who made you, saved you, loves you, lives in you; a God who can do anything, everything, as long as you let Him, as long as you are open to His love.

My prescription, then, for a love that never ends? Never take each other for granted, and never take God for granted. It's strange but true: God's own Son-in-flesh could walk willingly to a cross; what he could not bear was to be ignored; what he needed was to be needed. God can indeed get along without you; but He doesn't want to. And you cannot get along without Him, without the God within you.

Which brings me, finally, to you dear friends in the pews. I've said it before, and I shall say it time and again: This is not JFK Stadium, and you are not spectators. Though God can do everything, He really prefers to have us help. In this world where love and hate meet in daily deadly duel, Jeannie and Richard cannot make it without you. Not only your sterling silver, your spode pottery, your Limoges porcelain (keep them coming, of course). More importantly, you yourselves: your selfless lives, your hard-nosed love, your open doors when life closes in on them, the touch of your hand, the affection in your eyes, the courage in your hearts.

Such is your supreme wedding gift to Richard and Jeannie. It alone is priceless; it alone is ageless; it alone is deathless. And so, when in a few short moments these two, so beloved of us, link their hands for ever in God's own hand, cover those hands with your hands, and tell them in your hearts what our Lord Jesus told his dear disciples: "As the Father has loved me, so do I love you" (Jn 15:9). So will I love you till death do us part.

Holy Trinity Church
Washington, D.C.
November 8, 1986

29
WHEN TWO COVENANTS WED
Wedding Homily 5

- Tobit 8:5–7
- 1 Corinthians 12:31—13:13
- John 15:9–16

Joan and David: Today is not a time for prolonged preaching; it calls rather for profound praying. A prayer particularly of thanksgiving. Thanksgiving to the God of Abraham, Isaac, and Jacob, to the God who is the Father too of Jesus Christ.[1] Why thanksgiving? For two exciting reasons.

First, thanksgiving because your love is so *ordinary*. Not ordinary in a base sense: mediocre, middle-of-the-road, dull, dreary. Ordinary in that your love shares in the wonderfully human love that has bound man and maid together since a loving God shaped two images of Himself in Eden, strikingly alike but never the same, each incomplete without the other. Each of you, David and Joan, each of you says this day to the other: "It is not good for me to be alone; and so our good God has made me a helper fit for me. Therefore I leave father and mother and cleave to you, and we shall become one" (cf. Gen 2:18, 24). In this, your love links you to the billions of men and women who have ever fallen in love—a glorious tradition where to be ordinary is to be human, to live the way God has fashioned you to live ever since Eden, to live as "I and thou" without "mine and thine."

Second, thanksgiving because your love is *out of the ordinary*, extraordinary. As you especially know so well, one of the most mystifying mysteries of the past 2000 years is the history of Jew and Christian. Two historic peoples who have covenanted with the same Lord, two religions of love each under the same command "You shall love your neighbor as yourself" (Lev 19:18, 33–34; Mt 22:39), have found it dreadfully difficult to love one another.

Your love is out of the ordinary, extraordinary, because it is a striking symbol of the love that should link our two peoples. Your very faces tell us more vividly than words that our love too, the love of our two peoples, should be "patient and kind, not jealous or boastful, not arrogant or rude, not irritable or resentful," that neither Christianity nor Judaism should "insist on its own way, rejoice at wrong," that between us "these three abide: faith, hope, and love—but the greatest of these is love" (1 Cor 13:4–6, 13).

For so extraordinary a love, dear David and Joan, I welcome your wedding with a singular thanksgiving. This is not to imply that your life and your love will be "a piece of cake." Because you are shaped not simply of intelligence but of flesh and blood, because behind you and within you there lie two powerful traditions often locked in mortal combat, you may well face problems other couples need not confront: when dear ones find your love difficult to understand; when children come in response to your love; when you try to carry your love to two communities, to two worlds severed by centuries of strife, of misunderstanding, of tragic isolation.

Even so, my hopes for you are high. Your adult years, your experiences ecstatic and depressing, have already taught you that lasting love is a tough, hard-nosed proposition. But the same years have also proven to you that Jew and Christian *can* love one another as the God of *both* Testaments has loved you. Otherwise you would not be here hand in hand, stars in your eyes. As always, what Yahweh, your Father, asks of you, above all else, is fidelity to Him. Faithful to Him, you will keep faith with each other. Keeping faith with each other, you will reveal to our troubled world, reveal to us, that love is not only stronger than death; love is stronger than hate, stronger than the hells that surround us.

Joan and David: For your extraordinary love, all of us are in your debt; you compel us to be better than we are. As for myself, I am, believe me, much the better for this day: a more human man, a more loving Christian, a more compassionate priest. You see, your love has already borne fruit!

Georgetown Visitation Convent
Washington, D.C.
November 22, 1986

30

OUR HEARTS ARE RESTLESS
Homily for a Mass of the Resurrection

- Daniel 12:1–3
- Colossians 3:12–17
- Luke 10:25–37

"Thou hast made us for thyself, O Lord, and
our hearts are restless until they rest in thee."
St. Augustine

Two weeks ago, Mary Marg, I placed a call to you on Jupiter Island
in Florida. My latest book of homilies, due out next month, would
be dedicated to you and Al.[1] I needed data to update what Al had
provided a year before. I wanted what I shall call in my dedication
your "living homilies." I mean the sermons you two have delivered
over the years, not in spoken words but out of your flesh and spirit.
The information came instantly and impressively:

17 children,
75 grandchildren,
7 great-grandchildren.

To preach to you, Mary Marg, and to these 99 living homilies
crafted by you and Al is a rude intrusion. Without a single syllable,
each of you says so much more about this dear man than celibate
Jesuit rhetoric can supply. I dare to speak only because you have
asked me—asked me to sum up at this unexpected moment not simply why *you and I* loved him but, more importantly, why *God* loved
him through seven decades and will love him days without end. Five
reasons you may recognize.

I

First, our Lord loved Al because Al was for ever restless. The only human I ever knew who could sit on his hands and not be still: at the table of the Lord and the table at home, in board room and on the 19th Hole—a jet stream between Philly and West Palm. There was simply too much to do and too little time to do it. Cynics might call him paranoid, but in my more perceptive moments Al's restlessness reminded me—far more persuasively than George Burns ever did—reminded me of God: the Father who could not rest in His heaven until He had shared His life and love with people of flesh and blood; the Jesus who could not rest even on the Sabbath because there were friends and enemies to be healed. A second-century Christian bishop[2] used to say that God the Father had two hands to work with: His Son and His Spirit. Al himself had two unusual hands: Mary Marg was his right, a telephone was his left.

II

Second, our Lord loved Al because Al loved people. He was not a pushover; he could be short, gruff, hard as a nine iron; he was a realist from head to toe; he knew his politicians, the just and the grafter; his likes and dislikes he wore on his bulging sport shirt. And because he loved so intensely, he sometimes expected more than we were ready to give. But only because the Lord expected him and us to love God above all else, to love our fellows as much as Jesus had loved us. Paradoxically, I found him divinely patient with people who bored me unbearably, who tempted me to toss my unpriestly cookies. In return, the Lord who is never outdone graced Al literally a hundredfold: a gracious lady whose love rested his restlessness, and 99 others who gifted him with 99 lives. These above all he loved with a restless love, never satisfied because he had not given all, could still give more.

III

Third, our Lord loved Al because Al was faithful. Faithful in two scriptural senses. Like the God of Israel and the Jesus of Jerusalem, Al was faithful in that he was dependable. You could rely on him, trust him—with your money or your wife, with your love or your life. And Al was faith-full; I mean, full of faith. He had put his trust in God and he never took it back—in life's rough and on the fairway, when God laid a burden on his back and when God let him fly high Tegler-style. Like Job in the Old Testament sitting unhappily on dung, Al could wonder at times why the God he served so faithfully could prove so unpredictable; but he never took back his hard-nosed "Father, into your hands I entrust my spirit." Whatever you want, Lord.

IV

Fourth, like our Lady's husband Joseph, Al was a just man. Not a wimp; just in the strong sense of the word. His justice was not merely a thesis from philosophical ethics: Give to others just what they deserve. Al's justice was a remarkable image of Old Testament justice, where the Lord God told His chosen people: Do to your neighbors, do to the stranger, as God has done unto you—the God who rescued you from Pharaoh, dined you in the desert, led you to a land of milk and honey, forgave your every idolatry, adultery, infidelity. And so Al fed the hungry and gave drink (all sorts) to the thirsty; he clothed the naked and housed the homeless (even Jesuits); he sat with the sick (ask our dear nonagenarian, ageless Dennis Comey) and strengthened unnumbered men and women imprisoned in discouragement or despair.

V

Fifth, our Lord loved Al because he was a man of joy—unlimited joy. Oh yes, he suffered—from smaller spirits and finite flesh; and only Mary Marg really knows what dark nights shattered his soul. But to our face and before God, he took all this as he took a golf slice or intestinal gas: This too would pass! I loved him because he loved life, lived life with relish and gusto, because he loved God and Mary Marg, loved his special 99 and a thousand others, with the same zest as at dinner he gobbled any forbidden snacks within arm's reach.

Mary Marg and Al's beloved 99: We lay this restless lover of life to rest in a week he might well have picked for himself: the Holy Week of the loving Lord who died for him. It contains the paschal mystery Al lived so vibrantly. Thursday's Last Supper will recall the Eucharist that bent him low in awesome adoration—especially at home Masses, when Mary Marg and I always had the good sense to recognize his divine right to the first reading. Friday's three hours will always symbolize the cross he carried with Christ, for Christ, far more joyfully than poor Simon of Cyrene. And on Easter Sunday, Al's 72nd birthday, we shall listen for his boisterous laughter when the risen Christ embraces him and murmurs to our restless friend: "Al, welcome into my rest!"

Good friends, we have good reason for tears. Not indeed for Al; he is at last where God created him to be. It is we who are the poorer for his passing. Still, a twin consolation covers our tears. On the one hand, there is our vivid remembrance of a man who lived and loved and laughed: lived prayerfully, loved passionately, laughed powerfully. On the other hand, there is our Christian conviction, beneath this week's two crosses, that the man we mourn is at this moment alive. Not merely in our memories. He is as alive as our Christ is alive—alive with the risen life of his Christ—for ever. Do you believe that? *I* do. And Al will be terribly restless if you don't!

Cathedral Basilica of SS. Peter and Paul
Philadelphia, Pa.
March 26, 1986

31
UNLESS A GRAIN OF WHEAT DIES. . . .
Celebration of Beatification
of Diego de San Vitores, S.J.

- Isaiah 61:1–3
- Revelation 3:14, 20–21
- John 12:24–26

Today two remarkable moments in history meet. In one sense, they are worlds apart—separated by thousands of miles and more than 16 centuries. One event took place awfully far from here, outside a sacred city called Jerusalem, near the Mediterranean Sea; the other quite close to where you are standing, near your own Tumon Bay. One event happened in the distant past, around the year 28; the other much later, as close as 1672.

But time and tide are not important here. Across these waters, across these centuries, two remarkable men meet. One was a Jew, the other a Spaniard. Each died young: one 33, the other 45. Each died a bloody death: one because his hands and feet were fixed to a cross, the other because his head was mauled with a machete and his chest pierced with a spear. One was taken down tenderly and laid in a fresh grave; the other was flung brutally into an unfriendly sea. Before dying, one murmured "Father, forgive them"; the other, "May God have mercy on you."

If this were all, our celebration would be interesting for history but little more. What rips it out of history books and touches it to each one of you is this: What happened to those two men can be, should be, the most important feature in your life . . . *if*. If you understand who each was, why each died, and how this reaches you in 1985. So, let me talk to you about three persons: about Diego, about Jesus, and about you.

I

First, Diego Luis de San Vitores.[1] You know far more than I about your father in the faith, about the Jesuit who first carried Christ to the Chamorros. But a homily is not a biography, not a day-to-day diary of Diego. And I come to you not as a historian but as a pilgrim. I wing 9000 miles not so much to preach as to pray. I come to share your joy, to celebrate with you, to thank God for the wonders He has worked for you through your dear Diego. Still, it may help if I, a stranger to you and your islands, tell you very simply how *I* have come to see him.

First, I see an adolescent Diego, a youngster not yet in his teens. Three passionate desires burned within him even then: He wanted to be a Jesuit, he wanted to bring unbelievers to our Lord, and he wanted to die a martyr. I don't mean that he had a death wish, that all he wanted was to vanish from this vale of tears. If I saw anything like that, I would suspect not only his sanctity but his sanity as well. I mean rather that he had an insight far ahead of his years, a realization that if he was to live like Christ he had in some deep sense to die: die to himself, to all that was small and self-centered, to anything and everything that did not somehow speak to him of Christ. How do it? Join a society consecrated to the salvation of others; spend his whole life for those who did not know their God; end his life as his Lord had done, on a cross of love.

Second, I see a very young Jesuit. Some of the things Diego did, personal penances, do not turn me on: beating himself to blood, standing on one foot, never allowing himself any pleasure. But remember, Diego was not yet 13 when he entered the Society of Jesus; and I blush to recall what I myself did as a novice eager to subject the rebellious flesh. Much more significant is how he reacted when God did not seem to be there for him, when for seven or eight months the God he loved left him in utter loneliness, completely without consolation, when God was deaf to all Diego's cries and tears. Through all this dark night of his soul he never felt sorry for himself, never stopped praying, never sulked in some corner, never ceased doing what a God he could not see wanted him to do. I find it particularly impressive that this young Jesuit found Christ in the poor, the underprivileged, the disadvantaged. Not only in theory, not only as an abstract theological principle. I shall never forget one blind old man our records have passed down to us. Not only did Diego pray with him, talk to him about God; Diego made his bed, plucked the bugs from his body, cleaned out his chamber pot. Greater love than this few people have—even Jesuits!

Third, I see a missionary. I see a Diego whose first eight or nine years as a priest were restless years. He did well, and with enthusiasm, all he was asked to do—taught high school, taught philosophy and theology, preached retreats and missions—preached so powerfully that his own father broke down and cried. But a large part of Diego's heart was far from Spain, far from Oropesa and Madrid and Alcalá de Henares. His heart was overseas, with the countless children of God the gospel had not touched. In a moving letter he begged his Father General to yield to his yearning, told him how on three occasions when close to death he had vowed his life to the missions if he recovered. His superiors, sensible men indeed, said yes, sent him to the Philippines. But five fruitful years in the Philippines were only a preparation. Crossing the Pacific five years before, he had lost his heart—to Guam. And one grace-filled day, June 16, 1668, that heart was filled to overflowing: Diego set foot on the shores of Agana, to the joy of the Chamorros waiting there to welcome him. Imagine the Mass out there that first day of new life for the Marianas; Diego's first sermon out there, so fervent, we are told, that it seemed he had been given the spirit of St. Francis Xavier and the gift of tongues; the ecstasy of Diego as he baptized 23 children after the Mass and sermon.

Fourth, I see a martyr. Through those four all-too-short years in this paradise of the Pacific, I see a cross slowly coming to completion. I see this thin priest living like the poorest of his people, because he had come "to preach the gospel to the poor" (Lk 4:18). I see him, terribly nearsighted, led along by a rope at his waist to avoid trees and rocks. I see him ever ready to die, praying for a martyr's end, persuaded that the islands he loves will be blessed in his blood. I see him a prisoner on Saipan, threatened with death. I see him raising a crucifix of peace before 2000 hostile warriors. I see him coming to Tumon, pouring saving water over an ailing child, knowing full well her father will be furious. I see him falling to his knees, murmuring a prayer for forgiveness, kissing his crucified Christ just before his skull is split and his heart speared.

II

Now let me move from Diego to Jesus. You see, the more I read about Diego, the more convinced I am that your dear deceased

Archbishop Flores[2] sensed the essence of the adolescent and the
Jesuit, of the missionary and the martyr, when he requested the
Gospel reading you heard a few moments ago, the solemn words of
Jesus not long before he died: "Truly, truly, I say to you, unless a
grain of wheat falls into the earth and dies, it remains alone; but if
it dies, it bears much fruit. He who loves his life loses it, and he who
hates his life in this world will keep it for eternal life" (Jn 12:24–25).

You see, Blessed Diego's life makes Christian sense not because
he loved his brothers and sisters deeply enough to die for them. You
can do that without being a Christian. Diego's life was Christian because he was reliving the life of Christ. Jesus was born to die. Not
just like you and me, in the sense that all of us who are born of
woman will one day die. No, the only Son of God took our flesh, was
born of the Virgin Mary, because He wanted to die for us. John's
Gospel puts it simply and magnificently: "God so loved the world
that He gave His only Son" (Jn 3:16). St. Paul phrased it with equal
brevity and power: Christ "loved me and gave himself for me" (Gal
2:20).

Jesus did not have to die for us; he could have saved us from
sin and from ourselves in so many bloodless ways. Then why did he
die—and in agony, imprisoned with nails on two beams of wood?
He hinted at an answer when he told his disciples: "Greater love no
one has than this, that one lay down life itself for one's friends" (Jn
15:13), for those you love. But in today's Gospel he reveals so much
more of God's mystery, the ways of God that we find so different
from our ways. Do you think it strange, he asks in effect, that I must
die in order to bring you life? Don't you see the same paradox in
nature, in your very planting and harvesting? Leave a grain of
wheat to itself and it will never be anything more than that: a single
grain of wheat, alive perhaps but terribly alone. But bury it in the
earth, where to all appearances it is dead and gone, and that small,
insignificant seed will amaze you with the fruit it produces. And so,
he says, so it is with me, Son of God in flesh. "I, when I am lifted up
from the earth, will draw all men and women to myself" (Jn 12:32).
If I am crucified, if I die for love of you, then in God's mysterious
providence you can flower to a fresh life; the whole world can come
alive in a way sheer reason could never imagine. If I die, you can
live my life; the very life of God will pulse within you.

Precisely here is Diego's inspiration; this is what he saw so
clearly. This is what sparked the adolescent, the Jesuit, the missionary, the martyr. His baptism, he knew, had not only bathed him
clean of sin, had not only destroyed the devil's power over him, had

not only consecrated him personally to Christ. Baptism had sent him on mission, had commissioned him so to live the gospel that in him the command of Christ would find fulfilment: "You are the light of the world. . . . Let your light so shine before men and women that they may see your good works and give glory to your Father who is in heaven" (Mt 5:14–16).

In brief, Diego had to relive Christ. Oh, not in Nazareth or Jerusalem; not the robe Jesus wore, the fish he ate, the language he spoke; not even the exact cross on which Jesus was crucified. To relive Christ, Diego had to be "a man for others," a man who loved passionately, loved all that was human, loved especially the poor and the underprivileged—and the poorest and least privileged were those who had never heard of Jesus, did not know he had poured out his blood for them. So profoundly did Diego love them, so totally did he want to play Christ to them, that he yearned with all his heart to lay down his life for them, if . . . if death would bring life, if Diego dying for them would mean Christ living in them.

And so it has been. Three centuries of Chamorro history bear witness to this. Linked to the blood of Jesus, the blood of Diego has seeded the Church in the Marianas, has flowered in your faith, in your hope, in your love.

III

Your faith, your hope, your love: Diego and Jesus lead me to you. For what happened in far-off Jerusalem and what happened in Tumon close-by are not just marvelous memories, at once painful and joyful. And what happened last month in Rome[3] is not simply something you celebrate here at home. Indeed you are right to rejoice; this is indeed a day that the Lord has made. Let heaven and earth resound with your singing, flame up with your feasting. The danger is, all this may deafen you to what Jesus and Diego are whispering to you, the lesson they leave to you about living and dying, *your* living and dying, the grain of wheat that is each one of you.

You see, the grain of wheat that was Jesus was only the first to fall into the ground and die. And Diego, for all his holiness, was only one stage (splendid indeed) in the Christian harvest. What began in Jerusalem with the death of Jesus did not end on Guam with the blood of Diego. If the gospel they died to bring to you is not itself to die, if the faith and hope and love that grace you today are not to "remain alone," each of you has to become a Diego. Not a Jesuit;

even Jesus, believe it or not, was not a Jesuit! But a missionary, each of you. Not a missionary to the States, though God knows we could use you. Still, a missionary. I mean, a man or woman on call from God to give to others what you have been given, to share what countless Diegos have handed down to you since 1672. To bring Christ to the Christless. To touch your living faith to those who doubt, your trusting hope to those who are discouraged or in despair, your lovable love to those who are lonely or unloved, bitter or bewildered.

Am I asking you to be a martyr like Diego? Only if the Lord Jesus calls you to it. But remember, Diego was not a martyr all of a sudden, on a single day, only on April 2, 1672. He died to himself—which means he began to live for others—from his youth. And there you have the positive side of the coin, the profound meaning of martyrdom. If you think of each day as a slow dying, you may not like it very much; you may even turn in on yourself. But if you see each day as another birthday, a fresh opportunity to serve Christ in your brothers and sisters, you will thrill to each moment as Diego did. If your heart and your hands are for ever outstretched to the "little ones" so dear to Jesus—the hungry and the thirsty, the naked and the stranger, the sick in spirit or flesh and those who lie in chains—then the tiny grain of wheat will die only to spring to life in a rich harvest: God's life in God's dear children.

My dear brothers and sisters: When I started this sermon six weeks ago in Washington, D.C., only two figures were in the forefront of my thinking. As I was closing my sermon this wondrous week on Guam, you made me aware that Agana's grain of wheat is incomplete without a third person. What the Lord Jesus began for you 1950 years ago, what Blessed Diego brought to you three centuries ago, you have seen with your own eyes, heard with your own ears, in Felixberto Flores. Each has been for you a grain of wheat; each has fallen into the ground for you, died for love of you. But the end is not yet. If Agana is to live, if the Marianas are to bear God's fruit, a cross on Calvary, a machete and spear at Tumon Beach, a deathbed in San Francisco are not enough. It is now you who must fall into God's earth, you who must die God's death, you who must enliven this land with God's life. If not you, then who?

Tumon Beach, Guam
November 10, 1985

A PRIEST FOR EVERY MOMENT
Feast of St. Francis de Sales

- Isaiah 52:7–10
- Ephesians 4:1–7, 11–13
- John 15:9–17

For the patronal feast of your seminary, a roguish temptation lures this Jesuit homilist. I am tempted to use Francis de Sales as a persuasive proof that a young man can attend a Jesuit college, have a Jesuit for spiritual director, found a Jesuit school, and still become a saint! Despite the influence of Marquette on your past and present, I shall resist the temptation and move into fields dotted with different land mines.

I shall not bore you with a biography; a homily is not a history. In a homily that is not simply a eulogy, one question leaps high above all others: Does this saint speak to our needs? Not broad generalities: "Love your enemies." "A priest is another Christ." "You did not choose me; I chose you" (Jn 15:16). Very concretely, can we tear a saint out of Savoy and post him 400 years later in Wisconsin?

I believe we can. Why? Because in his priestly existence de Sales says something significant to three facets of priesthood that raise neuralgic problems for priests today. (1) Identity: Who am I? (2) Preaching: What shall I say? (3) Loneliness: Whom do I love? In each case, let me raise the problem, touch it to Francis, and suggest how he helps.

I

First, the problem of priestly identity: Who am I? What does it mean to be ordained a priest? As I grew up, the answer was easy. The emphasis was on functions, on roles. We defined an ordained priest in terms of what he could *do* which an unordained person could *not* do. And here the crisis of identity has torn the guts of uncounted priests. They search for priesthood in terms of something specific to themselves, powers proper to priests, functions which distinguish them from the laity. They do indeed discover such powers, such functions—what they alone can do: "This is my body." "I absolve you." These powers are awesome, unique, crucial to Catholicism. But for all their significance, these functions take terribly little of a priest's time. The rest of their existence? Many suspect, to their dismay, that some man or woman in the pews could do it better. "Of all social roles," it has been observed, "the priest's calls for the widest use of his untrained capacities, and calls into play, more than any profession, his personality dispositions."[1]

Here Francis de Sales breaks in—not with his lips but with his life. Of course he grasped the centrality of the Sacrifice, of the Eucharist. "Unless I am mistaken," he wrote, "nothing more difficult nor more dangerous can happen to a man than to hold in his hands and bring to be, through his words, him whom the angels . . . cannot comprehend or sufficiently extol."[2] Of course "the weeks of Lent were one long uninterrupted ministry in the confessional and the service of souls. . . . "[3] But what impresses me even more in Francis is that for him *everything* he did fell under priestly ministry. He played with children and debated with the octogenarian Calvinist Beza. He distributed food to the poor and played the diplomat with prince and pope. He gossiped with the simplest of folk and directed a diocese with 450 parishes. He instructed a deaf-mute and established an academy he hoped would blossom into a Christian Athens. He rebuilt churches and wrote books, tracts, volumes of letters. "I am so overcome by business," he sighed, "that I can scarcely steal here and there quarters of an hour for these spiritual writings."[4]

So too for you. In the wake of Francis, I ask you to fix your eyes not so much on functions that distinguish you from the laity, as on a new relationship of responsibility to the Church, a relationship sealed by a sacrament. You are empowered, privileged, to represent the Christian community in its faith and its love, and in so doing to act "in the person of Christ." I ask you to expand your priestly horizons, to recognize priestly activity not simply in the cultic—"I baptize you," "I absolve you," "This is my body"—but in every action, every role, to which the Church summons you at this moment in her history, in fidelity to her mission and yours. I ask you to see no work of yours as secular—with the exception of sin and possibly subpar golf—because *whatever* you do in response to the call of Christ and his pilgrim bride is caught up in that solemn sacramental moment when you pledged to them your total self, your every waking hour, your agony as well as your ecstasy, your routine as well as your excitement, your failure as well as your success—your daily living *and* your daily dying. You are not only "a priest for ever," not only a priest "for all seasons"; you are a priest for every moment.

II

Second, the problem of preaching: What shall a priest say? I am not divulging an ecclesiastical secret when I submit that our people are rarely enraptured by the way we proclaim God's word. In dark moments I find it a tribute to the faith of our flocks, and to their Christian courage, that when we open our lips to preach they do not rush posthaste, pell-mell, to the nearest pub. A priestly tragedy, a tragedy for the body of Christ, for the task of redemption. For, as that remarkable French theologian-in-a-wheelchair Yves Congar once wrote, "I could quote a whole series of ancient texts, all saying more or less that if in one country Mass was celebrated for thirty years without preaching and in another there was preaching for thirty years without the Mass, people would be more Christian in the country where there was preaching."[5]

De Sales sensed that. He took seriously a sentence of Trent we've stowed away: "The first and principal duty of the bishop is to preach."[6] And so he did: more than 4000 sermons, to all manner of people. He even wrote a letter on preaching to the archbishop of Bourges—9000 words!

How did he preach? Contemporaries speak of him as a preacher of power and charm. Not high oratory; that was not his way. Not classical eloquence; such was not his strong suit. His power was his simplicity; his charm, drawing hearts to God by gentleness and love. Pius IX did indeed declare that Francis was a "master of sacred eloquence," that he restored a degraded art "to its ancient splendor."[7] But he did it in his singular fashion. He practiced what he advised. "The sovereign artifice," he stressed, "is not to have any artifice. Our words should be burning words, but because of what we are truly feeling, not because of our cries and our extravagant actions. They must come from the heart, not the mouth. Say what you will, the heart speaks to the heart, the tongue only speaks to the ears."[8]

De Sales does not demand that we copy his elements of style. The rhetoric of 17th-century Geneva is not the rhetoric of 20th-century Milwaukee, and in the last analysis the style is the man. But he does lay two heavy demands upon us—demands the Church herself makes on us, demands we can refuse or belittle only with peril to our priesthood. First, we must preach. And not just any message, some spiritual pap. We are to proclaim, Vatican II insisted, "God's wonderful works in the history of salvation . . . the mystery of Christ." Not just read the works, not just remember the mystery. The sermon must make the mystery of Christ "present and active within" our people.[9] This can happen only if de Sales's second demand takes flesh in us. Our words must be "burning words," and that means my heart must be aflame with what I preach, afire with Christ crucified, Christ risen, Christ alive with the Father and within us.

It will cost you dearly—for at least four reasons. (1) You must bury yourself in Scripture, plunge into God's word, make it the air you breathe, the prayer you pray—not feel, as some do, that the exegetes "have taken away my Lord, and I know not where they have laid him" (Jn 20:13). (2) You dare not be ignorant of theology, because theology is not primarily an ivory-tower science open only to an Aquinas or a Rahner, but the whole Church's endless effort to grasp the meaning of God's word, the whole Church's ceaseless search for a God who wore our flesh for love of us. (3) You must see your preaching not as an interruption in liturgy but as itself liturgy, an act of worship, your public prayer in the midst of God's people. (4) It is not sufficient if your sermon is the very model of Cartesian clarity. To preach is to imagine, to let loose your creative powers, to make the material an image of the immaterial, to use symbol and story, to do for preaching what artists do for painting and poetry, sculpture and architecture, music and dancing, stage and screen. Why? Because a picture is indeed worth a thousand words. Because your people are not yearning for sheer knowledge: This you have to believe, this you have to do. They want what the Greeks asked of the apostle Philip: "Sir, we would like to see Jesus" (Jn 12:21). You must bring the mystery of Christ from the Holy Land to your land, to this time and clime, to this congregation. You must tell the story afresh—to people who are not particularly moved by "the Lamb of God," by parables that seemingly do not speak to their needs, by a gospel of love that must compete with "Love Boat," with "Dallas" and "Dynasty."[10]

To preach like this, you pay a price—sweat and blood and tears. Are you ready to pay it?

III

A third priestly problem: loneliness. I know whereof I speak. I have played priest for 45 years. And *I* am uncommonly fortunate. I share a home with 85 other Jesuits (a blessing, but not unmixed). I live amid several thousand students (at night they murder sleep). Editing and writing, lecturing and preaching, crossing country and ocean, I cannot count the thousands I meet and greet. And still I must live much of my life alone: at my desk, in a library, on my knees, in bed.

Focus on only one facet of the problem. In a famous conference 40 years ago at old Woodstock Seminary in Maryland, John Courtney Murray spoke to the Jesuit community on "the danger of the vows." As for chastity, he told us that the vow we had taken endangered us, put us in mortal peril. We risked refusing to enter the world of Eve, risked a premature senility (sex is dead), thinking ourselves whole when we were not. We risked remaining the proverbial bachelor, "crotchety, emotionally unstable, petulant, and self-enclosed."[11] And some priests are. For them, woman is indeed a soul to be saved, but a mysterious, perilous species. They are uncomfortable with women, prefer the macho, high-fives, slap-your-rump relationship of the locker room. And so they live the first half of St. Jerome's pithy advice to a priest in 394: As for women, "either skip them all or love them all."[12]

At the other extreme, some enter the world of Eve all too enthusiastically. I mean, with passion, without reserve, either arrowed by a boyish Cupid or maturely convinced that only intimacy on every level can fulfil them as men and as Christians. I am not passing judgment; I am simply reporting on what you already know.

How does de Sales enter the picture? In two significant ways. First, his very life makes a significant distinction: He could be alone without ever being lonely. How was that possible? Because he had experienced God. His day-to-day relationship with his Lord reminds me of the powerful words Karl Rahner put with good reason on the pen of St. Ignatius Loyola:

All I say is I knew God, nameless and unfathomable, silent and yet near, bestowing Himself upon me in His Trinity. I knew God

beyond all concrete imaginings. I knew Him clearly in such near-
ness and grace as is impossible to confound or mistake. . . . I knew
God Himself, not simply human words describing Him. . . . I
mean God really and truly . . . the ineffable mystery, the darkness
which only becomes eternal light for the man who allows himself
to be swallowed up by it unconditionally. It is precisely this God,
He and none other, whom I personally experienced as the God
who comes down to us, who comes close to us, the God in whose
incomprehensible fire we are not, in fact, burnt away but become
ourselves and of eternal value. . . . Through Him, if we allow ourselves to be taken up by Him, we are not destroyed but given to
ourselves truly for the first time. . . . This experience is grace indeed and basically there is no one to whom it is refused.[13]

To be alone without being lonely, simply ask and accept what God
offers to each and all of us. Not a vision, not an ecstasy, not an experience "out of this world." Ask for the knowledge that is love—
oneness in love with a God who is terribly real. Such was Francis'
whole life. As a recent writer put it, "He was free . . . free to love.
All the rest was unimportant, for what was most essential for him
was the *pure love* of God."[14]

   Second, this very intimacy with God made possible an intimacy
with women that was wonderfully warm. The friendship of Francis
de Sales and Jeanne de Chantal tells us vividly that we priests have
within our power not two choices only: either crotchety bachelors
or passionate lovers. We are capable of an intense love that transcends passion, that links two human beings in a friendship so rich,
so deep, that it images the love wherewith Father and Son love each
other in the very heart of the Trinity. We are capable of it . . . if . . .
if we love God as Francis did: with all our mind and heart, with all
our soul and strength. But isn't that what we are called to do?[15]

   My brother priests, I can end on no higher a note than to repeat
a paragraph that decades ago appeared quite often on the ordination card of new priests. It stems, I believe, from a 19th-century
French Dominican preacher, Jean Baptiste Henri Lacordaire, and
it runs like this:

   To live in the midst of the world without wishing its pleasures; to
   be a member of every family, yet belonging to none; to share all
   sufferings; to penetrate all secrets; to heal all wounds; to go from
   men to God and offer Him their prayers; to return from God to
   men to bring pardon and hope; to have a heart of fire for charity
   and a heart of bronze for chastity; to teach and to pardon, console

and bless always—what a glorious life, and it is yours, O priest of Jesus Christ!

Saint Francis Seminary
Milwaukee, Wis.
January 23, 1987[16]

33

MIDDLEMAN FOR CHRIST
Feast of St. Barnabas

- Acts 11:21–26; 13:1–3
- Matthew 10:7–13

It's a long way from Antioch to Philadelphia, from an apostle to a theologian, from Barnabas to the CTSA.[1] Rather than erode your liturgical time with lame apologies, I shall suggest a connection in three stages: (1) the bare bones of Barnabas' bio; (2) his significance then; (3) his pertinence now.

I

First, some bare bones from the Acts of the Apostles. There Barnabas strides on stage in a striking contrast. His foil is Ananias, a wheeler-dealer tempted to inside trading. Ananias sells a piece of property, brings part of his profit to the apostles, pretends it's the whole shooting match, is lectured unsparingly by the prince of the apostles on lying to the Holy Spirit, ends up lying lifeless at Peter's feet; so too for his short-term widow, Sapphira (cf. Acts 5:1–11). In sharp contrast, Barnabas. He too sells a piece of property, a field he owns. But he has no secret Swiss account; he simply brings in the whole bag, lays all the proceeds before the apostles for the needy of the community (cf. 4:34–37). Little wonder Luke sums him up as "a good man, full of the Holy Spirit and of faith" (11:24).[2]

But it is not Barnabas' integrity that intrigues me. I am fascinated by a facet of his personality, of his apostolate, that flows indeed from his integrity but is more specific than sheer honesty, had important implications for the infant Church, and may well speak to today's theologian. Three concrete examples.

Item 1: Barnabas pleading for proselyte Paul. Paul has come from Damascus to Jerusalem, tries to join the disciples there. But they are in mortal fear of him, do not believe he is a genuine disciple of Christ. Barnabas intervenes. He brings Paul to the apostles, declares to them "how on the road [Paul] had seen the Lord, who spoke to him, and how at Damascus he had preached boldly in the name of Jesus" (9:27). From that critical moment for Christianity Paul "went in and out among them at Jerusalem, preaching boldly in the name of the Lord" (9:28–29).

Item 2: Barnabas apostolic nuncio to Antioch. He has been sent there by the leaders of the Church in Jerusalem, an "official visitor to the new, partly Gentile Church."[3] It is a delicate mission; for Barnabas is sent by the mother Church to a community founded by Hellenists, is commissioned not only to encourage and advise it, but to "bring it under the supervision of the Jerusalem community."[4] As this young community grows, Barnabas seeks out Paul in Tarsus, brings him to Antioch, labors with him for a full year there—there where "the disciples were for the first time called Christians" (11:20–26).

Item 3: the fateful council in Jerusalem (15:1–12). Barnabas is sent by the Church at Antioch, sent with Paul and others, sent to Jerusalem to discuss with the apostles and elders a crucial issue for the Christian Church, an issue that divided not Antioch alone but Jerusalem as well: "Does salvation depend on faith in Christ, or on faith *with* circumcision and observance of the Mosaic Law?"[5] Peter's voice prevailed, yes: "Why do you make trial of God by putting a yoke upon the neck of the disciples which neither our fathers nor we have been able to bear?" (15:10). But perhaps just as vital as the voice of Peter was the witness from Antioch: The assembly "listened to Barnabas and Paul as they related what signs and wonders God had done through them among the Gentiles" (15:12).

II

So far, bare bones from Barnabas' bio. But how put flesh on those bones? What was his significance then? Exegete John Meier put his finger on it when he called Barnabas a "middle-man."[6] He was an intermediary, a mediator, that arduous role where you struggle to reconcile varying visions, opposite opinions, passionately opposed parties or persons—yes, good Christians in conflict.

Item 1: Barnabas mediated between a feared persecutor of the

Church and the apostles of that Church. He did it not only with a story—the unlikely story of a convert preaching Christ fearlessly in the very city where he had gone to take Christians captive. He did it by bringing that ex-persecutor face to face with the top men in the Church. "Here he is. Look at him, look into his eyes, listen to him, and then tell me what you see, what you hear." It was not an easy task for Barnabas; it called for courage. The atmosphere was fear; *all* the disciples in Jerusalem, Luke tells us, were afraid of Paul (9:26). I shudder to speculate what the face of the Church would have been like, had not an imaginative convert from Cyprus dared to confront the apostolic curia.

Item 2: Barnabas mediated between Jerusalem and Antioch. On the face of it, it sounds simple enough. The mother Church wanted the Gentile converts on the shores of the Orontes to know that Jerusalem rejoiced in their gospel joy. "When [Barnabas] came and saw the grace of God, he was glad; and he exhorted them all to remain faithful to the Lord with steadfast purpose" (11:23). But Barnabas had also to make Antioch aware that if the Church's heart was everywhere, its head was in Jerusalem. Oh, not the jurisdiction of canon law. A much looser supervision—but perhaps for that very reason more difficult to explain to fervent new Christians converted by "men of Cyprus and Cyrene" (11:20). I am impressed when I read, possibly between the lines, that Barnabas was revered by Jerusalem and Antioch alike.

Item 3: Barnabas had to mediate within Antioch itself and in Jerusalem, had to mediate between converted Pharisees who insisted on circumcision for all and those who resisted such obligation. Here mediation could not mean compromise. Discussion, of course; persuasion, if possible. But the two sides stood in flat contradiction; only one theology could be authentically Christian. Here mediation ended in a definitive directive—what Barnabas and Paul saw as clearly as did Peter: no imposed circumcision, freedom from Mosaic law. Only thus could "the young Church" be "freed from its Jewish roots," be "opened . . . up to the world apostolate then confronting it."[7] Even for the apostle Barnabas, mediation was a means, not an absolute in its own right.

III

So much for Barnabas; so much for his significance then. But what is his pertinence now, for a society of Catholic theologians?

Very simply, the theologian is a mediator. It may not be our total task, but it is a crucial role.

Item 1: We are called to mediate between the People of God and the People's God. Not quite after the manner of the Hebrew prophets. Not ours, precisely as theologians, to castigate, to whip into line, to threaten with hellfire. And still, in a sense, it is ours to struggle to the point where we can assert with due humility "Thus says the Lord." Not definitively. But it is our task to help the People understand what the Lord God has spoken, from the silent fashioning of one world and two divine images, through the burning bush in Midian and the "still small voice" on Horeb (1 Kgs 19:12), to the shaping of God's Son in flesh and the signs of today's times. We are indeed "middlemen" and "middlewomen," invited by God and implored by the People to make a transcendent God and an ascended Christ come alive for the human mind, so as to be loved by the human heart.

Item 2: We are called to mediate between the authoritative magisterium and the rest of God's People. Here we are middlemen and middlewomen in a sense specially appropriate and potentially perilous: We are caught in the middle! In large measure, teaching from the Tiber and the "sense of the faithful" are in fair accord, particularly where doctrine does not disturb daily living. But we are expected by authority to pass on "the tradition" as understood in Rome even when, as with Murray and Congar, we are convinced that such is not the Church's genuine tradition, may think it inadequate, short-sighted, in error. And we are expected by more and more of the faithful to crystallize their own understanding of what God is asking of them, from control of birth to justice for women, even when they differ from those "whom the Holy Spirit has made [their] guardians" (Acts 20:28). The sanctuary is not the site for a solution. I simply say that, as men and women "in the middle," we have a difficult duty to shepherds *and* flock, and we must be prepared for crucifixion from one side or the other—at times from both.

Item 3: We are called to mediate within our own fellowship; I mean the fellowship of theologians. In one way we've done well. Whatever our ecclesial stripes, ecumenism has compelled or persuaded us to be more Christian, Christians in the middle, striving to reconcile, to bury the bias and bitterness of the past through the openness and love of the present. I only wonder, I only question, whether within our own Catholic theological body we are capable of disagreeing without disliking, of taking exception without excommunicating, of searching together for the truth the Son of God died to give us. In the twilight of my own existence, I ask myself often: Am *I* a force for reconciliation, or have I given up on those who find me less than Catholic: Catholics United for the Faith, the Fellowship of Catholic Scholars, the *Wanderer,* perhaps Opus Dei? It is not only the theologically unsophisticated for whom Christ prayed "that they may all be one . . . I in them and thou in me, that they may become perfectly one, so that the world may know that thou hast sent me and hast loved them even as thou hast loved me" (Jn 17:21–23). Experience tells me that the body of Catholic theologians will never be perfectly one in mind. What agonizes me much more is the fear that we shall never be one in heart.

Good friends: I suspect that, to be a theologian who reconciles, I must be a good bit more like Barnabas: "a good man, full of the Holy Spirit and of faith" (Acts 11:24). St. Barnabas, middleman par excellence, pray for us!

Old St. Joseph's Church
Philadelphia, Pa.
June 11, 1987

NOTES

Preface

1. From Gerard Manley Hopkins, "As kingfishers catch fire ... ," Poem 57 in W. H. Gardner and N. H. MacKenzie, eds., *The Poems of Gerard Manley Hopkins* (4th ed.; New York: Oxford University, 1970) 90.

Homily 1

1. Marguerite Duras, *The War* (New York: Pantheon, 1986). Actually, this is a collection of six texts; it is the first text that details the suffering (*La douleur*, the original French title) of Marguerite.
2. This and the two following quotations in this paragraph are taken from the review of *The War* by Frederick J. Harris in *America* 155, no. 13 (Nov. 8, 1986) 288–90, at 288.
3. Catholic preachers should be aware of a difficulty here that stems from our age-old inability to grasp exactly what Mary's "virginity in parturition" (*virginitas in partu*) meant in terms of her corporeal integrity; cf. L. G. Owens, "Virgin Birth," *New Catholic Encyclopedia* 14 (1967) 692–97, at 693–95. My own brief sentence in this homily is not in line with a tradition that exempts Mary from woman's punishment for sin as expressed in Gen 3:16, but I believe it is theologically defensible.
4. See Samuel Beckett, *Waiting for Godot* (New York: Grove, ©1954).
5. Act II (Grove ed. 58b).

Homily 2

1. In this and the following paragraphs of my first point, I am borrowing freely from an Advent sermon of mine more than two decades old, "St. Andrew: Advent and the Search for Christ," published in my *Saints and Sanctity* (Englewood Cliffs, N.J.: Prentice-Hall, 1965) 191–99, at 193–96.

Homily 3

1. New York: Hawthorn, 1973.
2. A reference to a Broadway play by Christopher Durang that was less than gracious to parochial-school education in his more tender years.
3. See the homily "Forgive Us As We Forgive," in my *Sir, We Would Like To See Jesus* (New York/Ramsey: Paulist, ©1982) 47, as well as my booklet *Towards Reconciliation* (Washington, D.C.: United States Catholic Conference, 1974).
4. See John L. McKenzie, in *The Jerome Biblical Commentary*, ed. Raymond E. Brown, S.S., Joseph A. Fitzmyer, S.J., and Roland E. Murphy, O.Carm. (Englewood Cliffs, N.J.: Prentice-Hall, ©1968) 43:25–26.

Homily 4

1. Sallie M. TeSelle, cited by Urban T. Holmes, III, *Ministry and Imagination* (New York: Seabury, ©1976) 166, from the *Journal of the American Academy of Religion* 42 (1974) 635.
2. St. Augustine, *Confessions* 8, 12, tr. F. J. Sheed, *The Confessions of St. Augustine* (New York: Sheed & Ward, 1943) 179.
3. Here I am following Raymond E. Brown, S.S., *The Gospel according to John (i–xii)* (Anchor Bible 29; Garden City, N.Y.: Doubleday, 1966) 178–79, itself admittedly dependent on F. J. McCool, "Living Water in John," in J. L. McKenzie, ed., *The Bible in Current Catholic Thought* (New York: Herder & Herder, 1962) 226–33.
4. For the record, this homily was actually preached on the *Second* Sunday of Lent, Cycle C, at which the Gospel is customarily the Transfiguration. With an eye to the candidates for baptism or for full reception into the Church, and an eye on the "scrutinies" for that Sunday, the liturgical committee for the Dahlgren 12:15 Mass thought it appropriate to use the Samaritan-woman Gospel from the *Third* Sunday of Lent, Cycle A.

Homily 5

1. See Peter C. Craigie, *The Old Testament: Its Background, Growth, and Content* (Nashville: Abingdon, ©1986) 164–67.
2. Ibid. 167.
3. I am not claiming that Ezekiel is speaking simply or primarily of temporal life; but it is true that life in Jerusalem, life in the temple, is intrinsic to his prophecy.
4. Joseph A. Fitzmyer, S.J., *Pauline Theology: A Brief Sketch* (Englewood Cliffs, N.J.: Prentice-Hall, ©1967) 62.
5. Karl Rahner, "Following the Crucified," *Theological Investigations* 18: *God and Revelation* (New York: Crossroad, 1983) 157–70, at 169–70.

Homily 6

1. In using the word "preludes," I am not playing down the events of Jesus' life before his resurrection. All are important; Calvary can be termed "central"; and still the redemptive work of Jesus may be said to reach its peak on Easter morn.
2. See Joseph A. Fitzmyer, S.J., *The Gospel according to Luke (X–XXIV)* (Anchor Bible 28A; Garden City, N.Y.: Doubleday, 1985) 1521.
3. See Joseph A. Fitzmyer, S.J., "The Ascension of Christ and Pentecost," *Theological Studies* 45 (1984) 409–40, esp. 421–25.
4. Very pertinent here are the observations of Robert N. Bellah, "Religion & Power in America Today," *Commonweal* 109, no. 21 (Dec. 3, 1982) 650–55.

Homily 7

1. For useful information on this "appearance story" and the Lucan redaction, see Joseph A. Fitzmyer, S.J., *The Gospel according to Luke (X–XXIV)* (Garden City, N.Y.: Doubleday, 1985) 1554–60.
2. Gerald O'Collins, "The Appearances of the Risen Jesus," *America* 156, no. 15 (April 18, 1987) 317–20, esp. 318.
3. I am not implying that the supper at Emmaus was necessarily Eucharistic; see Fitzmyer (n. 1 above) 1560.
4. Augustine, *Confessions* 8, 12.
5. *Flannery O'Connor: The Habit of Being*. Letters edited by Sally Fitzgerald (New York: Farrar, Straus, and Giroux, ©1979) 348.
6. *The Long Loneliness: The Autobiography of Dorothy Day* (New York: Harper, ©1952) 107, 140, 141, 286.
7. From Henri J. M. Nouwen, *The Wounded Healer: Ministry in Contemporary Society* (Garden City, N.Y.: Doubleday, 1972) 25–26, apparently only one version of a very ancient story.

8. Taken from a "letter to the editor" by John R. Sheets, S.J., in *America* 156, no. 15 (April 18, 1987) 332.
9. From Gerard Manley Hopkins, "S. Thomae Aquinatis Rhythmus ad SS. Sacramentum," in W. H. Gardner and N. H. MacKenzie, eds., *The Poems of Gerard Manley Hopkins* (4th ed.; New York: Oxford University, 1970) 211–12.

Homily 8

1. References to popular TV serials.
2. On this see Joseph P. Fitzpatrick, S.J., "Justice As a Problem of Culture," in *Studies in the International Apostolate of Jesuits* 5, no. 2 (December 1976) 18–19.
3. See Avery Dulles, S.J., "The Symbolic Structure of Revelation," *Theological Studies* 41 (1980) 51–73, at 55–56.
4. Cf. Raymond E. Brown, S.S., *The Gospel according to John (i–xii)* (Anchor Bible 29; Garden City, N.Y.: Doubleday, 1966) 385.

Homily 9

1. Second Vatican Council, Decree on the Apostolate of the Laity, no. 5.

Homily 11

1. For useful information on the glad tidings brought to Mary, especially some of the more difficult phrases and words, see Joseph A. Fitzmyer, S.J., *The Gospel according to Luke (I–IX)* (Anchor Bible 28; Garden City, N.Y.: Doubleday, 1981) 334–55 (on Lk 1:26–38).
2. A reference to the actual "life situation" of this sermon, preached as it was in the Duke University Chapel.
3. Cf. Fitzmyer (n. 1 above) 422–23, 429–30.
4. I am supposing that Mary was in the synagogue that day, although Luke does not say so (cf. Lk 4:16–30).
5. Dogmatic Constitution on the Church, no. 63.
6. My quotations are borrowed from a column by John Kavanaugh, S.J., " 'Pagan' Madonna's Success Shows Money Is What Counts," *St. Louis Review*, Aug. 16, 1985, 14.
7. A TV-serial character, wealthy, glamorous, manipulative.
8. J.R. is J. R. Ewing, shrewd, selfish, domineering focus of TV's "Dallas." J.C., of course, stands for Jesus Christ.
9. Title of a popular cookbook.
10. Nicknames for Duke and archrival North Carolina.

11. Eugene O'Neill, *Lazarus Laughed*, Act 1, Scene 1; in *The Plays of Eugene O'Neill* (New York: Random House, 1955) 280.

Homily 12

1. Such a description of Paul's physical condition, "found in the apocryphal *Acts of Paul*, derives from the legend of Paul and Thecla and is unflattering enough to be authentic" (F. Schroeder, "Paul, Apostle, St.," *New Catholic Encyclopedia* 11 [1967] 8).
2. Decree on Ecumenism, no. 3. Actually, Vatican II stopped short of calling our separated brothers and sisters "members" of the Church, probably to avoid clashing with Pius XII's *Mystici corporis*.
3. Cf. William F. Orr and James Arthur Walther, *1 Corinthians: A New Translation* (Anchor Bible 32; Garden City, N.Y.: Doubleday, 1976) 279–89.
4. Decree on the Apostolate of the Laity, no. 5.

Homily 13

1. Much of this first point, and a bit of the second, I have presumed to borrow from a wedding homily I preached in 1984; see "Salt of the Earth, Light of the World," in my *Grace on Crutches: Homilies for Fellow Travelers* (New York/Mahwah: Paulist, ©1986) 155–59, at 156, with some fresh ideas added. The third point takes a different direction from the nuptial sermon.
2. I deliberately avoid "Isaiah" here, because only chapters 1–39 can be assigned to Isaiah's time; chapters 40–66 stem from the time of Cyrus of Persia (539 B.C.) and later.
3. Cf. W. Hill, "Isaia, Book of," *New Catholic Encyclopedia* 7 (1967) 666–71, at 670.

Homily 14

1. In my effort to make Christian sense out of the parable of the Dishonest Manager (or Unjust Steward), I am deeply indebted to the research and interpretation of Joseph A. Fitzmyer, S.J., *The Gospel according to Luke* (*X–XXIV*) (Garden City, N.Y.: Doubleday, 1985) 1094–1111.
2. Second Vatican Council, Decree on the Apostolate of the Laity, no. 5.
3. See Fitzmyer's own recapitulation of the essentials of this parable in his article "The Story of the Dishonest Manager (Lk 16:1–13)," *Theological Studies* 25 (1964) 23–42, at 40–42. Note Fitzmyer's observation towards the close of the article (42): "At the beginning of this article we men-

tioned a growing consensus of exegetical opinion about this Gospel story. We hope that we have made it clear that this is a consensus about the composite nature of it. Unfortunately, the same consensus is not found about the interpretation of it. The understanding of the parable which we have presented, however, has the advantage of giving an intelligible and coherent meaning to the whole. It is not, moreover, without some foundation."

4. "Happy Birthday, Fair Harvard!" *Time* 128, no. 10 (Sept. 8, 1986) 54–60.
5. Ibid. 57.
6. Augustine, *Confessions* 13, 38 (tr. F. J. Sheed, *The Confessions of St. Augustine* [New York: Sheed & Ward, 1943] 354).

Homily 15

1. See "Easier for a Camel," in *Still Proclaiming Your Wonders: Homilies for the Eighties* (New York/Ramsey: Paulist, ©1984) 134–38.
2. Here I have been helped by observations in Vincent Taylor, *The Gospel according to St. Mark* (London/New York: Macmillan/St. Martin's, 1959) 408–13; Alexander Jones, *The Gospel according to St. Mark* (New York: Sheed & Ward, 1963) 150–53; M. J. Lagrange, O.P., *The Gospel according to Saint Mark* (London: Burns Oates & Washbourne, 1930) 100–102; Henry Barclay Swete, *Commentary on Mark* (Grand Rapids: Kregel, 1977) 208–13.
3. The verb "scope" on Georgetown's campus refers to a pleasurable pastime where students eye with discrimination members of the opposite sex.
4. For the exact English translation, see Louis J. Puhl, S.J., *The Spiritual Exercises of St. Ignatius* (Chicago: Loyola University, 1951) 12.
5. Second Vatican Council, Decree on the Apostolate of the Laity, no. 5.
6. "Yuppie" is an acronym for "young urban professional."
7. See Carin Rubinstein, "Money & Self-Esteem, Relationships, Secrecy, Envy, Satisfaction," *Psychology Today* 15, no. 5 (May 1981) 29–44, esp. 40–44.

Homily 16

1. This homily was given at the liturgy during the Inter-Seminary Day of Reflection and Fellowship for the three major Roman Catholic seminaries of the New York metropolitan area: St. Joseph's Seminary, Yonkers, N.Y.; Immaculate Conception Seminary, Seton Hall, South Orange, N.J.; and Seminary of the Immaculate Conception, Huntington, L.I., N.Y.

2. For fuller but still summary discussion, see, e.g., Joseph A. Fitzmyer, S.J., *The Gospel according to Luke (I–IX)* (Garden City, N.Y.: Doubleday, 1981) 154–56, 556–57, and *The Gospel according to Luke (X–XXIV)* (Garden City, N.Y.: Doubleday, 1985) 1191–94; Peter Hünermann, "Reign of God," *Sacramentum mundi* 5 (New York: Herder and Herder, 1970) 233–40; M. J. Cantley, "Kingdom of God," *New Catholic Encyclopedia* 8 (1967) 191–95.
3. Fitzmyer, *Luke (X–XXIV)* 1193.
4. Ibid.
5. Herbert Mitgang in the *New York Times,* Oct. 2, 1985, B9.
6. Quoted by Mitgang, ibid., from *Poems and Sketches of E. B. White* (1981).

Homily 17

1. This homily was preached at the close of the Western New York Conference on Catholic Education, sponsored by the Department of Catholic Education of the Diocese of Buffalo, Oct. 3–4, 1986. The theme of the conference was "Tell the Next Generation."
2. Note that Matthew also has "if you say to this mountain, 'Be lifted up and thrown into the sea,' it will be done" (Mt 21:21). On these texts see Joseph A. Fitzmyer, S.J., *The Gospel according to Luke (X–XXIV)* (Garden City, N.Y.: Doubleday, 1985) 1141–44.
3. The sonnet is not really from the pen of Xavier. The original Spanish text may be found in James Brodrick, S.J., *The Origin of the Jesuits* (New York: Longmans, Green, 1940) 181; the English translation is my own.
4. From Gerard Manley Hopkins, "God's Grandeur," in W. H. Gardner and N. H. MacKenzie, eds., *The Poems of Gerard Manley Hopkins* (4th ed.; New York: Oxford University, 1970) 66.

Homily 18

1. See "Easier for a Camel," in *Still Proclaiming Your Wonders: Homilies for the Eighties* (New York/Ramsey: Paulist, ©1984) 134–38.
2. Here I borrow, with some changes, from two previous homilies: "The Man Who Lives with Wisdom," in *Tell the Next Generation: Homilies and Near Homilies* (New York: Paulist, ©1980) 100–101, and "From Wisdom to Wonder," in *Grace on Crutches: Homilies for Fellow Travelers* (New York, N.Y./Mahwah, N.J.: Paulist, ©1986) 186–87.
3. Alan M. Kriegsman, "Balanchine's Ballerina," *Washington Post,* September 29, 1985, G1, G5, G6, at G1.
4. Ibid. G1, G5.
5. Ibid. G5.
6. Ibid. G6.

7. Ibid.
8. Ibid.
9. Ibid.

Homily 19

1. See my homily "A Kingdom for the Shrewd" elsewhere in this volume (Twenty-fifth Sunday of the Year).
2. See Joseph A. Fitzmyer, S.J., *The Gospel according to Luke (X–XXIV)* (Garden City, N.Y.: Doubleday, 1985) 1175–82, at 1178–79, note on 18:3.
3. See ibid. 1318, note on 20:47.
4. See ibid. 1180, note on 18:6.
5. A well-known University of Maryland basketball player, killed suddenly by cocaine after signing a lucrative contract with the Boston Celtics.
6. In this section on Job, I am borrowing, often verbatim, from my homily "In God We Trust," in my *Tell the Next Generation: Homilies and Near Homilies* (New York/Ramsey: Paulist, ©1980) 39–43.
7. I say "Luke's Jesus" because "Holy Spirit" is apparently "the Lucan redaction for the more original *agatha*, 'good things,' preserved in Matt 7:11" (Fitzmyer, *Luke* 915–16, note on 11:13).

Homily 20

1. See Joseph A. Fitzmyer, S.J., *The Gospel according to Luke (X–XXIV)* (Garden City, N.Y.: Doubleday, 1985) 878, 880.
2. See ibid. 884.
3. I am indebted here to a sentence put on the pen of St. Ignatius Loyola by Karl Rahner, S.J., in an imaginative but defensible "letter" to a modern Jesuit in his *Ignatius of Loyola* (London: Collins, 1979) 13: "This [direct] experience [of God] is grace indeed and basically there is no one to whom it is refused."
4. Quoted by George W. Hunt, S.J., "Of Many Things," *America* 153, no. 11 (Oct. 26, 1985) ii.
5. Edward K. Braxton, "Black Catholics in America: Where Do We Go from Here?" *America* 153, no. 12 (Nov. 2, 1985) 273–78, at 276.

Homily 21

1. In point of fact, I incline to the view that interprets Lk 21:7–24 of the destruction of Jerusalem, and only vv. 25–36 of the end time; cf., e.g., Joseph A. Fitzmyer, S.J., *The Gospel according to Luke (X–XXIV)* (Garden

City, N.Y.: Doubleday, 1985) 1323, 1348. Since, however, I am convinced that the liturgy for the Thirty-third Sunday of the Year is far
more concerned with the end of the world and Christ's final coming
than with the destruction of Jerusalem, my homily proceeds in that direction. The reading from Malachi supports this approach.

2. See my homily for this same Sunday back in 1983, available in my collection *Still Proclaiming Your Wonders: Homilies for the Eighties* (New York/
Ramsey: Paulist, ©1984) 155–59.

3. The references are to Jn 6:5–14 and Jn 2:1–11.

4. Archibald MacLeish, "The End of the World" (1926), as reproduced in
Lynn Altenbernd and Leslie L. Lewis, eds., *Introduction to Literature:
Poems* (3rd ed.; New York: Macmillan, ©1975) 714–15, reprinted there
from *The Collected Poems of Archibald MacLeish* (Houghton Mifflin,
©1962).

5. Robert Frost, "Fire and Ice" (1923), in *Complete Works of Robert Frost
1949* (New York: Henry Holt, 1949) 268.

6. The reference is to the main character in a popular TV series called
"Dallas."

7. Elizabeth Barrett Browning, "The Cry of the Children," in *Complete Po-
etical Works of Elizabeth Barrett Browning* 1 (New York: Thomas Nelson,
n.d.) 356–61, at 356.

Homily 22

1. A reference to a demonstration, on the grounds of Georgetown University in the spring of 1986, against GU's financial investments in
South Africa.

2. "Byte" and "Apple" are computer terms.

3. The next three paragraphs are borrowed substantially from my sermon "The Trinity: Mystery of Love," in my first book of sermons, *All
Lost in Wonder: Sermons on Theology and Life* (Westminster, Md.: Newman, 1960) 3–8, specifically 5–7.

4. A popular TV serial.

5. See Robert N. Bellah, "Religion & Power in America Today," *Commonweal* 109, no. 21 (Dec. 3, 1982) 650–55.

6. Ibid. 652.

Homily 23

1. Individuals at the center of recent brouhahas: Gary Hart, Jimmy Bak-
ker, Ivan Boesky, and Lt. Col. Oliver North.

2. *Union Seminary Quarterly Review* 21 (1965–66) 121.

3. See Robert N. Bellah, "Religion & Power in America Today," *Commonweal* 109, no. 21 (Dec. 3, 1982) 650–55.

4. See *Time* 128, no. 10 (Sept. 8, 1986) 57.
5. The last two items are references to contemporary films.
6. Jeff Kaczorowski, "Reaching Out," *The Colgate Scene* (Colgate University), January 1986, 7.

Homily 24

1. Tom O'Brien, review of the film in *Commonweal* 111, no. 17 (Oct. 5, 1984) 536.
2. The rest of this paragraph takes its stimulus from, but adds to, similar paragraphs in two earlier homilies: "Look, Love, Laugh," in *Tell the Next Generation* (New York/Ramsey: Paulist, ©1980) 109–15, at 110–11, and "Zapping the Zelig," in *Still Proclaiming Your Wonders* (New York/Ramsey: Paulist, ©1984) 189–94, at 190.
3. John Donne, *Holy Sonnets*, no. 15.
4. It should be noted that, for this particular Mass of the Holy Spirit, the Scripture readings remained the readings for that Sunday, the Twenty-third Sunday of the Year (Isa 35:4–7; Jas 2:1–5; Mk 7:31–37).

Homily 25

1. For the text of the third passage, not from Scripture, see my third point.
2. Elizabeth Barrett Browning, *Sonnets from the Portuguese* 43.
3. I am adopting one of the two possible interpretations of verse 5; the other: Have for one another the attitude which Christ Jesus had. See Joseph A. Fitzmyer, S.J., in *The Jerome Biblical Commentary* (Englewood Cliffs, N.J.: Prentice-Hall, ©1968) 50:16.
4. See Monica Furlong, *Merton: A Biography* (San Francisco: Harper & Row, 1980) 294.
5. Thomas Merton, *New Seeds of Contemplation* (New York: New Directions, 1961) 67.

Homily 27

1. For more detailed consideration of the first two readings, see my homily "Above All These Put On Love," in *Grace on Crutches: Homilies for Fellow Travelers* (New York/Mahwah: Paulist, ©1986) 160–64. In the present homily I have compressed my treatment of those passages into two paragraphs, in order to focus on the text from John.

Homily 28

1. The reference is to several bargain stores in Washington, D.C., that sell all sorts of items apparently acquired from other, larger firms, because these latter must periodically clear their stock or the items have small, fairly obvious defects.
2. I am not claiming that my third point emerges totally or clearly from 1 Corinthians 13. As I ask later, "What do Paul's *epistles* promise?" Still, the springboard for my "promise" is in the passage on love.
3. A reference to the father of the bride, at once an outstanding obstetrician and a gifted golfer.

Homily 29

1. To grasp fully the meaning of my brief remarks, one should be aware that Joan is Jewish, David a Roman Catholic.

Homily 30

1. The collection of homilies dedicated to Albert and Mary Margaret Tegler is *Grace on Crutches: Homilies for Fellow Travelers* (New York/Mahwah: Paulist, ©1986).
2. St. Irenaeus, bishop of Lyons in Gaul,

Homily 31

1. For the historical facts about Blessed Diego and his activities, I am indebted to an unpublished article by Francis X. Hezel, S.J., "Diego Luis de San Vitores," and the monumental work *Manila and Agaña on the Beatification or Declaration of Martyrdom of the Servant of God Diego Luis de San Vitores, Professed Priest of the Society of Jesus (+ 1672): Deposition on the Life and Martyrdom Officially Presented Rome MCMLXXXI,* translated from the original Spanish by Juan M. H. Ledesma, S.J. (Baguio City, Philippines: San Pablo Seminary, n.d.).
2. Archbishop Felixberto Flores, who had given so much of his time and energy to Diego's beatification, died in San Francisco on October 25, 1985, on his way back to Guam from the beatification ceremonies in Rome, and was buried in the Guam cathedral on November 9, the day before the Guam celebration for Diego. Archbishop Flores had explicitly requested this Gospel (Jn 12:24–26), which was also the Gospel read at his funeral Mass.
3. A reference to the beatification ceremonies on October 6, when two

other Jesuits were also beatified: Father José Maria Rubio (1864–1929) and Brother Francisco Gárate (1857–1929).

Homily 32

1. See B. R. Wilson, "The Paul Report Examined," *Theology* 68 (1965) 89–103.
2. Quoted by Michael de la Bedoyere, *François de Sales* (London: Collins, 1960) 46.
3. Ibid. 187.
4. Ibid. 201. The "spiritual writings" were, or at least included, the *Treatise on the Love of God.*
5. Yves Congar, O.P., "Sacramental Worship and Preaching," in *The Renewal of Preaching: Theory and Practice* (Concilium 33; New York: Paulist, 1968) 62.
6. Quoted from de la Bedoyere 102.
7. Quoted from E. J. Carney, "Francis de Sales, St.," *New Catholic Encyclopedia* 6 (1967) 35.
8. Quoted from de la Bedoyere 103.
9. Vatican II, Constitution on the Sacred Liturgy, no. 35.
10. Three popular contemporary TV serials.
11. John Courtney Murray, S.J., "The Danger of the Vows," *Woodstock Letters* 96 (1967) 421–27, at 427.
12. St. Jerome, *Letter 52*, no. 5.
13. Karl Rahner, *Ignatius of Loyola* (London: Collins, 1979) 11, 12, 17, 13.
14. Wendy M. Wright, *Bond of Perfection: Jeanne de Chantal & François de Sales* (New York/Mahwah: Paulist, ©1985) 59.
15. See the whole of Wright's work (n. 14 above) for details.
16. For the historical record, be it noted that this homily was not actually delivered. A heavy snowstorm in Washington, D.C., on January 22, 1987, denied air travel to the homilist. Note also that the homily was to be addressed not to seminarians but to priests of the Archdiocese of Milwaukee.

Homily 33

1. This homily was delivered at the Mass celebrated during the 1987 convention of the Catholic Theological Society of America. The date of the liturgical celebration was June 11, the feast of St. Barnabas, apostle and companion of St. Paul.
2. On the problem of the generalized sharing of possessions in the early Jerusalem community, as well as the factual foundation of the Ananias-Sapphira story, see Edward J. Mally, S.J., "The Gospel according to

Mark," *The Jerome Biblical Commentary*, ed. Raymond E. Brown, S.S., Joseph A. Fitzmyer, S.J., and Roland E. Murphy, O.Carm. (Englewood Cliffs, N.J.: Prentice-Hall, ©1968) 45:31–32.

3. B. M. Ahern, "Barnabas, St.," *New Catholic Encyclopedia* 2 (1967) 102.
4. John P. Meier, in Raymond E. Brown, S.S., and John P. Meier, *Antioch and Rome: New Testament Cradles of Catholic Christianity* (New York/Ramsey: Paulist, ©1983) 33. For problems on the beginnings of the Christian Church at Antioch, see ibid. 32–36.
5. Joseph A. Fitzmyer, S.J., "A Life of Paul," *JBC* (n. 2 above) 46:29.
6. Meier, *Antioch and Rome* 34.
7. Fitzmyer, *JBC* 46:30.